## REVIEWS OF 'CHEER UP PETER REID'

★ ★ ★ ★ ★

*'Bought this book yesterday and decided to have a scan of it when I got home. This ended up a full reading, finishing at 5am. Great book, could not put it down. A must for all football fans and, in particular, Evertonians. Reidy comes across as friendly but firm, a lovable rogue. The sort you want on your team and by your side in the bar'*

*'I can thoroughly recommend this book – a welcome change from most football autobiographies'*

*'Not very often in the high profile football world do you get a real insight and true reflection of a real professional... a good down to earth read which gives the reader a look into the world of football both as a player and a manager'*

*'Brilliant, like the man himself'*

*'A soccer legend with wit and grit'*

*'Smashing book, writes it in the same way he played, very honest, hundred per center. Would recommend it to anybody'*

*'I found it hard to put down. Brought back many memories...'*

Peter Reid has collaborated
on this book with
award-winning journalist Tony
Barrett. Tony has written for
the *Liverpool Echo* and was
*The Times'* north-west football
correspondent.

From Amazon.co.uk

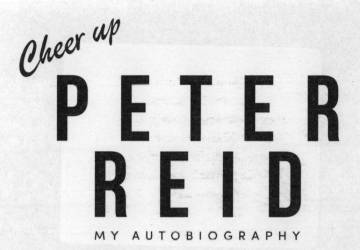

*Cheer up*

# PETER REID

## MY AUTOBIOGRAPHY

Sport Media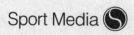

| BRENT LIBRARIES | |
| --- | --- |
| 91120000369781 | |
| Askews & Holts | 23-May-2018 |
| 796.334 | £8.99 |
| | |

*For Barbara, Louise, Freddie*
*and the people of Huyton.*

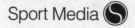

Sport Media

Copyright © Peter Reid
The right of Peter Reid to be identified as the owner of this work has been asserted
in accordance with the Copyright, Designs and Patents Act, 1988.
All Rights Reserved. No part of this publication may be reproduced,stored in a
retrieval system, or transmitted in any form, or by any means,electronic, mechanical,
photocopying, recording or otherwise without the prior permission in writing of the
copyright holders, nor be otherwise circulated
in any form of binding or cover other than in which it is published
and without a similar condition being imposed on the subsequent publisher.

Written with Tony Barrett.

Paperback edition first published in Great Britain and Ireland in 2018 by
Trinity Mirror Sport Media, PO Box 48, Old Hall Street, Liverpool, L69 3EB.

www.tmsportmedia.com
@SportMediaTM

Trinity Mirror Sport Media is a part of Trinity Mirror plc.
One Canada Square, Canary Wharf, London, E15 5AP.

1

Paperback ISBN 9781910335918.
Hardback ISBN: 9781910335741.
eBook ISBN: 9781911613046.

Photographic acknowledgements:
Mirrorpix, Getty Images, PA, Peter Reid personal collection, Tony Woolliscroft.

Design and typesetting by Trinity Mirror Sport Media.
Editing: James Cleary
Production: Roy Gilfoyle
Design: Rick Cooke

Printed and bound by CPI Group (UK) Ltd,
Croydon, CR0 4YY.

# CONTENTS

# THANK YOU:
# IN IT TOGETHER

*'Hopefully this book will serve as a reminder that*
*for individuals to thrive they almost always need an*
*army of people to help them along the way'*

WHEN I committed to telling the story of my life in this book, the one thing that I didn't fully appreciate was just how much the process would stir up a profound sense of gratitude to the countless people who inspired, nurtured and created the conditions for me to have a career in football. From the days when I kicked a ball around the streets of Huyton, through to domestic and European glory with Everton and stints managing some of English football's biggest clubs, I have been blessed to be surrounded by family, friends, team-mates, opponents, managers, coaches and medical staff who brought out the best in me.

What would I have been without them? All I can say for sure is it's hard to imagine that I would have made it as a footballer because, as much as individual talent is important, without the right environment to thrive in and the right kind of encouragement at the right time, it can easily be wasted. There was never a chance of that in my case and while I accept that part of the reason for that is because of my own competitive nature, I also know that without those individuals I would not have been half the player that I became. That is why I can't thank them enough. It was Margaret Thatcher who once infamously claimed that there is no such thing as society. I know from experience that this isn't true and hopefully this book will serve as a reminder that for individuals to thrive, they almost always need an army of people to help them along the way.

First and foremost, in my case, are my mum and dad. By creating a loving family and bringing up five children with the right outlook on life, and giving us the opportunity to fulfil whatever potential we had, they set an example that continues to stand me in good stead. My parents were not rich and ours was not a household in which anything could be taken for granted because money never came easy, but we never felt poor and what we lacked in pounds, shillings and pence was more than made up for in affection, guidance and warmth. My dad is no longer with us but his influence lives on, and any time I get to spend with my mum is never anything other than wonderful. As you know Mum, I will never stop loving you.

The childhood I shared with my three brothers, Michael Patrick, Gary Anthony and Shaun, and one sister, Carol Elizabeth, was magnificent. I know lots of people say that but mine really was, and the support that each of them has given me throughout my career is more appreciated than they will ever know. I might have won a few medals along the way but the silverware belongs to my family as a whole, rather than to me as an individual.

If there is one thing from my career that I cherish more than anything else, it is a photograph of me with my mum and dad and the FA Cup, taken after Everton overcame Watford at Wembley in 1984. That trophy meant the world to us and every time I look at that picture on the wall at my mum's house it reminds me of how fortunate I am, not just to have won what I still regard as football's greatest trophy, but to have a family that made it possible. That doesn't just apply to the Reids either, it also applies to the Murphys and all of the rest of the extended clan.

Going back to my school days and my formative years as a footballer, Tommy Evans, who I played alongside for Huyton Boys and Bolton Wanderers, was always more than a team-mate, and the laughs we had travelling to Bolton when we were still only kids will live with me forever. Tommy was one of a circle of friends who accompanied me on my journey, in his case literally as well as metaphorically, and along with the likes of Stephen Pearson, Phil Kennedy, John Fargin and Ted Roberts, who is sadly no longer with us, they provided a network of individuals who brought out the best in one another in so many different ways. The friends I made as a kid are the friends I still have today which tells you everything you need to know about them, and about the area we came from.

I would need another book to list all of the team-mates who brought something to my life, both professionally and personally, and also the opponents who unintentionally helped take me to another level by making me rise to the challenge that they set. That I can count so many from both groups as close friends and drinking partners to this day is something I regard as a great privilege. Then there are the people who have supported me behind the scenes, none more so than Mike Morris, John Camilleri and Peter Cowgill, who in their own different ways have made life easier for me than it might otherwise have been. Thanks also to my great mates Derek Hatton and Tommy Knox.

Without the brilliance of Jimmy Headridge, the physio at

Bolton who saved my career, I would not have gone on to win two league championships for Everton and appear at a World Cup for England, so my appreciation for everything he did for me is absolute. His efforts meant I never needed any reminders of the wonderful work that people in the medical profession do on a daily basis but I got one recently when I saw the way that my daughter, Louise, was cared for when she became ill.

My gratitude for the doctors and nurses who have looked after her and her husband, Danny, a cracking lad who has been through a tough time, is immense. It has reinforced my view that by setting up the NHS, Nye Bevan created something that we should all cherish.

Last, but by no means least, thank you to the publishers of this book, Trinity Mirror Sport Media, for wanting my story to be told and to Steve Hanrahan, Paul Dove, James Cleary and all of their colleagues for making it happen.

# FOREWORD: SIR ALEX FERGUSON

*'Peter has always been someone who is held in the highest esteem and I am fortunate enough to class him as a friend and not just a former rival'*

AS a Scotsman, one of my favourite memories of Peter Reid was the famous occasion when he tried – and failed – to keep up with Diego Maradona when England lost to Argentina at the 1986 World Cup. It was like watching an old racehorse chasing Frankel.

As the manager of Manchester United, I was rarely happier than when a team I was in charge of defeated Peter's Manchester City. But as someone who was fortunate enough to work in football for many years my respect for him, as a player and a manager, is absolute. Whenever we meet, there is a spark and a fair bit of mickey taking, but Peter has always been someone who is held in the highest esteem. I am fortunate enough to class him as a friend and not just a former rival.

The first time I saw Peter in the flesh was one of the greatest nights of his career. Everton were playing Bayern Munich in the semi-final of the European Cup Winners' Cup at Goodison Park and I was in the stands. The atmosphere was terrific and all of the Everton players responded magnificently, Peter more than most.

There are times when you watch games and you can just tell that an individual isn't going to allow his team to lose. While I'm not taking anything away from his Everton team-mates, who were brilliant to a man, there was not a chance that Peter was going to walk off the pitch at the end of the game without having reached the final.

He had a bloodied sock and his ankle was in such a state that it would have been understandable if he had gone off but players who are built like Peter was don't stand aside when the going gets tough; they play even harder. That was exactly what he did and I still regard it as a privilege that I was there to see him help Howard Kendall's greatest team to reach a European final that they would go on to win.

It was only one night but it was a game that summed up the way Peter approached football. He wasn't the quickest, injuries had cost him some of the pace that he had, but if there was a loose ball you could put money on him being the first to reach it due to a combination of a fierce will-to-win and an ability to read the game. On the few occasions when he didn't get there first, he would be straight in with a tackle, playing as if his life depended upon winning a single tackle and when he had the ball, he would use it quickly and accurately.

He was the kind of player I loved as a supporter, somebody who I would have wanted in my team as a player, and respected as a manager. Passion and determination can sometimes be underrated qualities in the modern game but Peter had them in abundance and that was one of the main reasons, along with his natural football talent, why he was able to enjoy such a distinguished playing career.

If anything, his talent has become under-estimated with the passage of time. The same can be said for the Everton team of which he was a key part, a side that was undoubtedly one of the strongest in Europe during the mid-1980s when Howard had them playing some brilliant football. When people talk about the job that I took on at United in 1986, one of the first things that is often highlighted is the challenge we had to overhaul Liverpool but I have always thought that was disrespectful to Everton, who won the championship for the second time in three years in my first season in charge.

Howard's decision to leave at the end of that campaign probably stopped Everton in their tracks a little bit but when I first went to United there is no question that they were a top side, and I knew full well that getting the better of them was going to be a big job in itself.

It was when Howard left another job, this time at City, that Peter's chance to break into management arrived. I can remember the sequence of events clearly. I was in bed on the morning of a game and my phone went. I picked it up and Freddie Pye, the City director, was on the other end. "Howard's gone back to Everton," he told me. I was surprised at the timing because, like everyone else in football, I hadn't seen it coming, but I wasn't shocked that it had happened because I knew just how much Everton meant to Howard.

Freddie then asked me for my advice. "Do you think Peter Reid could do the job?" he asked, and I didn't even need to think about it. "There is absolutely no doubt about it," I said. Freddie told me they were hoping to make the decision that day and I told him not to think any further; they had their man.

Every manager needs a club to give him a chance but anyone who had seen the way Peter works would have seen that he had the qualities to take charge of a club. He is a natural leader, an organiser who demands that everyone is as committed as he is and who has no interest in doing anything but win football matches. The excellent job that he did at City didn't surprise me and I couldn't believe it when they decided to get rid of him after just four games of the 1993/94 season.

I know he won't thank me for the part I played because United were not making it easy for whoever the City manager would have been but he had proven himself to be a very good young manager, and the decision to sack him is one that I still can't fathom, even after all these years.

Peter could have let that setback affect him but he isn't made that way and he went to Sunderland and was the most successful manager that they have had for decades. Like at City, his team played in his image: tough, uncompromising and hard to beat. He made some magnificent signings, Kevin Phillips was one of *the* great bargains and Niall Quinn was the perfect foil. Everything he achieved there was done on a limited budget and his will-to-win was as evident on the touchline as it had been on the pitch as I, and every other manager who came up against him, can testify.

It is as a human being, though, that he most excels. I have got to know him well and he has a wonderful sense of humour, but he is also astute and has a natural ability to make people feel at ease in his company. When he was manager of City the rivalry between the two clubs was never anything other than tense but we were able to strike up a rapport, which we maintain to this day. On one occasion, we had agreed to do an interview with Joe Melling and Bob Cass, two national newspaper journalists, in the build-up to the derby. I was only there briefly when I was called away on club business and on the way out I swiped Joe's tape recorder.

I got back three hours later and they were all still there and I asked if they had got any of the interview done. "No," Joe said. "I don't know where I've left my recorder." "Here you go," I said. "Use my one," and put his on the table.

We all fell about laughing but Peter didn't think that was the end of the practical jokes. "Never mind that, where have you been?" he asked. "I've just signed Eric Cantona," I told him, and I could tell he didn't know whether or not I was having him on. It was only when my chairman, Martin Edwards, turned up and confirmed the story that he realised I was telling the truth. Peter being Peter, he then turned the air blue. I won't repeat the exact words he used but the basic gist of it was that I could have at least waited until after the derby before signing him.

It is that sociable, human side of Peter that I love. As managers you can go months without having the chance to spend time with one another, but Peter was always one of those who would make himself available whenever anything was going on. A mutual friend, Keith Pinner, would organise lunches that I would attend with Peter and other managers including Joe Royle, David Moyes and big Sam Allardyce. They were always great occasions and they were important, too, because they allowed us to understand the problems that one another were having and also recognise the pressures that we were working under. We might have been at rival clubs but that didn't prevent us from establishing the kind of camaraderie and mutual respect that is always important in a profession like football management.

Calling them lunches is probably a loose description and there is one that I recall which Peter, Sam and myself enjoyed in particular. Later that night, Big Sam was on television and I said to Cathy, my wife, "Just wait until you see this," but he was perfect. I'm not sure Peter would have done quite so well but, as a footballer and as a manager, he made the most of himself and that is all that any of us can ever do. He came up the hard way and had to work for everything, which is why he deserves all of the accolades he has received, and many more for all that he has achieved in the game.

# PROLOGUE: LOUISE REID

*'He was always there for me more than he
will ever realise. I know he credits my mum
with bringing me up because he worked away a lot,
but, in my eyes, they brought me up together and
I will always be grateful to them for that'*

TO millions of people, at home and abroad, Peter Reid is a footballer, a manager and a character who they might associate with because of how he played the game, or because of the way he is as a person.

As a kid at primary school, I would be astonished when the sight of my dad at the school gates would prompt loads of my friends, especially the boys, to race out to see him on the rare occasions that he would be able to come and pick me up.

I was too young to understand it then but whereas I was seeing the father who would look after me when I was poorly and hug me when I was upset, they were seeing an Everton and England star, someone they dreamed of emulating and wanted to know.

At times, it can be a surreal experience to be the daughter of someone who is in the public eye, although I enjoyed it when my friends showed their support for him, as they did when he was managing Manchester City and they all came into school wearing City pin badges.

And it was definitely strange when he appeared on *Wogan* singing "E-v-e-r-t-o-n" and my mum got asked at the school gates if my dad was in a pop band!

It was also a bit different for me than it was for most other children because my dad's job meant that he wasn't always around. He was always there for me more than he will ever realise, though. I know he credits my mum with bringing me up because he worked away a lot, but, in my eyes, they brought me up together and I will always be grateful to them for that.

I have always been a proper daddy's girl and that's just the same now as it was when I was little. If I have any kind of grown-up problems I always speak to my dad first, and ask him to tell my mum. He is the one I ring when I'm scared or upset.

Knowing that he is there for me has always been a massive reassurance and never more so than at the end of 2016 when I was diagnosed with cervical cancer. I had got married to Danny in October and my dad had given me away so, as a family, we went from a big high to a massive low in a short space of time.

At first, the signs were more positive. Some abnormal cells had been picked up during a smear test but I was told that they were pre-cancerous and to go back to work. Everything seemed pretty normal and then I went into Hope Hospital for a seemingly routine procedure and the message was exactly the same: "There's nothing to worry about, go home and enjoy Christmas, there's nothing cancerous here."

The cells were removed in the January and the hospital told me I wouldn't hear from them again until my six months' check but, the following day, they called me and asked me to go back in.

Obviously, alarm bells start to ring then and sitting in the waiting area was probably the longest few hours of my life. I went into a room and there was a Macmillan nurse sat there, I was told that I had a tumour.

They booked me in for an MRI scan, which was due to take place the following week, but my husband said I wasn't waiting that long, because the worry we had after being told was that the cancer might have spread to my liver or kidneys. I was told to come back at 3 o'clock the same day so, in the meantime, we drove straight to my mum and dad's to tell them the news.

Of all the things I have ever done in my life, this was undoubtedly the hardest. I went into my dad's room, where he watches football and cricket, and as soon as I walked in he saw my face and just said: "It is, isn't it?" I'm a parent myself now so I could tell he was doing that thing where you try to appear strong, when the reality is that you're absolutely devastated. He and my mum both told me that I was in good hands and everything would turn out okay.

I then had to make a decision about whether I would have a full hysterectomy or a trachelectomy and the specialist basically advised that, with the size and aggressiveness of my tumour, to take no chances. I already have a son, Freddie, from a previous relationship but Danny and I had been planning to have children so that made the decision even more difficult. Ultimately, the decision was made for me because I couldn't take any chances.

I went in to have the hysterectomy and after the operation was over, the first person I asked for was my dad. He came in and gave me a kiss, but then he started crying. The only time I can recall seeing him cry before then was at my grandad's funeral. I was in a bit of a state because I was just coming around off the anaesthetic. I was squealing in pain and I was very emotional, which must have been difficult for him, but he was there for me.

When I was discharged from hospital, he was at my house every single day, even sitting downstairs for hours on end while I slept upstairs, just in case I might need him. Every chance he got, he reminded me of how lucky we are to have a wonderful NHS and magnificent doctors and nurses, like the ones who had looked after me at Hope and at the Christie in Manchester. My dad is very political and he has a strong sense of what is right and wrong so he never missed an opportunity to show his gratitude to the medical staff because he knows the pressures that they work under, and how much they care for patients like me.

It hasn't been an easy process and when I first had chemotherapy I had a bad reaction to the drugs. I ended up with an oxygen mask on with my dad by my side, rubbing my back and my shoulder. When the drama was over he sat in the corner of the room looking relieved. "Is it hot in here?" he asked with a bright red face. "You got a right panic up then." I hadn't been the one panicking though; it was him!

He stayed at my house the night before he was taking me to my next chemotherapy. I took my wig off to go and wash my head and he saw it on the side. After I had finished, I put the wig back on, and he said: "Go on, are you showing me then?" I didn't want to because I was a bit embarrassed and I didn't want anyone else to see it but he just said: "Louise, you're my daughter, take it off."

So I took it off. "Louise, you look beautiful," he said, gave me a big hug and told me how proud he is of me. That's my dad. That's the Peter Reid I know and love.

# 1. IN BED WITH MARADONA

*'In my dreams I'm still running but there's a wind against me. No matter how hard I try, I can't get there. I could have been the player who stopped the world's best, the one who prevented England from being eliminated from a World Cup that we could have gone on to win'*

"GLENN HODDLE plays a long pass trying to find God, it gets intercepted, the ball bounces between Peter Beardsley and myself, Diego Maradona turns and goes at pace. I run after him but Beardsley just stands there, although you can't blame him with that hunch on his back. He goes past Terry Butcher, Terry Fenwick, Peter Shilton and scores. It had fuck-all to do with me."

That is how I've described arguably the greatest goal in football history whenever anyone has mentioned it over the last 30 years or so. It is tongue-in-cheek and I doubt the lads I mention will be too happy with me, but I know the truth: I, Peter Reid, was as powerless as the rest of the other England players to prevent one of the finest footballers of all time from delivering the signature moment of his career.

A witness to Maradona's genius, I was also a victim of his deception. The biggest game of my career, a quarter-final at the 1986 World Cup, was defined by one man – and it wasn't me. Argentina's greatest sporting hero remains a villain in the eyes of the English public. I have more reason than most to regret being on the receiving end of both his brilliance and his deviousness at Mexico City's Azteca Stadium. It still hurts that he finished us off with his feet after opening the scoring with his hand. I have had to come to terms with the fact that I may never get over it.

That I was out there at all, playing in such an iconic game, was a minor miracle. Seven years earlier I had been told that my career might be over after suffering a badly broken leg while at Bolton Wanderers. Although I recovered from that injury, the physical scars it caused remain and so, too, do the mental ones inflicted by Maradona. I knew when I went to the World Cup, having already conquered England and Europe with Everton, that it would be an unforgettable experience, but I had no idea that the impact of a single opponent would be so profound.

Maybe I should have realised before kick-off, when all eyes were on him? His name had been mentioned in the dressing room beforehand and the question that was asked was, how were we going to deal with him? Bobby Robson's solution was that whoever was closest to him would have responsibility for picking him up, which I thought was the right approach because if we had gone man-to-man we would have lost our shape, and that would have prevented us from playing how we wanted to. We had an experienced group of players and we all knew our jobs so there was no point in disrupting that for the sake of one player, no matter how brilliant he undoubtedly was. I always admired

Bobby for that. We were on the biggest stage of all and, win or lose, we were going to play the way that suited us best.

The problem was that Maradona could be unplayable, no matter how the opposition set up. As soon as the pre-match warm-up started there were signs that this could be his day. I was looking at the state of the pitch, which had been repaired with slabs of turf instead of the divots being put back, and wondering whether the surface might affect the game when he caught my eye.

He was just going through his routine but it was as if he was a street performer on Las Ramblas who didn't have a care in the world. While I was stretching my thighs and knocking the ball about, he was keeping the ball up with his left peg, knocking it high and low, putting back spin on it. Every time it landed on his instep he wouldn't have had to move. It was mesmerising. Here was this short, stocky fella with a touch from heaven and even though he was probably only doing it to get himself ready for the match, this was one game of keep-ups that inevitably attracted the attention of the 11 English lads in the other half of the pitch.

We had all seen skill before and some of us even had skill, but never had we seen it demonstrated so effortlessly ahead of such an enormous game. He was marking our cards and, in that respect, it was a case of job done for Diego because, even if we hadn't have known what we were up against beforehand, we certainly did after seeing his one-man show.

There were more Argentinians in the crowd than there were England fans but whether you had come to support him or were there in the hope that he would fail, Maradona was one of those rare players who attracts attention, even when he's doing basic things. I can remember thinking to myself, 'I'm only little and a bit chunky, why aren't you all looking at me?' A smile briefly flickered across my face as I had a vision of tens of thousands of football supporters being captivated by my shuttle runs and heel taps as 'Fred Karno' was doing his thing 50 yards away.

I was quite happy that everyone was focusing on him because attention brings pressure and, while we knew all about his talent, we didn't know how he would cope with being the man who *had* to win the World Cup for Argentina. Up to that stage, the signs had been that he was coping with that burden but, as you go further in the competition and the stakes and the standards become higher, so too does the pressure. That's difficult enough when it is spread throughout a team but when it is trained on an individual it can become suffocating. Not that we were of the opinion that all we had to do was stop Maradona. We knew that Argentina were a solid side which had enough quality to trouble most opponents, even if they were a bit dependent on him.

They also had a different approach to us, which became apparent soon after kick-off, as they looked to go man-to-man whenever we were in possession. They would go tight on Gary Lineker, tight on Beardsley, tight on the wide men and it was difficult to get space to play in. Argentina were clever and their game plan was clearly to stop us in the belief that, at some point, Maradona would do his thing and the game would be taken away from us.

We wanted to get Hoddle on the ball and we were looking to get Links in behind but they were preventing us from doing those things. I suppose that was a back-handed compliment because it showed how much Argentina respected us, but it meant the game was cagey with few chances being created and not too much good football being played. We went in at half-time and I stood in the dressing room and told everyone who would listen that if that was the best that Argentina could do, we would beat them if we found a way to play our own game.

Then everything changed when the man who had mesmerised

everyone with his tricks beforehand showed that he was also a conman. Cheat is a strong word to use in football and players hate it when they are accused of being one so I do not use it lightly, but I can say without fear of contradiction that Diego Armando Maradona is a cheat. He deliberately used foul means to deceive the referee and to unfairly damage England so how could I see him as anything else? We all cut corners and take advantage of situations and I've never knocked anyone who does that, because I know full well that I did it myself. But there are boundaries to what is acceptable as a competitor and he crossed them.

The build-up to one of the most infamous moments in football was mundane as he tried to play a give and go that came to nothing and Steve Hodge knocked the ball into the air. Maradona was on the move and followed the ball in but Peter Shilton was coming out of his goal. I was in no doubt that he would get there first but, as he went up, Maradona knocked the ball into the net. It was obvious what had happened. It was impossible for Maradona to score without using his hand because everything about his jump, and Shilts' positioning, indicated that Argentina's number 10 just wasn't in a position to win a header above our keeper. I knew straight away that it wasn't right and that feeling grew when Shilts and Hod ran past me to remonstrate with the Tunisian referee – but he remained unmoved and the goal was given.

If it would have been Harald Schumacher in our goal, Maradona wouldn't have got the chance to use his hand because he would have been smashed to the ground and the only thing he would have ended up picking up would have been his teeth, rather than the World Cup, but Peter had gone about things in the proper way and got punished for it. Maybe it was a difficult one for the referee to spot and, like us, he had been caught out by a cheat.

Years later, Maradona tried to justify his actions by setting them against the backdrop of the Falklands War four years earlier. "Whoever robs a thief gets a 100-year pardon," he said, but was he really thinking of a disputed territory in the South Atlantic when he led with his hand? Was he fuck! The only thing on his mind was doing whatever it took to score a goal at the World Cup and hope that he would get away with it. I certainly don't call it the 'Hand of God'. It was the hand of a cheating bastard.

From there we went from the ridiculous to the sublime as he scored what I believe is the greatest goal of all time. It all started innocuously, with us losing possession in a non-threatening area deep inside the Argentina half and, as the ball was played to Maradona, Beardsley and myself went to close him down but, before we could, he went up a gear and burst away.

Could I have done the professional thing and fouled him there and then to prevent him from breaking into our half? If I could have got close enough I would have done, but the afterburners were on and I was trailing in his wake.

From that moment, that first pirouette away, I was a spectator to what followed, an eyewitness to a moment of genius that I was powerless to prevent. I went with him in so much as I trailed in his wake but it was like a kid racing his dad in the back garden, knowing he wouldn't be able to get close. For every yard I ran, he was running a yard-and-a-half and he had the ball at his feet.

Terry Butcher was the first to engage but he went past him like a slalom skier going around a gate, keeping the ball on his left foot as he cut inside towards goal. Terry Fenwick was next to have a go and I had mixed feelings as their confrontation loomed because Terry had already been booked. I thought he might catch him and get sent off – but he couldn't even get close enough to do that. The Argentinian bull was going through English matadors as if they weren't even there but, by then, he had picked up so much speed that every shift of balance and every touch could send him sprawling so I was thinking, 'Go down, fall over.' But he kept on going, charging into the penalty area as if there was nothing and no-one that could stop him.

Shilts came off his line and closed him down but Maradona just danced around him with the ball still tied to his left foot and then finished, despite Butch's despairing last-ditch tackle. From start to finish, the whole run took just under 11 seconds. That was over about 70 yards on an unbearably hot day and with England's best players doing everything they could to try and stop him. As much as I detested what he had done for his first goal, I couldn't help but admire him for his second.

Something that had occurred at high speed had seemed to happen in slow motion. It was as if we were in a sci-fi movie, where one of the characters has superpowers and the rest are mere mortals, powerless to prevent this superior being from using them. It is a goal that had a profound effect and it still wakes me up to this day. In my dreams I'm still running but there's a wind against me. No matter how hard I try, I can't get there.

A psychiatrist would have a field day with that one but I don't need anyone to tell me why I have these kind of visions when I'm asleep – it's because, even now, more than three decades on, I'm still incredibly disappointed that I couldn't lay a glove on him. I could have been the player who stopped the world's best; the one who prevented England from being eliminated from a World Cup that we could have gone on to win. Ultimately, I was neither of those things. I just had a walk-on role in one of sport's most celebrated scripts. As much as I am willing to hold my hand up and recognise his genius, it hurts me that I was unable to stop him from demonstrating it in such devastating fashion.

Things happen on a pitch and you have to try and leave them

there, but that is easier said than done with those goals because, for different reasons, they were both monumental. There were only 21 other people on the pitch when Maradona scored them and I was one of them, so I wasn't really in a position to put them out of my mind. I tried to because no-one likes reliving occasions when things haven't worked out but Maradona is such a huge figure in football history that his name comes up all the time. Whenever Lionel Messi scores a wonder goal, people ask whether he is as good as Maradona. Whenever anyone cheats, as Thierry Henry did against Ireland in their 2009 World Cup play-off, the question is what can be done to stop players like him and Maradona from taking advantage of the officials?

There is no escape, so I have to deal with it in my own way. I got a bit of revenge a few years ago when I was in Dubai and discovered that Diego was coaching nearby. I went to watch and he was showing off a bit, pinging amazing free-kicks into the top corner while smoking a cigar, and I have to admit I was impressed, even though he had a bit of a belly on him. When he had finished I went over to speak to him through an interpreter and I went to bite his hand. The press got the wrong end of the stick, suggesting that I was kissing his hand as an act of forgiveness but I was actually pretending to take a chunk out of it. I told him that if I had caught him when he went on that run I would have kicked him. He just smiled and said: "No, no, no." It was amicable but at least I had made my point after all those years.

If only I had been able to get that close to him in 1986 I might not have needed to, and my dreams might be of a wonderful English victory, rather than a controversial defeat. I can't change it now, though. I just have to accept that our hopes of World Cup glory were ended by a genius and a cheat.

# 2. THE HUYTON TALENT FACTORY

*'Had I grown up somewhere else I might not have become a footballer, let alone one who was fortunate enough to go on and enjoy a successful career with some of England's greatest clubs'*

PEOPLE often say they were born lucky and, in my case, that is undoubtedly true. By sheer good fortune – or, more accurately, a population explosion in Liverpool that led to new estates being built in places like Kirkby, Speke and Huyton on the outskirts of the city – I spent my childhood in a place that I will always regard as one of the best, and most natural, football academies in Europe.

I'm a great believer that the environment makes the individual and I couldn't have had a better one to grow up in, and it was all down to my mum and dad's decision to move the family to Huyton. Had they gone elsewhere things might have turned out differently but, before I was even born, they made a choice that would shape my life in a way that they could never have imagined.

There were areas with more wealth, places with better houses and districts with more amenities but we had football morning, noon and night. Not only that, it was home to kids who had the kind of winning mentality that top clubs are crying out for these days. If you went out with a ball and got involved in a game you had to win, it was that simple. I was a bad loser then and I'm still a bad loser now. I put that down partly to my dad, who passed that attitude on to me but he wasn't the only one who saw football that way; so did almost all of the kids who I played against every day. It wasn't enough just to play or to show your skills, every single pass and every single tackle had to count. The pressure was on from an early age and I loved it.

Had I grown up somewhere else I might not have become a footballer, let alone one who was fortunate enough to go on and enjoy a successful career with some of England's greatest clubs. Huyton was the making of me. It wasn't only me, either. You could field a team of top players who have come from there. Steven Gerrard is the one who most will think of, and rightly so, when you consider what he achieved. I've got a lot of admiration for Steven. He might have played for Liverpool but he was one of the greatest English midfielders of the last 20 years and for someone from the same area as me to lift the European Cup is magnificent, even if it was for the wrong team. I've got something that he hasn't though – a league title medal. In fact, I've got two but I don't mention that too much because that would be rubbing it in, and he's also younger and fitter than me.

Then there's the likes of George Telfer, Joey Barton, Tony Hibbert, Tony Kelly, Jay McEveley, David Nugent, Lee Trundle; you could go on and on. It always makes me laugh when the media focus on academies at top clubs and how many players they've produced. They should come and have a look at the estates in Huyton: the Bluebell, Mosscroft, St John's, Fincham, Longview and the rest, to discover why these narrow streets with cheek-by-jowl housing have been the starting point for so many professional football careers.

They could have a look at Kirkby while they're at it, too. When I was a kid, Kirkby seemed a world away to me because I spent almost all of my time in Huyton and nowhere else mattered, but it was the area right next to the one that I grew up in and it is very similar. That's why it's no coincidence that so many footballers come from there as well. Dennis Mortimer and Phil Thompson, two European Cup-winning captains, Terry McDermott, Leighton Baines, Alan Stubbs, Mike Marsh, Tommy Caton and Rickie Lambert to name but a few. That's why I'm not jealous of the kids of today and the exposure they get to superior facilities, with 4G pitches and the like. I know that football has to move on and progress is almost always a good thing, but I wouldn't swap the football education that I got for anything.

Huyton, like Kirkby, was a place where you learned not just how to play, but how to be a competitive footballer. If I could change one thing about youth development in the modern game it would be to reintroduce some of the values that we took for granted on the streets and on the playing fields, but which are no longer as prized as they once were.

The football culture was ultra-competitive. There were basic rules that existed outside of the laws of the game but, in a way, they were just as important. The one that stuck with me most was that if someone kicks you, don't let them see that you're hurt and don't, no matter what, get beat. You had to win at all costs. I know people talk about the result being secondary in terms of player development but that makes no sense to me. Maybe I'm old fashioned but I think you can pass on that winning mentality with development. Why can't that happen? If you want to be a winner you have to know how to win. That attitude, that basic belief isn't enforced as much as it should be at academies, and I think that leads to sanitised footballers playing sanitised football. That desire to win every tackle, to be better than the player you're up against, to win every game, should be at the top of the list when it comes to creating the footballers of tomorrow. That's why my era produced leaders and the current one struggles to do so.

It was certainly top of my list growing up on Wimbourne Road in the Murphy household. My first memory is of playing football in the street with a lad called Joey Myers, who was a bit older than me. I absolutely loved it. But as soon as it started getting competitive my pitch, well the street in front of my house, became out of bounds because the council put tarmac down and we had to wait for it to set.

It was probably only a few days but it seemed to take forever, and we had to play in the alleyway at the side of the house. But once the tarmac had set it became the scene for some of the most exciting games I've ever had. Every kick mattered. You can't grow up in a place like that and not want to win. It just isn't possible. I was always one of the worst for it. I couldn't take losing. It would literally make me feel sick. People think I'm exaggerating when I say that but I'm not. I would have an indescribable feeling in the pit of my stomach that made me want to vomit. It probably isn't healthy to be like that but it's the way I am, and I didn't choose to be that way. I wouldn't change it for the world though. It helped me become the player that I was.

On those days, when I couldn't play football from the moment I got up until the moment I went to bed, I had to go to school. My Auntie Eileen used to take me with her mates and they'd all be singing Beatles songs on the way. I hated it. I was growing up in the city that gave us Merseybeat and at the height of Beatlemania but, for me, those songs were the soundtrack to being taken to school at St Dominic's and being taken away from playing football. It was like being hooked on a drug and then being put on cold turkey for six or seven hours every day.

I was born at Sefton General Hospital in Liverpool on June 20, 1956, the first son of Patricia and Peter. Like many other natives of the city where I was brought into the world, I had Irish ancestry. Where my background was different, though, was that my grandfather on my dad's side, Patrick Reid, and his brother, John Joe, had been involved in the 1916 Easter Rising when Irish republicans used force to try and bring an end to British rule.

Paddy, who was also known as "Whacker," was only 15 at the time but he was stationed at Boland's Mills in Dublin during the insurrection, having smuggled guns into the city beforehand. John Joe, who was alongside him, ended up being sentenced to death by court martial but later had his sentence reduced to 10 years of penal servitude. The two brothers ended up serving on opposite sides in the Civil War that followed, with Whacker fighting for the Irish Republican Army and John Joe declaring his allegiance for the Free State.

My grandad ended up being promoted to lieutenant but he was on the losing side, which was why he fled to Liverpool via Dublin docks, where he had worked, and started a new life on this side of the Irish Sea. He went on to become active in the trade union movement before taking over as chairman of the Labour Party's Huyton constituency, a role which allowed him to become close to Harold Wilson, the local MP who had two terms as Prime Minister in the 1960s and 1970s.

From an early age, I was aware that Whacker had been involved in the conflict in Ireland but he never talked to me about it. I had to pick up details and anecdotes from other family members, so it was a big deal for all of us when he travelled to Dublin in 1966 to be presented with a medal by Eamon de Valera, the Taioseach, whom he had fought alongside at Boland's Mills. Even though he was reluctant to tell us about his experiences, it was obvious that he had stood up for something that he believed in and fought for what he felt was right, and that set the standard for the rest of the Reid family to follow. I had a lot to live up to.

At first we lived in the attic of my grandparents' home. There is only two years and nine months between me, our Michael and our Gary, so the three of us and our mum and dad lived and slept in the top floor of a small house. It was survival of the fittest but luckily I had this insatiable desire to improve. Mum always tells me about the moment she realised I was like that – I was only 12 months old and I'd hold her hand and walk up one flight of stairs, across the landing and then up another flight.

That's the thing about having a tough upbringing – and I mean that only in the sense of how and where we were growing up – you have no choice but to try and stand on your own two feet, literally in my case. That's how it was for most of the kids in the area, which is why I say it's not a coincidence that Huyton has produced so many great footballers.

I remember my childhood being magnificent. There was a space in the middle of Mosscroft and we would play football there all day, whenever we could. The only time that changed was in the summer, when we'd play cricket but it was football mainly, and all of the streets on the estate had a team. We even had a tiny cup that would be presented to whichever street won the tournament.

Our street was Gloucester Road and the others were named after places like Lincoln, York, Essex and Warwick. You'd think we were representing those places in a championship of England, that was how much it meant. I'd put absolutely everything into it and it was when I was playing in that competition that someone first took notice of me as a footballer. A fella who lived on the estate had watched one of the games and he went straight round to my mum and dad's just to tell them that I was a good player. I was only six or seven.

The problem for my mum was that I was going through shoes like Imelda Marcos and she was constantly having to find the money to get me a new pair because I'd wrecked the ones I had. I couldn't get enough though. I loved cricket – and I still do – but I knew straight away that football was the game for me. It meant everything and I wanted to learn as much about it as I could.

As a young boy my dad said to me that if someone kicked me I wasn't to let them know I was hurt, I was to get up and nail him as soon as I got the chance. When I got into the school team he told me that if any of my team-mates pushed forward I should try and fill their position. Those messages stuck with me. Nowadays people go on about tactical innovation and all that kind of stuff but I was getting the benefit of that as a kid in the 1960s, we just didn't have fancy names for what we were doing. But those two lessons from my dad – about being as competitive as you possibly can and being willing to fill in for your team-mates – are as relevant now as they were then. I didn't realise it at the time but I was getting a good football education.

Think of the great players. If you kicked Kenny Dalglish when the ball was played into his feet, which I did more than once, he was as hard as nails. He wasn't looking to go down and win cheap free-kicks. He wanted to hold you off and use his strength and ability to get the better of you. The same went for George Best. Diego Maradona might have handballed it but if I'd been able to catch him – and that's a big if – he wouldn't have gone to ground.

I don't want to sound like an old man who's always going on about everything being better in his day but I look at how easily players go down in the modern game and it saddens me. It's not the game that I grew up playing.

People talk about players feeling contact and going down, and of players winning fouls, but what they're doing is cheating. It's a side of football and the way that the game has gone that I just can't identify with, and I think the only way to get rid of it is to hit players with bans when they're guilty of diving, or simulation as some call it. I love that the game's evolved but there are basics that we should all cherish, and one of those is that you try to stay on your feet. If I'd have gone over my dad would've battered me, and I mean battered me. I'm not advocating that but, as parents and as people who watch and love football, we should be doing everything we can to try and ensure that kids aren't going down as easily as some of the professionals do.

By the time I was playing for the school I thought I was the best in the team. There was a lad called Steven Speed who was a good player. Tommy Evans was another. I was playing for the year above and I was a June baby so I was the youngest by a distance, but I'd never let that put me off. My mum always tells me that I was running through people's legs with a ball when I was two or three so by the time I was in the school team I knew what I wanted to do with it. I also knew that the only thing I wanted to be was a footballer and our Mick has kept something that I wrote when I was nine, where I said that I was going to play for Liverpool and England. I only turned out to be half right but, even at that age, I knew exactly what I wanted to be.

I've always suffered for my art though. People think I only started picking up injuries when I became a professional, but I was finding weird and wonderful ways of hurting myself even when I was a kid. At St Aidan's our kit was Wolves gold. It looked great and we won the Dimmer Cup wearing that, beating St Luke's and St Dominic's, but I hadn't realised at first that the nylon shorts we had on were basically attacking my legs. The chafing was unbelievable but I played on, and when I came off at the end I had friction burns on my thighs and around my groin.

Thinking I knew the best way to treat them, I put talcum powder on the burns but they got infected and I was in agony. That was my career in medicine over before it had even started, and I had to leave it to the specialists to make them better. The only problem was it was a nurse who would come around to treat me and she had to put me into a hot bath. I know it won't have even entered her mind but as a young lad I was mortified, knowing that she'd be able to see everything, not that there was much to see. I was only 10 but I'd be in bits before she came around and all because of those stupid nylon shorts. That was my first injury and undoubtedly my most embarrassing – but it wouldn't be my last.

Another memory from my childhood was of the family going for a drink on a Sunday afternoon. There'd be murder when they got home and it was always over football. My dad was a Liverpudlian. Five of my mum's brothers were Evertonians and five were Reds, and it would go off. No one would give an inch or take a backward step. I'd be at home with my mum waiting for them all to come back, knowing that there would be fireworks when they did. You had to take a side, you couldn't be neutral or show any willingness to accept that the person you were arguing with might have a point. Colours had to be nailed to the mast – Red or Blue – and that didn't apply only to human beings; even the budgie, which belonged to Whacker, was called Dixie.

You were either a Blue or you were a Red and I was the latter.

When I was playing in the street I wanted to be Ian St John. I liked his name and I liked his aggression. My dad always used to tell me about Billy Liddell and no one else compared to him in his eyes but, for me, it was all about St John. I'd be recreating his winning goal in the 1965 FA Cup final, the first time that Liverpool had won the competition, and in my imagination I was him. Running with the ball, going past my mates, getting a chance and finishing it off; whatever I was doing, the commentator in my mind was saying: "And it's St John. He beats one man. He beats another. He shoots. St John scores for Liverpool."

The voice I heard was definitely Kenneth Wolstenholme's because, even now, I can close my eyes and hear him say "Sinjun" as if St John was all one word. I was the Sinjun of Wimbourne Road, a tenacious little nark who saw football as a game that had to be won. Talk about typecasting.

When I wasn't pretending to be my favourite footballer I'd be at home, but life was tough. I remember having custard without sugar because we didn't have any. I remember hiding behind the couch when the rent man knocked at the door, although Mum insists that never happened. But there were good times, too, like when Dad found a few bob in his coat pocket that he'd forgotten about and he went to the chippy, got fish and chips and woke us up for a late feast. I've been lucky enough to have some wonderful meals since then but not many have tasted as good as that.

We were a religious family. Like my dad, my mum was also from Irish Catholic stock and we would go to Mass on Sunday mornings. At one point, I had a test to become an altar boy at St Aidan's and we had to balance the bible on our heads, but mine fell off accidentally on purpose. Trust me, you didn't want to be seen wearing a smock around Huyton!

I ended up going to St Augustine's secondary modern school

because I also unluckily failed the 11-plus. If I'd passed I would have had to go to a school that didn't play football and that would have been a waste of time. I can't say I failed on purpose because I didn't, but my heart wasn't in it.

As was the case for many people from a similar background, football was my escape. But I also loved other sports, too. We'd go to the rugby club at Alt Park on Fridays in the summer. I wasn't a bad scrum-half but it was hard. I played for the town cricket team and I also played baseball for Liverpool. But in the main it was football. My first pair of boots had nailed-in studs with steel caps. The caseys were the brown leather ones with the lace in. Once they got wet they were so, so heavy. That's why it's a fallacy that we played the long ball in those days. You couldn't kick it that far!

We'd make goals wherever we could, whether that meant playing between a couple of lampposts, bins that had been left outside, a pillar box at one end and a coat on the other, you name it, we used it. We had to be resourceful because we weren't blessed with facilities. If needs be, someone would paint a goal on to the gable end of a house, anything so that we could have a proper competitive game. If enough of us had boots we'd play on the fields and that was always better, because it meant you could make slide tackles without taking the skin off your knees. Not that it mattered too much. If the ball was there to be won, you had to win it, no matter what kind of surface you were playing on.

Nowadays, if a young player shows promise he is whisked off to an academy and given the best of everything, whether it's boots, kit, pitches or even education. We had none of that but, against the odds, Huyton became an area synonymous with football. The only drawback was that it wasn't a natural finishing school, there were too many drawbacks for that. Whether it was the pull of local pubs like The Bluebell, The Quiet Man or The Eagle & Child, the attraction of girls or the potential to get drawn into things that you shouldn't, there was no shortage of temptations and distractions to drag even the most talented teenage footballer away from playing the game.

I was part of the Huyton Boys' team that won the English Schools Cup in 1971, a magnificent achievement and a fantastic side, which some claimed was the finest ever seen in junior football in this country. But a lot of my team-mates didn't make it, even though they had more than enough talent. I often ask myself why and I keep coming back to a story that Colin Harvey tells about seeing Wayne Rooney out with a gang of his mates when he should have been at home, and Colin pulled him the next day and asked him if he wanted to be a footballer. I don't think a lot of the lads who I played with ever got asked that kind of question, not by someone like Colin anyway.

They were good players, really good players. I went on the ale myself but it never stopped me from working my bollocks off in training. That might seem strange nowadays but that's the way it was. You could have a drink as long as it was at the right time. The attitude – and it was a good one – was that if you had a good dressing room then you had a chance of winning the game.

That worked for me but it didn't work for everyone, and the ones who fell by the wayside will have their regrets that things did not turn out differently. I think of them and the talent they had and I know they should have gone on to join the list of footballers to emerge from Huyton. As with other academies, not everyone was destined to make it but I was one of the lucky ones. Huyton had given me the perfect opportunity to develop my talent; after that, it was up to me to make the most of it.

# 3. ONCE A RED ALWAYS A BLUE

*'I look back now and I realise how lucky I was to have been part of that environment. Everything that was happening, every little thing that I was picking up then, was going to stand me in good stead for what followed. At the time you're just thinking, "It's great, this." You didn't even realise you were learning but you were'*

HAD my mum got her way I would have become an Evertonian long before I signed for them and finally saw the light. Being a Liverpudlian, my dad used to go to every home game at Anfield but my two grandads, five of my uncles and my mum were Blues, and they all wanted me to follow in their footsteps.

When my mum married my dad her own father said to her, "It's like a mixed marriage", and in a football sense it was. It meant I grew up with a choice of who to follow, but one that left me knowing that I'd upset one of them, depending on which way I went. My dad got in first by taking me to the game and that made my mind up. Not that nailing my colours to the mast stopped my mum showing hers: if anything, it made her worse.

There was a famous FA Cup tie in 1967 that was watched by over 100,000 people: 65,000 at Goodison Park, and another 40,000 watching the game on a big screen at Anfield, and it was decided in Everton's favour when Alan Ball smashed the winner right into the top corner. I vividly remember thinking, 'I hate you, Mum' because her team had beaten mine. Little did I know that I'd end up sharing her passion for Everton.

My dad used to take me on The Kop. I'd take a wooden stool and stand on it so I could see, and my first game was Alan Ball's Blackpool debut at the start of the 1962/63 season. For some reason we went in the Kemlyn Road for this game, probably because Dad thought I'd be too small to see past the big lads on The Kop. It was also Liverpool's first game back in the First Division for eight years after being relegated in 1954 so it was a huge occasion, especially with Bill Shankly in charge, and there was a definite sense that anything was possible with him as manager. It wasn't going to be an easy start to life back in the big time though and Liverpool lost 2-1 on a blazing hot day.

Obviously I was only a kid so Ball didn't mean anything to me then, other than being the 17-year-old lad whose bright orange hair matched his team's kit, but looking back I was lucky enough to see one of the greatest players of all time, and someone who would later become a great friend, play his very first game. Things like that mean a lot to me. It was similar when I went to Bolton and Roger Hunt and Peter Thompson, two of my biggest boyhood heroes, were there. It doesn't get any better than that.

Going to Anfield became a ritual. It wasn't like it is now in that it was possible for working-class men like my dad to take their kids to the match, without needing a small fortune to get in. We used to stop at a pub in West Derby on the way to the match and I'd have a bottle of pop and a packet of crisps while my dad and his mates had a hevvy

When I was a bit older, there were certain games when we used to get the bus from Huyton to Old Swan, where we got a special football bus to the ground. Then, when I went with my mates, we used to get over the wall of The Quiet Man to steal the empty bottles, and take them to the off-licence to get the deposit back on them. That was how we got the money to pay for our bus fare and to get in the match. It wasn't long before we got sussed doing that, though, and then we had to hitch a lift to Anfield.

We had to get to the ground early because the queues were massive, so we'd get fish and chips and wait until the gates opened a couple of hours before kick-off. It was heaven. Standing there, eating a chippy dinner knowing it wouldn't be long before you saw Shankly's Liverpool. As a kid, those were my best days.

I was in the boys' pen at Goodison when Sandy Brown scored his famous own goal in December 1969. I was also at the Anfield derby nearly a year later when Everton were 2-0 up and Liverpool came back to win 3-2, with Chris Lawler scoring a late winner. Now it's all corporate and we know about the importance of safety but I loved being in crowds then. We would stand up and sway but I never felt in any danger. It really was fantastic.

I've got to be honest, I felt like I hated Everton then. It wasn't a real hate, it was how a kid hates someone or something. They were simply the wrong club, the wrong team and they wore the wrong colours. Liverpool were the only team for me and it was the same for my dad, who was a really rabid Red.

Fast forward 15 years and I went on *A Question Of Sport*, the BBC television quiz show. They showed an old picture of me with my dad and we were holding a red scarf. I was mortified. I didn't hate Liverpool then and I don't now but I have an irresistible sense that they are the *other* team, not my team. I couldn't have imagined that as a kid but it's the way things have turned out and I wouldn't change that for the world. I might have been the boy who would walk to Melwood with dreams of getting Tommy Smith's autograph, but as a man I would have walked over broken glass if it meant getting a win against Liverpool. When people talk about the zeal of the convert I know exactly what they mean because I have felt it, and I still feel it to this day. Once a Red, now always a Blue. My mum had been right all along.

The irony is that it was my love for football which would take me away from Liverpool. From the moment I started playing for my school, it set in motion a chain of events that would lead to me changing my allegiance by taking me into the arms of Everton. That journey began with me being selected to play for the Huyton Boys' team, a side that won national acclaim and which put me on the path to becoming a professional footballer.

I was playing for St Augustine's against other local schools like St Aloysius, St Dominic's and Seel Road, and the teachers who were in charge of the Huyton team were able to run the rule over me and the other young lads, before selecting a group of players that would represent the town against other teams from across the country. Getting into the squad was the hard thing but when I was 13 I was invited to train with them, and that was a massive achievement for me at that point.

I was close but I still wasn't in the team, so me and the rest of the new lads would go and watch Huyton Boys play at the King George V playing fields on a pitch at the top that we called Wembley. Our aim was to play on that pitch because it was magnificent, but a lot of the lads went even further than that ambition because most went on to sign for professional clubs.

But, at the outset, that was our dream – to be considered good enough to grace Wembley. There were no Twin Towers but, locally, that field was the pinnacle for a young footballer. I used to go to sleep dreaming of playing there but, for that to happen, I had to convince the coaches that I was ready.

Eddie Kilshaw, an ex-professional footballer who'd had a great career at Sheffield Wednesday and Bury before seeing his career cut short by injury, was central to the process of transforming us from hopeful youngsters into fully-fledged players. So was Alan Bleasdale, who went on to have an even more renowned career, just not in football. They would pick the squad after speaking to other teachers, and the team would sort itself out from there.

Luckily, I was one of the players they both liked and I got in. What helped in the year I made the breakthrough was that it was the first time we'd been able to pick lads from Prescot Grammar and that made a big difference, because they had some really good players. On top of that, Frank Pimblett, who went on to play for Aston Villa, came into the side late and, like the other new additions, he was the icing on the cake.

Alan was a teacher at St Columba's. He was only a young man, and the best thing about the way he approached things was that he didn't try to blind us with science. He recognised that we had ability and that we knew what we were about, so he just told us to go out and play. That approach has always been a bit undervalued because coaches might want to make a name for themselves by showing what they could do, but he gave the responsibility to us and, with that particular set of lads, that was the right thing to do.

What he recognised was if he gave us basic guidance and encouragement at the right times then we would more often than not find a way to win. That's good management. He knew his players and he knew how to get the best out of them. That even extended to training, which all of us looked forward to, because it was so enjoyable. We'd do a warm-up, some basic skills games and then play. Simple but effective.

It was also clever because it allowed us to mix and, seeing as we were all coming from rival schools who'd usually kick hell out of one another, it was a good way of breaking down any barriers that might have been built up. Some of those games were more like battles, especially when our school, St Augustine's, which was Catholic, played Huyton Hey, which was Protestant, so it was important that any bad blood wasn't carried over when we met up. By making training as enjoyable and uncomplicated as they could, Alan and Eddie made sure that lads who might not have been on the best of terms at other times, got on like a house on fire when we were all together.

The game when I thought something big was happening with Huyton Boys was when we played Derby Boys in the English Schools Trophy in the 1970/71 season. The game was played on the pitch at Huntley and Palmer's biscuit factory on Wilson Road, and it was absolutely mobbed. There was a real fervour surrounding the tie. We were only a gang of kids but we had the backing of hundreds of people who were all desperate for us to do well, not just for ourselves but also for the town.

That was probably the first time that I realised what it is to play for other people, and the sense of pride and responsibility that gives you. When you first start playing you're just doing it for yourself because you want to show how good you are but, when you have people that you don't even know cheering every tackle you make and giving you all their backing, that's a really powerful thing. I'd seen it at first hand at Anfield, where Shankly had the supporters so wound up that they would sometimes power Liverpool to victory just through sheer emotion, but I'd never experienced what it was like to be on the receiving end of that kind of support. It was absolutely wonderful.

It was a horrible day, the rain was lashing down and the wind was blowing a gale. They were big favourites, mainly because they had a lad called Steve Powell, the England schoolboys' captain, playing for them. We were on a hiding to nothing but, with the group of lads we had and the backing we were receiving, none of that mattered. We were playing for ourselves, for our families and for our town, and it showed in everything that we did.

In front of the local media, we put on a proper team display. To a man, we worked ourselves into the ground and managed to win 1-0. That was one of those results that made the rest of the country take notice because Derby had been one of the favourites to win the competition. Powell was a great player though and shortly after that game he made his first-team debut for Brian Clough's Derby County at the age of 16, going on to win two league titles and play over 350 times for them. But on the day our team was better than his and we went on to the next round.

After that, the buzz in the town grew. I'd be walking down the street and strangers would be shaking my hand, patting me on the back and wishing me all the best for the next round. That's how much it captured everyone's attention. The feeling was that we had a real chance of winning it.

I was always learning at that stage. I was learning how to play competitive football in a team, that you only ever get out what you put in, and how much the game means to people. But the biggest lesson came when I went to Morecambe for a training break because that was the first time I'd been away with a team, and I realised how important that was for team spirit.

We were all up there together with no other mates or family around and the bonds that developed made a real difference.

I was only 14 years old but I was experiencing what a team competition is, and how it can bring players together. That made a real impression on me, and it was something that I would use later when I became a manager because I'd seen at first hand what a positive effect it could have.

The semi-final was huge. It was at Anfield. For me, a big Liverpudlian, it was better than playing at the real Wembley. In the quarter-finals we'd been away to North Kent and beaten them 4-1, which was a massive result because everyone was expecting them to win, but we went down there and turned them over. That was a great trip. It must have taken five or six hours getting down there on the coach on the day of the game but that was no hardship, because it allowed us all to have a laugh.

We knew North Kent were favourites and so did they but Eddie and Alan had an ace up their sleeve. Before the game they told us that if we got through, the semi-final would be at Anfield or Goodison Park. How could we lose? Here we were, a gang of lads from Huyton, a mix of Liverpudlians and Evertonians, but no matter who we supported, all of us knew how big it would be to have a game at one of the two great Merseyside stadiums. So we went out and turned it on. Some of the football we played was magnificent, and one of the main reasons was that one of the greatest carrots you could ever wish for as a young player from Liverpool had been dangled.

The day of the semi-final against Barking was the biggest of my life to that point. Forget Holy Communions and weddings, as a teenage lad this was the stuff that dreams were made of. Again, in the days leading up to the game you couldn't walk down the street without people stopping you to shake your hand and wish you well. It was the same for all of the lads, and it made us realise how important it was to everyone in the town.

You can't prepare yourself for something like that, though. I walked into the ground, the same place where I'd stood on a stool on The Kop to watch Liverpool play, and that was when it really hit me, that I was going to play there myself. The excitement was huge but so was the pressure. What if I play badly? What if I let the team down? Doing that on a playing field in Huyton would be bad enough, but you'd struggle to live with yourself if you failed to perform at a venue like Anfield.

I can't over-emphasise this, it really was intimidating. Everything about the place was massive, or that's how it seemed to us kids. The home dressing room, the place where my heroes got changed on a matchday, wasn't made for boys, it was built for men. We walked out on to the pitch before the game and I tried to touch the This Is Anfield sign in the tunnel but I couldn't reach. Then, when I walked out on to the hallowed turf, I looked up at the stands and at The Kop and another wave hit me – there were thousands there. I'd expected a few hundred to turn up but this was a proper crowd. It was just like a dream.

The only question then was how we would cope with the pressure. Imagine how we would have felt if we'd lost. There can be a thin line between being inspired and being intimidated and, at that age, when you've never experienced anything like it previously, it's probably as thin as it can be. The teachers realised this and, again, they recognised that this was a time to keep things simple and to remind us of how good we were. We had so much going on in our minds anyway with the stadium, the crowd and the chance of reaching a national final, that if they'd tried to be tactical or asked us to do anything differently, the message almost certainly would have got lost. So before kick-off they built us up, tried to take away at least some of the nerves that we all had, and then reminded us of how big an opportunity this was for all of us to go and show our talent. It was all about getting us focused on the game, rather than the occasion.

Eddie Kilshaw was clever. "You're playing at Huntley and Palmers, lads," he told us, reminding us that this was a day for playing as we always did, rather than focusing on the fact we were playing at Anfield. I didn't realise but this was good psychology. Eddie was brilliant for me. He was the older, shrewd one, the wise old head. He had bow legs like I've got now and you'd notice things like that as a kid, but as soon as he started talking he had your attention because he was one of those rare people who is brilliant at giving you the benefit of their experience. Alan was the younger, enthusiastic one, so as a pair they were ideal.

I look back now and I realise how lucky I was to have been part of that environment. Everything that was happening, every little thing that I was picking up then, was going to stand me in good stead for what followed. At the time you're just thinking, 'It's great, this.' You didn't even realise you were learning but you were.

Barking had a lad called Richie Powling, who went on to play for Arsenal, you could tell he was a good player, and another called Brian Bason, who later played for Chelsea. They were a good team and it was a tough game but we nicked it 1-0. There were around 10,000 people there for what was basically a kids' game and my abiding memory is of the noise they made. Playing in that atmosphere was totally new to me but, having experienced it once, I knew it was something I wanted to experience again and again. Luckily, I didn't have long to wait because although the final against Stoke Boys was over two legs and the first game was away, the second was to take place at Goodison Park. Another carrot had been dangled.

I wouldn't say the second leg was an anti-climax, because the venue meant it couldn't be anything but a special occasion, but some of the edge had been taken away by the result of the first leg, which we'd won 4-1 at Stoke's old Victoria Ground. That was another brilliant stadium and we graced it. As we were the visitors we were given the away dressing room, which would later be the scene of one of the most inspirational moments of my professional career with Everton, but on the day of the final it was about Huyton, and winning the cup for the first time.

There was always going to be a bit of tension because it was such a big occasion, and someone came up with the idea of having dinner at Trentham Gardens, a sprawling estate on the outskirts of Stoke-on-Trent. Someone told me that it had once been the site of an Augustinian priory, which I took as a good omen as a St Augustine's boy, but some of the other lads were busy taking other things. When we sat down to eat we saw there were four forks, four knives and four spoons, and we all looked at one another, thinking, 'What the fuck do we do with all these?'

There weren't four of each left by the end of the meal, though, and the game was given away afterwards when one of the teachers got on to the coach and said, "Come on, where's all the knives and forks?" All you could hear was the sound of cutlery falling out of pockets on to the floor. We hadn't won the trophy yet but we'd already got more than our fair share of silverware.

We had to give it all back, obviously, but having got one hand on the trophy in the first leg there was no way we were going to be releasing our grip on that. In my own mind we'd already won it. It's one of those things that you could never – and would never – say as a player, but my thoughts were already on what it would feel like when the final whistle went and we'd be dancing on the pitch at Goodison. I'd built it up so much that I just wanted to get the game out of the way. That's not like me because I absolutely love playing, but this was about being a winner.

It was about being able to look my dad in the eye and we'd both know that all the times he'd lectured me about the importance of winning had brought out the best in me. It was about being part of a team that had created history. But most of all it was about Huyton showing the rest of English football that we were a force to be reckoned with. There was so much motivation to succeed that winning became all that mattered. How I played, or how the team played, was irrelevant. It was just a case of winning and collecting the rewards. The excitement was unbelievable, local and national newspapers were all over it and if we'd got carried away by all of the attention we would have felt like local celebrities, but we were in 'get-the-job-done' mode.

At the time, Goodison was enemy territory for me but it was still revered. I'd been there before for derby games, but to walk in there as a young player was huge. Everyone builds up rivalries and we all stick up for our own side but how could anyone fail to be impressed by a place that was, at that time, home to the reigning champions, one of the most celebrated English teams of all time? This was the Everton of the Holy Trinity, Howard Kendall, Alan Ball and Colin Harvey, three players who would go on to have a massive influence on me and my career. I didn't need anyone to tell me how good that Everton side was.

My mate in school, Richie Harrison, was a massive Evertonian and he was always going on about the Holy Trinity, and there I was playing at their home ground. Whatever your allegiance, it doesn't get much better than that. The city of Liverpool had seemed like the centre of the world when I was growing up, whether that was through football or music, and Everton were a big part of that. I just hadn't fallen for their charms yet.

Before kick-off I sat in the dressing room just soaking it all in, and someone handed me the match programme that included pen portraits of the players from both teams. Obviously the first name I looked for was my own, and what I read gave me a confidence boost at exactly the right time. 'Peter Reid: Right-half. There isn't much of Peter but what there is can be described in two words – sheer class,' it said. 'Together with Frank Pimblett, he sews up midfield with precision ball play and hard work. Always wins more tackles than he loses. County trialist.'

Two words in particular stood out – 'sheer class.' I knew I could play because I wouldn't have been in the line-up of one of the best schoolboy teams in the country otherwise, but that description was a huge compliment. This was the biggest game of my life to that point and even the programme was filling me with belief.

Alan was keeping an eye on us all, though, and he had recognised that there was a risk of complacency setting in because we were all but home and hosed. He reminded us that we needed to win not just the tie, but the game itself. We did just that, 1-0 in the second leg, and we were always in full control. It was the first time I'd been a winner at Goodison but it wouldn't be the last.

Which member of that team went on to have the greatest career? Easy. Alan Bleasdale. After coaching us, he became one of the greatest television writers this country has ever produced. *Scully*, *Boys From The Blackstuff*, *The Monocled Mutineer*, *GBH*; he was responsible for writing all of them, and the numerous awards and plaudits he won are testament to his incredible talent. Which makes it all the more precious to me and the other lads from that Huyton Boys team that whenever Alan is interviewed, he makes a point of saying how special it was for him to manage us when we won the English Schools Trophy.

"Those boys were described by the football correspondent of the *Daily Express* as the greatest school football team that ever lived," he revealed to a national newspaper. "They were just astonishing.

And that's probably what I feel proudest of – because I didn't do it for myself."

In another interview, he was even more fulsome in his praise: "I have often said that anything I've done since doesn't stand comparison with that," he said. "The most enjoyable thing I have ever done as a teacher or writer was to run that team. I could wax poetic about Peter. Quite honestly, Peter Reid was the personification of everything worthwhile in schoolboy football. Peter was quite brilliant and stood out even then. Ten of that team were actually signed on by League clubs but only Peter made it.

"I think the reason was because he applied himself more than anyone else. He had great skill and application and tremendous heart. He really was an exceptional boy, never mind footballer. He was a bit skinny then, like a matchstick, which is why I think he never got international honours as a schoolboy. He looked as if a puff of wind would blow him down but he started to fill out when he went to Bolton."

Compliments don't come any higher than that. The man who created *Boys From The Blackstuff* admired us because we were boys with the right stuff.

# 4. GROWING UP AND GROWING PAINS

*"'You were going to be a good player," he said, in an attempt to be affectionate, but his words finished me off. I kept hearing them over and over again in my head. "Going to be." Not "will be," not "could still be," and not even "might be"'*

THE Bolton Wanderers dressing room was where I did most of my growing up. It was a brutal place and if you weren't ready for it, or you couldn't handle it, you'd soon be found out.

I'd ended up there partly because Huyton Boys had been so successful. From my performances I'd been able to get into the England schoolboys team, and had been invited for trials at several clubs. I went to Hull City, who wanted to sign me, to Stoke City, and I trained with Man United, Everton and Liverpool.

I wasn't afraid of going to a big club but two things swayed my decision in favour of Bolton. The first was that they were also going to take Tommy Evans, who was my big mate. The second was that I saw them as a club where I would have the best possible chance of making a mark. I didn't want to go somewhere, make progress in the youth set-up and then find that there was no way into the first team. I wanted a clear pathway and that meant I had to join a club that would offer me a route through the ranks, and then it would be up to me to prove that I was good enough.

My mind was made up when I was watching *The Big Match* with Gerald Sindstadt one Friday evening and there was a feature about the number of homegrown players who had graduated to the first team. That was enough for me and I finished school on a Friday in mid-July at the age of 15, in 1971, and started at Bolton on the Monday morning.

Everything about that environment was a test of character. In my case, it started with an initiation which involved giving a song, while everyone else lashed stuff at me. I chose *Band Of Gold* by Freda Payne, which had been a big hit but no sooner had I belted out, "Now that you're gone, all that's left is a band of gold," a football boot whistled past my ear. That was followed by socks, jockstraps, shorts, tops, anything the lads could get their hands on came my way. It was like being a coconut in a coconut shy. That wasn't the worst of it, though.

Once I'd done my turn, I was held down while they blackened my bollocks with boot polish. Something like that wouldn't happen today but it was the norm then. It was all very Darwinian because only the fittest would survive, and that meant surviving an aerial bombardment and an attack on the short and curlies. Thankfully, I came through it, and lived to fight another day. Although things became easier, the dressing room was never a place you could relax, you always had to have your wits about you.

When I joined I was also signing for a club with a World Cup winner on their books – and a Liverpool hero as well. I know Roger Hunt well now and he is such a gentleman. I actually can't put into words how much of a gentleman he is and always has been. This is one of *the* icons of English football, who played in the '66 final against West Germany, and yet he is still as humble as anyone that you could ever meet.

He didn't have to do anything for me during those early days because I would have still adored him no matter what, but he was never anything but superb with me. As a young Scouser making his first tentative steps into the world of professional football that meant so much.

He was lean but he had big veins in his calves and I'd be clocking his legs bulge when we were doing sprints on the shale track at Burnden Park. He had short strides but every one mattered and with each step his calves would seem to grow a bit more. This was all about physical dedication and getting himself in the best possible condition and he rammed that point home. "It's all about hard work," he said to me. "You have got to be dedicated."

I knew that already because just watching him train was enough but his words reinforced what I was seeing; this was the standard that I had to aspire to. I was skilful and I knew that I could play but when someone of that stature underlines the old adage about talent being nothing without hard work, it really hits home.

I'm not ashamed to say that I would hang on his every word, especially as Roger was one of those people who didn't talk for the sake of it. I asked him about winning the World Cup once and he just said it was like a dream, there was no embellishment and no attempt to talk up his own role in England's greatest triumph, he just left me with the impression that he felt fortunate to have been able to play his part. That wasn't the way I saw it. Roger was one of my heroes and, for me, England had been as lucky to have him as they had been to have him.

We would clean the players' boots and I would fight with Tommy to be able to do Roger's. Just getting my hands on them was special so I was in raptures when he actually gave me a pair. They were white, which was the style at the time, and Roger signed them for me. It was like being given untold riches. I took them home, kept them and looked after them but somewhere along the way they went missing, which I still kick myself about every time I think about it. They would be worth a fortune today but I would never have sold them because their value was much greater than any financial return.

Thankfully, I never lost the most precious thing that he gave me – the benefit of his experience. That stood me in good stead for my career. I can't speak highly enough of him. When you meet your heroes and you're not disappointed, it's a great feeling.

I didn't realise that my chances of breaking into the first team were being stalled by my diet – or lack of. The lads in the dressing room weren't shy about letting me know and after one comment too many I decided to have it out with the manager, Ian Greaves. I stormed straight into his office – a big mistake. "What the fuck do you want? Go back outside and knock before you enter," he ordered me. I did as he said and went back in, with my tail between my legs. Even worse, he confirmed pretty much what was being said – that I needed to start living like a professional, and that would start with shifting some timber.

I took the message on board and finally convinced Greavsey to give me a chance, making my debut as a sub against Orient in October 1974, with my first start coming at Hull City the following week. Greavsey pulled me out again, but a month later he put me back in – and I stayed in. That first season, playing alongside Big Sam Allardyce, Gary Jones, John Ritson, Warwick Rimmer and the rest was great, but what made it even better was that the system and the personnel that it exposed me to was like a dream come true for a young player. We played a 4-3-3 and, as a midfielder who was just starting to make his way in the game, I needed a good winger in front and a good left-back behind.

As it turned out, I couldn't have asked for any better because my full-back was Tony Dunne and my winger was Peter Thompson. You don't need any more coaching when you're learning from players like that. How could I not learn from players who'd honed their talents under Sir Matt Busby and Bill Shankly? 'This will do me' I thought, and I was determined to soak up every bit of information they gave. I would listen to whatever they said, watch their movements and soak it all up in the knowledge that, in terms of my own development, this was absolute gold.

One early match experience that stands out involves Big Sam, and a game when we got told not to pass to him. We were a possession-based team and were at home to Bristol City when Greavesy told us to miss Sam out when we had the ball. We were knocking it around but, in keeping with orders, it never went back to Sam. I could see him getting increasingly wound up and eventually he snapped. "Any chance of me getting a fucking pass," he shouted, and Roy Greaves turned around and said: "The manager's told us not to pass to you." Sam's face was a picture. There was no way that I would have told him. I'm not that brave.

I loved playing in front of Sam anyway. He was one of those uncompromising defenders who would take everything, as I discovered to my cost on more than one occasion. The worst thing you could do was ask why he hadn't won a ball. I did it once after I tried to head a long kick back towards where it had come from, only to get a slight touch off the back of my head because it was too high. I turned around and had a go at Sam for not dealing with it and it was like a red rag to a Bolton bull, as though I had questioned his masculinity. Soon after we were faced with a similar situation – and this time the outcome was very different.

As the ball dropped in between us I could hear the sound of his boots, which looked as though they'd been made at Cammell Laird, thundering behind me. I flinched because I knew what was about to happen but nothing could have prepared me for the impact. Sam hit me, hit the lad who I was supposed to be challenging, won the ball and left us both in a heap. It was the last time that I ever asked him why he hadn't come for a long ball.

Sam looked like a doorman, the kind who would turn you away for having your hair too short one week, and tell you that you couldn't come in a few weeks later because he didn't like hippies, but in some ways his appearance was deceptive. He could look after himself but he was also a great thinker on the game. From the word go, it was obvious that he didn't just want to play football, he was determined to learn and understand it.

He was only 28 when he went out to the USA to play for Tampa Bay Rowdies and it was while he was there that he became interested in the kind of sports science developments that he would later use to great effect as a manager. The best thing from my point of view, apart from seeing a great mate and a great professional go on to have a brilliant career in management, is that I'm still benefiting from his vision. The state-of-the-art training complex that he pioneered at Bolton is now home to Wigan, who gave me a job in the summer of 2017, and I get to enjoy the magnificent facilities every day. That's the least I deserve for him running me over on the pitch and leaving me in a heap!

During my early years with Bolton I quickly realised that when you don't have experience in your team, you have to make as much use as you can of those who do. In that respect, I was blessed to come in when I did. Greavesy was brilliant, too, because there are some managers whose egos prevent them from getting experienced players in because they're worried about their own authority, but he was the opposite. Realising he had a lot of young talent, the manager set about giving us the best chance of fulfilling our potential by bringing in another couple of pros who were proven at the highest level when he brought in Willie Morgan from Burnley, another former United player who'd worked under Busby, and the incomparable Frank Worthington.

I was only 21 when we signed Frank from Leicester City and early on Greavesy pulled me to one side and told me he wanted me to look after him. I had read all of the newspaper stories and been fascinated because, as a character, Frank was a one-off. While I enjoyed a night out I wasn't sure that I had what it took to be his sidekick, never mind keep him in check so that he would be in the best possible nick for training and games.

Like a lot of people, I was guilty of being taken in by his reputation and for all of the countless things that have been said and written about him, the reality was that Frank wasn't much of a drinker. We went out for a few meals and had a couple of nights out but while he was a party animal and young ladies found him attractive, he wasn't the type to drink until he could drink no more. Usually, he was the last off the training ground.

As a player, he was up there with any who I played alongside. He could pluck balls out of the sky with the deftest touch, come up with pieces of skill that took your breath away. Whatever he lacked in pace he more than made up for with skill and ingenuity.

On and off the pitch, he was flamboyant and charismatic in a cool way and, like me, he had a love for Elvis Presley, which helped us to hit it off. We even went to an Elvis convention in

Blackpool with Willie once. They both had long hair and could carry the look off but this little five foot seven inch Scouser looked more like Elvis's smaller and less talented brother. I had no chance in that company.

Greavesy was building a really good team around emerging and proven talent. For two years we were a real force but the problem was that the Second Division was a tough place to get out of. It might not have been the top flight but there was some incredible talent. Apart from our own team, there was Laurie Cunningham at Leyton Orient, Paul Mariner at Plymouth, Viv Anderson at Nottingham Forest, Ray Wilkins at Chelsea and Bobby Moore and George Best at Fulham. Look at the PFA Second Division Team of the Year for 1977/78; the midfield was Glenn Hoddle, Alan Ball and me! What company that is to be in.

I'd actually won the first of my six England Under-21 caps alongside Laurie, against Scotland in a friendly at Bramall Lane in April 1977. The first black player to play for England at any level, he scored the winner in a 1-0 win – and was sensational.

Despite how competitive it was, we came close to winning promotion on two occasions before we finally made it to the promised land of Division One. The second near miss underlined just how much quality we were up against, and also how well we were doing to compete. It was Brian Clough's Forest who pipped us by a point on the final day of the 1976/77 season to win the third and final promotion place, and leave us devastated.

What made it even worse is that we had our fate in our own hands with two matches remaining and Forest knew that we were favourites to finish third ahead of them. Wolves beat us at home and then we could only draw 2-2 at Bristol Rovers and our chance was gone. I can still feel the pain now because there's not many things worse in football than working your bollocks off, from August to May, only to miss out in a photo finish. I can say that without fear of contradiction, having suffered a similar fate with Everton less than a decade later.

Forest had beaten us by a short head but there was no shame in that because they were on the verge of something special; the following season they won the league, before going on to win the European Cup twice. Cloughie was a genius, a one-off, but Bolton could have stopped one of English football's great success stories in its tracks. Without our late implosion maybe the Forest miracle wouldn't have happened, although looking back maybe it wasn't all negative because they stopped Liverpool from winning another couple of trophies, and that's never a bad thing. Not that there was any consolation at the time, I was absolutely devastated.

We used our frustration at missing out to fuel us throughout the following season. It was a four-horse race between Southampton, Spurs, Brighton and ourselves, and this time it was us who got to the finishing line first. Forest might have been conquering the country but we had overcome our demons. We were able to celebrate at the Playmate Club in Bolton after winning 1-0 at Blackburn on the Wednesday to confirm promotion. Three days later, the final game of the season, we picked up the point we needed at home to Fulham to ensure that, this time, we were the ones who went up as champions.

The tone had been set on the opening day of the season when Roy Greaves' header gave us a hard-earned victory at Burnley and that told us that, mentally, we had recovered from the heartache that we had suffered just a few months earlier. We still had another major psychological obstacle to overcome, though, because Bolton hadn't been in the top flight for 15 years, so we had to prove we were ready to take the club back there. When we achieved that aim the overwhelming feeling was of relief. It goes without saying that there was joy and the celebrations lasted long into the night, but I just remember thinking, 'Thank God we've made it this time' because if we'd have missed out again, the psychological blow might have been too big to recover from.

We went up as a team but I'd already had chances to play in the First Division, not that I was aware of all of them. One opportunity I definitely knew about came when I was tapped up by Queens Park Rangers. They made it be known that they wanted to sign me and, at the time, they were a really good side, having only missed out on being crowned champions on the final day of the 1976/77 season when Liverpool won at Wolves, but there was no chance of me going there. It wasn't that I wouldn't have been interested but at that time the clubs held most – if not all – of the cards. If they didn't want you to go then you didn't.

It's very different now, with players forcing clubs to let them leave and agents getting up to all kinds of tricks in the media but, back then, players didn't call any of the shots. I know now that Bolton received a number of other approaches for me but they never told me about them, and that's just the way it was.

After QPR's interest came and went, I didn't let it get to me, I just knuckled down and it was at the end of that season that we won promotion. I wouldn't have missed being a part of that for the world. To be in a team that lifts an entire town is special, especially as Bolton had given me my chance. I was grateful and determined to repay the club and supporters for everything they had done for me. Helping them get back into the top flight wasn't a bad way of doing that.

I was improving with every game and the year we went up I scored nine goals, which isn't a bad tally. There was one that I enjoyed in particular when I scored against Brighton after playing a one-two with Frank Worthington. I loved that one because it showed what I could do when working with a top player, which Frank unquestionably was, and there were others in the team as well which was why we were able to win promotion.

After we went up, the manager looked to strengthen again, bringing in Len Cantello from West Brom and Dave Clement from QPR. You could see what Greavesy was trying to do, he was looking to build on the quality and the experience that we already had because he knew we were going to be tested, having gone up a level. We had no fears – I certainly didn't – and I was going to go into every game looking to prove myself because I was desperate to show that I belonged in the First Division. There was no point in getting there and sinking without trace, this was going to be like being a kid in Huyton again, having to prove that I could mix it with the big lads.

It doesn't matter what level you're at, you always have to earn the right to play but I'd done that since I was in reception class so it wasn't a challenge that put me off. Mentally, I was ready and physically prepared, or so I thought. That pre-season we entered the Anglo-Scottish Cup and were drawn against Sheffield United. The game was competitive but not overly so and, even though both teams wanted to win, our priority was to get some fitness in the bank ahead of another long, hard season. I was feeling good and then, out of the blue, a lad called Tony Kenworthy caught me on the knee and I knew straight away that I had a problem, although I had no idea how bad it would turn out to be.

Our physio, Jim Headridge, had a good look at it and decided to send me to a specialist who looked after the Manchester United players. My left knee was swollen and there was a fair bit of pain and discomfort but the specialist took out some fluid, which was mainly blood, and told me to rest for two weeks before starting jogging again. I'd had a right result because, by the way it was feeling, I'd been worried that I could be out for a lot longer than that but the big needle had done the trick, or so I thought.

Two weeks later it was still painful but I just thought that was normal because I hadn't had any injuries of that kind up to that point. So I started jogging again in the expectation that it would take a few days before the stiffness and inflammation died down, and then I'd be back playing. It didn't turn out that way though. Every step I took, my knee felt a little bit worse than it did on the previous one. I had expected discomfort but this was bordering on being unbearable. If I hadn't been brought up the way I had, not wanting to show anyone when I was in pain, I would have pulled up long before I did. I kept going until I could take no more and then stopped. I was in agony. "There's no way this is right", I said to Jim. "There's something wrong here."

Realising I wasn't the type to struggle unless there was a genuine problem, Jim took me to see another specialist called Mr Winston, who was based on Chorley New Road in Bolton. He X-rayed me and when he saw the scans he looked at me, and told me I'd broken my kneecap! I nearly fell off the bed in shock because, only a day or two earlier, I'd been trying to run around the training ground with my knee in bits. Mr Winston put me in plaster and that was me out of football for a few months.

At a time when I should have been taking my first steps in the First Division, I was struggling to walk around the house. It was a huge blow. I was only 22 but when you've worked so hard to get to the big stage it is demoralising to have it taken away, but all I could do was get my head down, recover and then work my way back to full fitness, while the rest of the lads were playing against Liverpool, Everton, Arsenal, Nottingham Forest and the rest.

Because I was young and hadn't had any real problems previously, I came back fairly quickly and, by October, I was ready to play again. I had a few games, felt alright, and we beat Man United 3-0 three days before Christmas 1978, which was one of those results that clubs like Bolton long for because they show that you are able to go toe-to-toe with the big boys. As Christmas presents go, they don't come much better. I was fit again, the team was winning and we had given ourselves a great chance of staying up, which was our objective no matter what Forest had done after winning promotion 12 months earlier.

As much as we believed in ourselves and as much as we knew we were an improving side, we weren't daft enough to start thinking that we were about to go winning league titles and European Cups. There was also a realisation that fate could intervene at any point and, if it did, then we would really find out whether or not we were good enough to stay up. Little did I know that when fate did intervene, I would be its victim.

New Year is supposed to be a time of new beginnings and fresh promise but, for me, the opening day of 1979 ended with me in a hospital bed with my career in the balance, and all because of a challenge on a snow-bound pitch in a game that perhaps shouldn't have been played. We were due to face Everton but when I woke up that morning it was obvious the game would be in doubt. It might have looked like a scene from Winter Wonderland but while it was great for riding sledges down hills and having snowball fights, it was less than ideal for football.

In the build-up to kick-off the news kept changing; first the game was on, then it was off, and then it was back on again. As a player, you hate that kind of uncertainty because that is the time when you're getting yourself in the right frame of mind to play. You don't want any doubts or distractions creeping in, you just want to get ready and get out there.

Finally, we were told that the game was on and we went out to warm up. The problem was we were wearing white tracksuits, and we literally couldn't pick each other out in the snow. It was as if we were all camouflaged. That would have been difficult enough for our opponents but it would have been an absolute nightmare for us, so the decision was taken for us to play in our red away kit rather than wearing our white home jerseys.

Everything was wrong. The weather was wrong. The build-up was wrong. Even our kit was wrong. But we went out to play, believing that we could beat Everton, even though they were a strong side at the time. The referee, Trelford Mills, blew the whistle to start the game and we went at each other in six inches of snow. It was never going to be a classic in those conditions but at least the fans could see us, and we could see each other.

As it turned out, for me red spelled danger. If I developed an aversion to that hue later in my career, that was the day when I realised that it wasn't my lucky colour. The game was ultimately abandoned at half-time with the score at 1-1 but it is remembered only for the incident in which I suffered a serious knee injury in a challenge with George Wood, the Everton goalkeeper. I slid in for a ball at the Railway Embankment End and tried to stop myself but George came hurtling out at me, and the next thing I knew I was in a crumpled heap on the floor.

I don't know whether shock kicked in straight away but I wasn't able to move. To this day, I still don't know how I got off the pitch, whether I was carried off or crawled off. I was put into an ambulance, which couldn't get out of the car park for what seemed like an eternity, and with every passing second my pain increased. By the time we reached A&E I was in absolute agony.

I'd had pain before but this was on another level to anything I'd experienced. I was put in plaster and given painkillers, but I didn't sleep a wink that night. I just lay in my hospital bed wondering if it was all over. I was in a haze, as much because of the lack of sleep and my state of mind due to the medication. It turned into one of the longest nights of my life. All I could do was wait to find out how bad the damage was.

The diagnosis came the following morning after scans revealed that I'd snapped my medial ligaments and partially torn my cruciate. At that time, those injuries were much more likely to result in your career being ended than they are now and I knew that, even if there was a chance of me recovering, it was going to be a long and painful road back to playing first-team football again. That journey began with me being moved out of hospital and into Newlands Nursing Home on Chorley New Road in Bolton, where I underwent surgery.

Afterwards, I was in a lot of pain again and the doctors made sure I was regularly topped up with morphine. I used to watch them putting it in, it wasn't supplied with a drip, they just used to come in and hit you with a shot and you'd be away with the fairies. It was the only time in my life that I knew how junkies felt because I loved that shot. I've had some great feelings in my life – the euphoria of winning trophies and the unrivalled pleasure of becoming a dad – but the sensation of morphine-induced relief was as good as anything I had ever felt. Anything to stop the pain, to stop me wondering if I'd pull a pair of boots on again.

Other than those fleeting moments of release, it was a torrid time. People would come to visit me but I couldn't really focus, either because of the physical pain or the mental anguish; they'd be in the room with me but my head would be somewhere else. I'd broken my kneecap previously but this one was different as the pain it caused kept reminding me that my career was in jeopardy.

To make matters worse, Bill Ridding, the former Bolton manager, popped in to see me one day and he said something that chilled me to the core. He only put his head around the door but the look in his eyes gave away what he was thinking before he said anything. Then the words came out and it was like being hit by a sledgehammer. "You were going to be a good player," he said, in an attempt to be affectionate, but his words finished me off. I kept hearing them over and over again in my head. "Going to be." Not "will be", not "could still be", and not even "might be."

I was being written off before I was even 23 and what hurt most was that I knew this hadn't been a throwaway comment. I knew better than anyone else how bad the injury was, and I'd had the same fears before Bill had articulated them. At that stage, all the morphine shots in the world couldn't have made me feel better. When you feel so low nothing can make you high.

I wouldn't say I was depressed because I would never demean the seriousness of that condition, but I was definitely on the floor. I'd worked so hard to get to where I wanted to be, given everything to work my way up from games with my mates in Huyton to playing in the First Division and here I was, after just a handful of games at the top level, with my career in grave doubt.

There was a moment when one of the doctors said to me that I might not play again, and asked me what I would do. I said I'd buy a gun and shoot George Wood – although my sister, Carol, did try and hit him after the game. I wasn't being serious, even though the situation was, because I know these things happen in football. But I shed more than a tear or two out of fear that I was finished. Football was all I could do. I'd devoted my life to it and had nothing to fall back on, having flunked carpentry classes I'd been forced to take by the club, and this was at a time when jobs were thin on the ground.

At times like that, you need people to lift your spirits because there is only so much that any individual can do for themselves.

In my case, the person who inspired me most was Jim Headridge. Jim was a brilliant character, a Scotsman full of life and full of stories, which meant it was a tragedy when he died not long after, having suffered a heart attack on the training pitch while working for Manchester United. The Football Medical Association later gave Jim a posthumous award for his outstanding contribution and I can say, without any hesitation, that he also made an outstanding contribution to my career. He was the person, more than anyone else, who made me believe that I would play again.

It was only a brief conversation but it was one that transformed my outlook, and reminded me of the qualities that had allowed me to become a professional footballer in the first place. I got straight to the point. "Jim, don't pull any punches, am I going to play again?" Immediately, he threw the question back at me. "Do you want to play again?" he asked, and I responded: "Of course I do." He just looked at me and said: "Well, it's up to you then."

In that one exchange, lasting no more than 30 seconds, he managed to put the responsibility back on me and also reminded me that I had the qualities to come back. It was up to me. It wasn't about the doctors, the physios, the club staff or anyone else, although they would all help me on my way. It was up to me to fight for my own career. That struck a chord straight away.

Jim had tapped into my character and delicately hit the nerve that he knew would make me respond positively. That's how good he was as a psychologist.

With others he might have gone down another route, offering comfort and coming up with plans that would show them the way back, but with me he knew he had to stop me feeling sorry for myself and make me react. That was the turning point. Every question I came at him with he came back at me with a better answer. There were no excuses and there was not going to be a hard luck story. I was going to get back playing no matter how long it might take, or how hard it might be.

For the next year I worked as hard as I could. As soon as I was able I was back in the gym, with my leg still in plaster, doing upper body work under Jim's supervision. I'd seen Nat Lofthouse do it with a medicine ball to the point that he was surrounded by a pool of sweat, so that was the standard I had to live up to. It wasn't as if I could go running or work on my technique, so I threw myself into weight training because I knew that by doing that, I would give myself the best chance of returning sooner, rather than later – and I'll always be grateful for Jim's support throughout this period.

I got myself in there early, starting first thing and leaving late in the afternoon. I would go in the drying room, put a mat down on the floor and go through the kind of routines that I'd seen Nat do on the dressing room floor. That's why the influence of former players like him made such an impact on me. I had seen what he would do to be in peak condition long after he had finished playing, and it made me realise that I would have to work just as hard – if not harder – if I was to give myself the best possible chance of coming back.

Before long, and quicker than many people had anticipated, I was back in full training and the next step after that was to play in a reserve game. I'd been in a similar situation before after my previous knee injury but the risks were greater this time because I'd been out for nine months so, before I made my comeback against Manchester United reserves, the manager and the medical staff all gave me the same guidance: "Just walk yourself through the game, get your legs and don't do anything daft."

It was good advice but, in football, it's easier said than done, and there's always a strong possibility that a situation will occur where you have no choice but to go in for a tackle. In my case, it was a bouncing ball, one of those that lands exactly halfway between two players and you don't even have a chance to think about whether to try and win it or not, because your instinct has already made your mind up for you. In this case, the other player was a lad called Steve Paterson, whose own career would end prematurely because of injury, and the two of us went in for the challenge in the only way we knew. I block tackled him.

I could have taken a step back and looked to nick the ball, but my nature dictated otherwise. As soon as I made contact I felt something but I stayed on and got through the game. As I was walking off the pitch, Jim came over to me to see how I was and, before he could even ask, I told him that I was struggling. He didn't believe me, half wondering if I was winding him up, and half worrying that I really did have a setback. But, after looking down at my knee and seeing for himself that it was swelling up, he realised that I had a problem.

Another visit to the specialist was arranged for the following day and after an x-ray, the diagnosis was that I had chipped a bone in my knee. It felt like I was going back to square one but the specialist told me it wasn't serious, and that I'd just need to rest for a month. I don't think he realised that 'just a month' would feel like an eternity to me after what I'd been through but I had no choice but to listen to what he was telling me, no matter how much I didn't want to hear it.

All I could do was count down the days and then get back to running again, only this time I knew that when I did come back, I would have to be a bit more careful.

I played a couple of reserve games and came through with no ill-effects. Then, the draw for the third round of the FA Cup was made and we were handed a tie at Sunderland. That was when

Greavesy took me up with the rest of the squad just for the trip, or so I thought, but then pitched me straight back into the team after a couple of glasses of lager the night before.

The problem was that the team that I was coming back into was a very different one – in terms of form and confidence – to the one that I had left behind after getting injured. At first, the lads had done well, and a promising return to the top flight became a good one when we managed to finish sixth-from-bottom, 10 points above the relegation zone (when it was still two points for a win), to keep ourselves in the elite. As a club and as a group of players, we had ambitions to go on and achieve more than just survival but, for the time being, that was more than enough.

Having kept ourselves in the division, we started off okay in the 1979/80 season, getting a couple of draws against Liverpool and Aston Villa, two teams who would go on to lift the European Cup in 1981 and 1982 respectively, before getting a good win at home to Southampton. But our encouraging start soon gave way to some really poor form and, after losing to Southend in the League Cup on August 28, we didn't win again until I made my comeback in the FA Cup at the start of January. Brighton, Forest, Coventry City, Derby County, Villa and Wolves all beat us comfortably and, not surprisingly given those kind of results, we found ourselves in the bottom three by the end of October. Once in the relegation zone we never managed to escape from it.

I'd found myself really frustrated watching the team struggle. It's bad enough being out on the pitch when things are going wrong but, at least when you're playing, you've got the chance to make a difference; when you're sat in the stands you're powerless.

Obviously, supporters and journalists were focusing on my absence and saying that the team missed me and there's probably a bit of truth in that. I'd been playing well before getting injured and I'd established myself in the team, but it's not so much that Bolton couldn't cope without me as an individual, it was that having been out of the First Division for so long, the club didn't have the kind of strength in depth that would allow it to thrive, when key players were not available. That was just a fact of life for us and, unfortunately, it made life very difficult.

People look at the manager and signings and whatever else, but sometimes you're just not built to cope with the demands, and that was the case for us. If we'd been able to keep everyone fit, had some luck and kept our confidence high we would have been okay but, when any one of those elements broke down it was going to be a big ask to stay up, and sadly it proved beyond us.

That last few months was a struggle for all of us because besides a few wins in March, when hopes rose that we might survive once more, there was a growing sense of doom that we wouldn't escape the drop again. It wasn't for the want of trying, either, because we gave it everything, but it just wasn't to be. There are some things you can overcome but when the odds are stacked against you, to the extent that they were for Bolton that season, events quickly conspire against you.

It was the opposite with my injury because, after my pep-talk from Jim, I knew I had enough to come back. It was a question of desire and wanting to play. My team-mates know what I went through and even though it was a really dark period in my life, there was always light at the end of the tunnel, even though when the plaster got taken off my leg after three months it looked like a wishbone. But whether I came back or not was always down to me and, no matter how tough things got, I knew I could do it.

I remembered Alan Waldron breaking his leg horrifically at Blackpool and coming back from that, and I thought to myself: 'If he can do it, I can do it.' I thought of Paul Hallows fracturing his skull against York City and going into intensive care but coming back from it, and that inspired me. My knee was probably only at 80 per cent of its previous capacity afterwards and I had to adapt my game, so that I tried not to go past people as much and read the game better, as well as taking up more good positions.

I also had to learn to avoid contact so when we played Halifax in the FA Cup and a player called Mick Kennedy, who was an over-the-top merchant, went for me I'd anticipated it, and was able to get out of the way just enough to ensure that he only skimmed me, rather than catching me full-on. As an individual, you can make all of these adjustments and you can overcome physical issues and even mental ones. But when things go wrong for a club like Bolton at the highest level it can become difficult to compete, because the other clubs have far greater resources.

So while I came back and got through, sometimes using anti-inflammatories, the team was limping while others were running and that can only carry on for so long. I had Jim and Mr Winston to thank for saving my career during this period, but there was no one to save us. We had done so well. We had been promoted, we had reached the semi-final of the League Cup and, for one season, we had held our own in the First Division. We had some big wins against top clubs and a lot of that was because Greavesy was so shrewd but little things went against us, and we found ourselves in a slump.

As I was to find out later in my career, managers come into the firing line as soon as results start going against you. Not many clubs are willing to take a step back, look at the progress that has been made and deal with a blip without making changes. When our form deserted us, I had hoped Bolton would deal with things differently; not just because Greavesy was like a second dad to me, it was mainly because of what he had done for the club.

At the very least, he deserved more time to try and turn things around because it wasn't as if he had inherited an established First Division club. Before winning promotion in 1978, Bolton had spent the majority of the previous 15 years in Division Two, even dropping into Division Three in the early 1970s. In that context, winning promotion is always going to be one thing, but turning the club into an established top-tier outfit was another.

It wasn't even as if he'd been handed a fortune to try to complete the transformation. He'd spent a club record £350,000 on Cantello and £150,000 to sign Clement, so the club did back him. However, this was in an era when Trevor Francis had become English football's first seven-figure signing and other teams were better placed to take advantage of the transfer market.

Such logic doesn't apply in club boardrooms when the pressure is on, though, and not long after he had been a serious candidate to succeed Tommy Docherty as manager of Manchester United, Greavesy was sacked with Bolton at the bottom of the table.

It was January 1980 and the new decade could not have got off to a worse start for me. Little did I know that it would turn out to be a turning point in my career for the right reasons.

# 5. EVERTON TO THE RESCUE

*'When Everton came in for me it was as if someone had flicked a switch. I was so determined to join them that I didn't even ask about personal terms. I just said: "Give me the deal and I'll sign it"'*

I TOOK Greavesy's sacking really badly. Part of me wanted to go in and have a big row but I was too gutted for that, so I decided to leave Bolton. That might seem like an over-reaction but it was nothing compared to the decision to get rid of a manager who had given us so much.

I knew I owed him a great deal and he deserved my loyalty, even if the club weren't willing to offer him theirs. My injury had been a big loss to him because, and I don't want to sound big-headed about this, I could make players play. In that sense luck had gone against him, although it's probably fair to say that his signings hadn't really worked out. If there's one thing that clubs don't like it's that.

When I came into Burnden Park on the Monday morning

after we'd knocked Halifax out of the FA Cup and found out that he'd been sacked, I was devastated. I went in to see him in his office as he was sorting out his stuff and he just told me to keep on playing but my mind was already made up, and not long after I told the club that I wanted to go.

The problem, for the club rather than myself, was that my contract was running out. The two-year deal that I was on was due to expire that summer and I had no intention of signing a new one. I was in a strong position to get a good move to another club – or so I thought. Manchester City, who were managed by Malcolm Allison, let it be known to John Doherty, a former Manchester United player who was helping me out at the time, that they were interested in signing me and that definitely turned my head. City had broken the British transfer record to sign Steve Daley not long before and were an ambitious club, with greater resources and more chance of success than Bolton.

I wanted to go but Bolton were keen for me to stay. They offered me a new contract worth the same money I was on, £800 per week, which wasn't bad in those days, but I turned them down. That was when things started to get messy. Because I'd rejected their offer and had no intention of signing any deal they put in front of me, Bolton decided that I was a contract rebel and stopped me from training with the team. It was one of those situations where a club tries to make itself look strong but just ends up cutting off its nose to spite its face, and that culminated in me being sent to train with Wigan Athletic. It was a strange situation because I was in demand at a number of First Division clubs but I found myself training with a team which had only recently come into the Football League.

At the end of the previous season, Bolton had played Wolves, who were captained by Emlyn Hughes at the time, and he tapped me up at the end of the game. Emlyn pulled me in the players' lounge and told me that their gaffer, John Barnwell, was going to come in for me. Wolves were a club on the up, they had Emlyn, a European Cup-winning captain at Liverpool, and Andy Gray, who'd cost them an English record £1.5m. They'd also just won the League Cup so their interest definitely excited me.

Negotiations with them seemed to be pretty straightforward, especially when they offered me personal terms worth £1,100 per week, which was much more than Bolton were offering, but Bolton dug their heels in on the fee and refused to accept anything lower than £600,000 for me. Nowadays, a player can just leave at the end of his contract but it was more complicated then because clubs held on to the players' registration even after his contract had expired, and that allowed them to demand a fee. Wolves wouldn't meet the asking price but then Arsenal and Everton came in so all hope had not been lost.

Arsenal had just sold Liam Brady to Juventus and were looking to invest the proceeds of his sale to strengthen Terry Neill's squad. Again, they were an exciting proposition for me. Neill was an up-and-coming young manager and Arsenal had just reached three FA Cup finals on the trot. They were also the kind of well-established, well-respected club that would interest any player so when I found out that they were sniffing around I hoped that I would end up at Highbury.

I went down to London to hold talks with them and everything went well with terms being agreed, which led to Arsenal informing Bolton that they were willing to meet their asking price. The move looked set to go ahead but then I asked Bolton for what I believed I was due and everything started to unravel.

In those days it was common for outgoing players to seek and, in most cases, get an ex gratia payment. As Bolton were about to bank £600,000 for me, having signed me for nothing, I told them I wanted one. I rang Reuben Kay, my accountant, to let him know what I was looking for. While that process was going on, John Doherty called Terry Neill to tell him to hang on because it would all be sorted once my payment had been granted, but Terry told him to forget about it. That was it, Arsenal had gone.

They would argue that I should have jumped at the chance to sign for them and I can understand that, but they were the ones who had come in for me and yet they weren't willing to wait a day or two for my situation at Bolton to be resolved. That has bugged me over the years because it doesn't stack up. Arsenal either wanted me or they didn't and if they did there was no reason for them to pull the plug, just because I needed to sort something out with Bolton before leaving. That they signed Peter Nicholas shortly after only makes me more suspicious.

It was around the same time that Everton came in for me. I'd been a Liverpudlian all my life but, by that stage, I was a professional footballer and allegiance didn't even enter my thinking. As a kid, I might have been a committed Red who would walk all the way from Huyton to Melwood in the hope of getting autographs from Tommy Smith and Ian St John, but that fanaticism hadn't blinded me to what a great club Everton were.

I met their manager, Gordon Lee, who was a nice fella but he asked me a strange question that I've never forgotten. He said to me: "If you had one team with 11 Sam Allardyces and another team with 11 Willie Morgans and they played a game on a small pitch, which one would win?"

Obviously, he was trying to suss out the way I thought about football and I was trying to second guess the answer that he wanted me to give him so I just said: "In my opinion, you've got to have a balance so you need a bit of a mix."

Gordon saw things differently, though, telling me he had no doubt 11 Allardyces would win. "I'm not saying they wouldn't," I answered, trying my best to be diplomatic at the same time as trying not to look weak by backing down, "but they might not get the ball." Anyway, that move broke down as well, although it was nothing to do with my tactical outlook, as Wolves came back into the picture and Everton backed away.

The Wolves deal fell down again though and I was back to square one. That was a really difficult time for me and the press didn't help. There were headlines calling me 'Greedy Reidy' and stuff like that, which missed the point entirely. Of course, I was looking to get the best move that I could and, like any player, I wasn't joining anyone for less than I was worth. But it was football reasons – mainly the sacking of Greavesy – that were pushing me into wanting to leave, and it was football reasons that made me want to join a club that had a better chance of being successful.

In the end, even that sense of ambition and desire to better myself made me have a re-think. It wasn't that I wanted to stay at Bolton because I didn't, but I was desperate to play. Even though I was training with Wigan I wasn't getting any game-time, and that killed me. I'd worked so hard to become a footballer and I'd already missed too many games through injury, so not being involved in matches when I was fully fit made no sense whatsoever. That really hit home and I can remember sitting at home one day just thinking, 'What are you doing?' That was the moment when I decided to resolve my differences with Bolton and I ended up signing a week-to-week contract with them.

I'd like to think that I left a lasting impression on Wigan in the short time I was there though. They were a fun club to be around at that time and I got on really well with the manager, Ian McNeill, and Micky Quinn, a fellow Scouser, in particular. We just used to have a laugh and I needed that, with everything else that was going on in my life. But the reason why I reckon I made my mark in the brief time I was there is caused by a training session that has gone down in infamy at the club.

All the usual faces were there but there was also a new player called Vic, who I presumed was on trial. We were doing a drill which involved playing one-twos but Vic was awful. We were up against one defender so all we had to do was give and go and we'd be in, but every time I knocked it to Vic it would bounce off him.

I got more and more worked up as he tried – and failed – to do the basics and, in the end, I lost it. I'd tried to keep my patience because he was obviously doing his best and trying to impress the coaches but this was one bobble off his shin too many, and I gave him the big one. "Fucking hell, you useless twat, is there any chance?" Before I could carry on with my tirade, one of the lads tapped me on the shoulder and said: "You need to go easy on 'Vic', he's the local vicar and he just comes around every now and again to join in with us."

I went crimson. There's the local clergyman trying to have a kickaround with his local team and one of the players, who isn't even playing for Wigan, is slaughtering him for not having a good enough first touch! All I could do was apologise but if falling out with a man of God wasn't enough to tell me to get back to Bolton, nothing was.

I'd be lying if I said I'd gone back willingly because the truth is it was with reluctance. Had any of the other moves come off I would have been out of there, but I was so desperate to play that I just knuckled down and got on with it. Bolton were back in the Second Division, having been relegated, but that didn't matter. It was just great to be back playing competitive games again. It didn't last long, though.

We went to Oakwell to play Barnsley and it was a tough game but nothing that I couldn't handle, at least that's what I thought. The day before, I gave an interview to one of the newspapers and I was asked about my ambitions. "Well, I'd like us to beat Barnsley tomorrow," I said. "I'm not looking any further than that because I could break a leg or anything." Talk about tempting fate.

It wasn't my own words that condemned me, though, it was a big lad called Ian Evans, who became the latest to put my bones to the test and discovered that they weren't unbreakable. We were pushing forward and I found myself out wide, looking to get a cross in but as I knocked the ball Evans came in and caught me, breaking my leg in two places. That left me facing another three months out injured.

To say I was devastated doesn't even come close but, even though it was a break, this time there was a consolation because it was clear straight away that I wouldn't be out anywhere near as long as I had been when I did my ligaments. There would be no dark nights of the soul, no fears that I might not play again; I just had to roll my sleeves up and get on with it. Whatever hand fate was dealing me, I had no choice other than to confront it.

I came back and started playing again but it wasn't long before my injury curse struck again. This time, my left knee just went in a game and it turned out I had what's called a bucket handle tear of the cartilage. In those days, they took your cartilage out if you had that kind of injury so that meant another spell on the sidelines. In the space of four years I'd bust my kneecap, torn my ligaments, broken my leg in two places and had my cartilage out. Luckily the injuries were shared between my two legs because if they'd just happened to one I might have had to stop playing.

As it was I came back again but at first I was struggling. I'd put a little bit of weight on while I was out and my morale, not surprisingly, had taken a knock. For the first time in my life, I was finding it hard to play football simply because the injuries had taken a toll on me. I managed to get my arse back in gear but then I got a stud in my knee against Watford and it opened up again. Thankfully, this time I just needed a couple of stitches and there was no lasting damage, which was just as well because I was starting to find my form again.

I started to attract interest from clubs again, with Sheffield Wednesday coming in for me in late 1982. They were managed by Jack Charlton at the time, so having started my career learning from one member of England's 1966 World Cup-winning team in Roger Hunt, here was a chance to continue it under another. As soon as I got the phone call from Jack I jumped into the car and drove straight across to Yorkshire in the hope of getting the move sorted. Jack wasn't there when I arrived, he'd either gone fishing or shooting, so I met his assistant, John Harris.

The talks went well. Wednesday had a good side then so on my way back to Atherton, where I lived, I'd pretty much made my mind up to sign for them. But as soon as I arrived home the phone started ringing. I didn't know it at the time but this was a call that would change my life. I answered it, and the voice at the other end said: "It's Howard Kendall here," so I answered: "It's about time." Howard was quick, though, and responded: "About time? From what I've heard about you, I'm lucky to catch you in, aren't I?" Straight away I thought, 'You'll do for me' and I went down to sign for Everton.

This was probably the first time in my life that my injuries worked in my favour. As I was seen as being injury prone, which wasn't really fair because it wasn't as if I was picking up strains and pulls all the time, my value had dropped. From being up for sale for £600,000, all of a sudden the asking price was just

£60,000. For that fee I was worth a gamble and Howard was the one who took the risk.

Actually, to say he took a risk probably doesn't do justice to just how much he went out on a limb to sign me. He insisted that the deal got done, even after I failed a medical, because after examining me, Everton's club doctor, Dr Irvine, said there was swelling on my knee and other problems that needed an x-ray.

Howard also made Everton change its bankers because their existing lenders wouldn't allow them to borrow the money to sign me. He was only a young manager making his way in the game and it would have been easy for him to back down in the face of that kind of opposition. But he stood up for me because he believed so strongly that I had something to offer.

I also had a secret – well, it was more of an open secret by then – in that I was a Liverpudlian. Even though I'd been making my own way in the game as a player with Bolton I hadn't stopped being a fan and I'd been to the FA Cup final against Newcastle in 1974, and I might have been at the European Cup final in Rome three years later as well, only I was away on tour with England Under-21s at the time. But when Everton came in for me it was as if someone had flicked a switch.

Unless you have been in that situation you wouldn't be able to understand it. It's not just about being a professional, it's much more profound than that and, after learning of their interest, I was so determined to join them that I didn't even ask about personal terms. I just said: "Give me the deal and I'll sign it." It was as simple as that.

By then, I was just so desperate to play at the highest level and for the best club I possibly could – and Everton were giving me that. It was down to me to prove that I was good enough for them because, after all the injuries I'd had, people understandably had doubts on that front. I can remember John Bailey saying to me that they weren't sure whether I could kick the ball from one side of the pitch to the other. I just said: "What does that prove?" But I knew that I had plenty to do to impress.

Football is a small family and people do talk. I was aware that there were people saying that I was shot and claiming that I couldn't handle it physically. I understood that; if the shoe had been on the other foot I'd look at things the same way as well but, because these things were being said about me, it just motivated me even more.

Like any player, especially one who'd had injury problems, I was interested to know what it was that had attracted Everton to me so I asked Howard, and he said it was Colin Harvey who had convinced him that I would be right for them. Apparently, Colin had watched me a few times and reported back that I'd done brilliantly, which meant a hell of a lot to me. I'd played against him when he was at Sheffield Wednesday and, even though he was past his best by then, he was still a brilliant footballer and I could tell that he had a fantastic football brain. Knowing that he'd recommended me made me even more determined to succeed.

I had so much to prove, to everyone who was doubting me but also to myself, and I also had to live up to the recommendation of one of Everton's greatest-ever players. It wasn't that I was doubting my ability because I'd shown that I could play and I knew that I was up to it physically because I hadn't had the same injury over again, I just kept getting different ones. This was still a step up for me, though, and it had come after one of the most difficult periods in my career.

When I first signed, my former Bolton team-mate, Neil Whatmore, came around to my house the night before and we ended up having a bit of a celebration. It wasn't planned but we got on the wine and the brandies and it turned out to be a good session. The problem was that, as ever, day followed night and this wasn't just any day either, it was my first day training with my new club. If there is a time for a hangover, this wasn't it. First impressions always matter – especially so in football. I knew full well that my new team-mates would be looking at me, weighing me up and making an early call on whether the manager had signed a dud, or someone who might actually make a difference.

Within a few touches I was making their minds up as the ball bounced off me over and over again. Now I knew how Vic felt at Wigan but the difference was I wasn't a trialist or a vicar, I was an Everton player. It was embarrassing. The lads looked at me and I knew they were thinking, 'What the fuck have we signed here?' I couldn't blame them. Things weren't about to get better, either.

Next up we had doggies, which are basically shuttle runs, designed to test and improve your fitness. My head was banging though and, on top of that, my stomach was lurching and my legs felt so heavy that I could barely lift them to move. But it didn't matter how I felt, I had to run in between these two trees over and over again, even if my gut instinct was to sprint behind one of them to throw up.

The gaffer must have seen that I was struggling. He could hardly have missed it, and he told me to do them with him instead of with another one of the lads. We went once, twice and on the third leg he lapped me. I would say in my defence that Howard was still only 37 and he was fit enough to still be playing but, if there's one thing you don't want to happen on your first day at a new club, it's to be shown up physically by your manager.

I felt like a bag of shite and I just wanted it all to end so I could get back home and go to bed but, as I was getting changed in the dressing room, Colin came over to me and said: "He wants to see you." Other than being told to go back out to do extra doggies, that was the last thing I wanted to hear. Reluctantly, I went into Howard's room where he was having a bath.

"What are you like?" he asked and I knew, if I didn't know already, that I'd let myself down and, worst of all, I'd let him down. I knew the very least I owed him was an explanation. "I've got to be honest, gaffer," I said. "Neil Whatmore came around last night. We had a few glasses of white wine and then we got on the spirits. It wasn't planned, it was just the way it worked out." I knew it wasn't a good explanation and it definitely didn't make me look like a brilliant professional. But things had gone so badly that I thought honesty was the best policy.

Howard's reaction stunned me. "Oh, you like a bevvy, do you? You've got a chance, son." He wasn't condoning my drinking, or the timing of it anyway, because he'd brought me in to give me a whack, having seen how badly I'd trained. But having subtly let me know that he expected better, he then acknowledged that I'd at least got myself in and had a go, no matter how rough I was. I'd been expecting a fine but I left his room believing that, not only had I joined the right club, I'd signed for the right manager.

I wanted to do it for *him*, I was absolutely desperate, but first I had to find a way of getting into the team. My cause wasn't helped by picking up a knee injury early on, which left Howard wondering if he had made a mistake in signing me. That wasn't an easy time and, at one stage, Colin actually apologised to Howard for recommending me to the club. But they gave me time to prove myself and, during that difficult period, my morale was kept up by my new team-mates.

I know Everton weren't flying when I joined but I can remember looking around the training ground during my first few days and being blown away by some of the players we had. Martin Hodge,

Neville Southall, Jim Arnold, Trevor Ross, Graeme Sharp, Kevin Ratcliffe, Mark Higgins, David Johnson, Kevin Richardson, Steve McMahon, Andy King, Brian Borrows, Billy Wright, John Bailey, Adrian Heath, Alan Irvine, Alan Harper, Gary Stevens; I could go on and on. We were a mid-table team but there were a lot of young lads with so much potential.

The problem was that, as a club, we were punching below our weight. It was hard to be an Everton player at that time, partly because of how well the other lot were doing over the park. I wouldn't say we were scared to play but there was a pressure that was hard to deal with. On top of that, the frustrations of the fans were spilling out on to the pitch and I could understand that. There was so much room for improvement. I was injured for the FA Cup quarter-final at Man United in March 1983, a game that sticks in my mind because we absolutely battered them – but got beat. Frank Stapleton scored the winner and United went on to win the Cup – but the lads were magnificent that day.

That showed me two things: one, that we had more quality than was widely believed and two, we didn't have the mentality to make it count as much as it should. I wanted to help change that and, without being big-headed, I thought this was one area where I could make a difference. First, I had to force my way into the team and that was proving much harder than I'd hoped.

I had a really good pre-season going into the 1983/84 campaign, probably the best I ever had in my entire career. It wasn't just about stamina and fitness, there was an unbelievable amount of focus on working with the ball and improving technique. I'd been used to running up hills for miles on end and doing all that kind of hard physical graft but Howard was ahead of his time in terms of sports science. He even gave us individually tailored programmes when necessary, like when Ratters said to him he was struggling running long distances and Howard told him not to worry because he didn't want him running long distances, giving him more sprint work to do instead.

Howard was only a young manager but he was so wise, and I got on board with his methods in a big way. Physically, I felt as good as I had in a long time but even that wasn't enough to get into the starting line-up on a regular basis and I was gutted about that. I'd played four games and in two of them, wins at Tottenham and Notts County, I'd scored. But soon after I got left out so I started to think that it might not happen for me at Everton. I went to see Howard and told him how I was feeling but he just told me to keep my head down, and to see how it goes.

There were no guarantees and Burnley were into me at the time as John Bond wanted to take me there, so I knew I had an option if things didn't work out. At that stage there was a strong possibility that I might have had to take it. I couldn't hide the way I felt and obviously my family knew that I wasn't happy about not playing. That was when my younger brother, Mick, decided to take matters into his own hands.

We'd just played Liverpool at Anfield in early November and lost 3-0; I'd been on the bench and hadn't got on so, naturally, I was absolutely gutted. I don't know what was making me feel worse, the result or the fact that I'd missed out again. Soon after a caller to a radio phone-in, hosted by Ian St John, went on air and said that Peter Reid should be playing. The Saint just thought it was an ordinary punter and he asked him, on what authority he had to say something like that. Our Mick responded: "Because I'm his brother!" At least I'd convinced him I was good enough, now I just needed the manager to see things the same way.

My chance finally came in a Milk Cup third-round tie against Coventry three days after the derby. I was named as substitute again and we were 1-0 down so Howard told me to go on with 20 minutes left. We turned it around, winning 2-1 with Sharpy scoring the 90th-minute winner at the back stick, and I stayed in the team from then on.

If that relieved a bit of the pressure that I was feeling, Howard wasn't so fortunate, and by the time we played them again in the league he was right in the firing line. There were only 13,659 fans at Goodison Park on that New Year's Eve afternoon and it felt like everyone who had turned up had come to see him off.

The game finished 0-0 and the tension was unbearable. I've never looked for excuses when I haven't played well but, as a team, it was extremely difficult to function that day because the atmosphere was so negative. With the ground being three-quarters empty you could hear the shouts from fans, and not many of them were in the mood to give us encouragement. We were getting the message loud and clear and it was fair enough because our results hadn't been good enough.

Just in case we were in any doubt about how the Everton supporters were feeling, leaflets were being handed out during this period calling for the manager and the chairman to quit or be sacked. 'Kendall and Carter out', they stated. '30,000 stay at home fans can't be wrong. Bring back attractive winning football to Goodison Park.'

These weren't just dark days – they were unremittingly bleak and, even though we were all behind Howard, we knew that the crowd going on at him could be the beginning of the end. How he coped with the pressure he was under – or didn't – would determine his fate but not many managers come back from the dead, and in the dressing room we were all too aware of that.

A 2-0 defeat of Birmingham City at St Andrew's two days later gave him a stay of execution but it had reached the stage when the next defeat could finish him off. As a result, our next game, a third round FA Cup tie at Stoke City, was massive. Lose that one and that might well have been it for Howard. Everton were at the crossroads.

**Schoolmates:** With Kevin Gattney, Stephen Pearson and Aiden Murrell at St Augustine's and (right) setting up camp with brother Shaun

**History Makers:** Me (front, third left) my Huyton Schoolboys team-mates and Mr Bleasdale (back, second right), 1971

**Beside The Seaside:** Stephen Pearson, me, Aiden Murrell, Tommy Evans and JJ Shiels on a day out in Rhyl

**LIVERPOOL FOOTBALL CLUB**

and Athletic Grounds Co. Ltd.

Manager: W. Shankly.
Secretary: P.B. Robinson.
Telephone: 051 263 2361/2.

ANFIELD ROAD,
LIVERPOOL, L4 OTH.

Date as postmark.

Dear Peter

You are selected to attend for extra coaching sessions during the school holiday period at our Melwood Ground, Melwood Drive, off Town Row, West Derby on _Sunday_ _17th January_ 10 Am.

Please report to the Ground, bring your own boots, stockings, shorts, ~~shirts~~ a ~~rubber~~ studded and towel.

If for any reason you are unable to attend please inform us as soon as possible.

Yours sincerely,

T. SAUNDERS,

for W. SHANKLY,

Manager.

**Fulfilling A Dream?** An offer to train with Liverpool from youth development officer Tom Saunders, 1970/71; (Right, back row, second left) On the bench for England Schoolboys v Scotland Schoolboys at my first managerial home, Maine Road, May 1971

ENGLAND v. SCOTLAND—Victory Shield, Main Road, Manchester, Saturday, 15th May, 1971
*Back row*—Mr. J. Morrow (Team Manager): P. Reid (Huyton SFA): J. Shepherd (N. Kent SFA): A. P. Clarkson (Altrincham and Sale SFA): C. Marshall (Liverpool SFA): J. S. A. Gordon (Stretford SFA): A. Cameron (Doncaster SFA): B. Odeje (Blackheath SFA): Mr. F. W. Coleman (assistant Team Manager). *Front row*—M. Wardrop (Salford SFA): A. M. Cahill (Crosby and Litherland SFA): J. T. Bowtell (Leicester SFA): S. Powell (Captain—Derby SFA): T. A. Spencer (Merton SFA): R. S. Morton (Warley SFA): B. Bason (N.W. Sussex SFA).

By Courtesy Manchester Evening News

**Leeds United**
Association Football Club Limited

President:
THE RIGHT HON. THE EARL OF HAREWOOD, LL.D.
Life Vice-Presidents:
E. J. BLEAKLEDGE
A. L. REYNOLDS                   J. H. SHICKLEY
Directors:
MANNY CUSSINS (Chairman)
SAM BOLTON
ALDERMAN G. ROBERTS
ROBERT B. ROBERTS
SIDNEY S. SIMON
ALD. PERCY A. WOODWARD
Team Manager:
DON PETER REVXXXX   J C ARMFIELD
General Manager & Secretary:
KEITH ARCHER
Public Relations Officer:
PETER FAY

LEAGUE CHAMPIONS 1968-9, 1973-4
F.A. CUP WINNERS 1971-2
F.L. CUP WINNERS 1967-8
FAIRS CUP WINNERS 1967-8, 1970-1
DIVISION 2 CHAMPIONS 1923-4, 1963-4

(INCORPORATED 1920)

Ground and Registered Offices
ELLAND ROAD — LEEDS LS11 0ES
TELEPHONE: 716037/8 LEEDS   TELEGRAMS: FOOTBALL LEEDS   VAT NO. 190 8484 88

P Reid Esq
Bolton Wanderers Football Club
Burnden Park
Manchester Road
BOLTON
BL3 2QR

29 October 1974

Dear Peter

I thought I must drop you a line to say how pleased I
was to see that you had managed to break into the First
Team.

I have always had faith you would make a regular first
team player one day and I am sure it will not be long
before that comes about.

I hope to read about you soon doing big things and I
shall watch your progress with real interest.

Please give my regards to your Mother and Father. I remain,

Yours sincerely

J C ARMFIELD

JCA/1961

---

THE FOOTBALL ASSOCIATION
LIMITED

Patron: HER MAJESTY THE QUEEN
President: H.R.H. THE DUKE OF KENT
Chairman: SIR ANDREW STEPHEN, M.B., Ch.B.

Secretary:
E. A. CROKER

Telegraphic Address:
FOOTBALL ASSOCIATION, LONDON, W2
Phone: 01-262 4542
Telex: 264159

16 LANCASTER GATE, LONDON, W2 3LW

Our Ref:    LC/JKR      Your Ref:        3rd May, 1977.

Mr. Peter Reid,
Bolton Wanderers F.C.,
Burnden Park,
Manchester Road,
BOLTON,
BL3 2QR

Dear Peter,

Just a short note to thank you for all
the hard work you put in to prepare yourself
for our game against Scotland last week.
This was very much appreciated, Peter, and
I am pleased we got a good result.

Best wishes, and thank you once again.

Yours sincerely,

Les Cocker

Registered Office: 16 Lancaster Gate, London, W2 3LW
Incorporated in London   Registration Number 77797

**Best Wishes:** A note from then Leeds United manager Jimmy Armfield, October 1974; (above right) a thank you from England Under-21s coach Les Cocker, May 1977

**Fresh Face:** Pictured below during the Bolton Wanderers photocall, August 1976

**On Target:** A scorer during a 3-1 home victory over Blackburn, January 1977

**Young Lion:** Kitted out in England colours ahead of my Under-21 debut, circa 1977

**Familiar Faces?** Here I am (front row, third right) in the Bolton Wanderers squad shot ahead of the 1977/78 promotion-winning season

**Blue Move:** In 1982 I made my big move to Everton. This (above) was my 10th and final appearance of 1982/83 before injury struck, at Aston Villa in February 1983

**Everton First:** Heading the opener in a 2-1 win at Spurs, September 1983

**Up For The Cup:** 'Celebrating' the second goal in a 3-0 defeat of Shrewsbury Town, FA Cup fifth round, February 1984

**Merseyside United:** (Front row, fifth left) I was part of the combined Everton and Liverpool squad picture following the drawn 1984 Milk Cup final at Wembley

**Boiling Over:** Words are exchanged with the sent-off Mal Donaghy during a 3-0 win at Luton, April 1984

**Friendly Face:** Referee George Courtney, a welcome presence at home and abroad

**Cup Glory:** Post-match memories from Everton's 1984 FA Cup success

**Best Ever:** The Everton squad, behind skipper Kevin Ratcliffe, ahead of the greatest season in the club's history, 1984/85. Left to right: Terry Curran, Andy Gray, John Bailey, Alan Irvine, Alan Harper, Kevin Richardson, Adrian Heath, Kevin Sheedy, Graeme Sharp, me, Trevor Steven, Jim Arnold, Derek Mountfield, Neville Southall, Paul Bracewell, Gary Stevens

**Vintage Year:** There was action, fun, effort and even kisses as we marched towards double trophy success in 1984/85

**Blood Brother:** One of my lasting memories from the European Cup Winners' Cup semi-final, second leg victory over Bayern Munich at Goodison: a bloodied sock...

**Here We Go:** Cup final song recording in '85 – ours was definitely better than United's!

**Victory Salute:** With Andy Gray during our lap of honour post-QPR, May 1985

**Champions:** Everton's class of '85 show off the Canon League Division One trophy following the home victory over West Ham at Goodison

**Picture Perfect:** Daughter Louise is a special person in a special shirt

**Silver Salute:** Team success in the Cup Winners' Cup – and there was personal glory (above) as I won the Players' Player of the Year award in 1985

# 6. TURNING THE
# BLUE TIDE

*'The look on his face gave away not only what it meant to him but also what it meant to Everton. If I live long enough to see a happier expression I'll be a lucky man'*

W HEN people talk about games that changed the course of history, the one that always springs to mind for me is that FA Cup tie against Stoke at the Victoria Ground on January 7, 1984.

The context was provided by what had happened during a Christmas period that was anything but festive as we failed to win any of the five games we played in a 21-day period to leave Howard fighting for his life.

Sat in the dressing room beforehand, we all knew what was at stake. Typically, Andy Gray was very vocal, making sure we were all right at it from the off. It's not always that straightforward though because in any team it's rare that there are no distractions ahead of a game. In this case, it was caused by Howard's decision to leave Andy King out. Kingy was absolutely devastated because he'd scored in our previous game at Birmingham and had expected to play in this one, so he shot out of the dressing room. We've all been in that situation as a player and it's hard to deal with it because, no matter how much you want the team to win, you're also having to cope with your own personal disappointment at not being involved in a big game.

Like the rest of the lads, I was gutted for Andy but we also had a job to do and that made it vital that the 11 of us who were going out on to the pitch for Everton didn't lose focus, because of what had happened to one who wasn't. That was what made what Howard did next such a masterstroke. When people talk about moments of genius by managers it usually involves a substitution, a change of formation or a player being used in a role that the opposition isn't expecting him to be in. Sometimes, though, simplicity is beauty and it certainly was in this case.

Opening the slats on the dressing room windows, Howard allowed the noise of the Everton supporters to flood into the dressing room. We could hardly hear ourselves think. Then the manager uttered those immortal words: "Go out and win it for them." That was it. There were no great instructions and no grand speeches, just a reminder of who we were playing for and what we owed to them.

Our performance wasn't great, it was never going to be after only one win in the previous month, but it was resolute from start to finish and that was exactly what was required. Andy and Alan Irvine scored the goals but, more than anything, it was the fans that got us through that day. I've sometimes wondered, when I've got the stomach to do so, what might have happened had the result gone against us. It's hypothetical but it's easy to see a chain of events starting with us going out of the FA Cup, Howard losing his job and then the success that followed being prevented by a single defeat. That's football. Careers turn on single results but what happened at Stoke was bigger than that – it was Everton's history that was being changed for the better.

It doesn't just happen, though. It takes bollocks to confront the kind of pressure that we were under at the Victoria Ground and not only cope with it, but actually go on and thrive on it. That goes for the supporters, who could have turned against the team; the players, who could easily have struggled to get themselves going due to a lack of confidence; the manager, who stood when there was a growing number of people who thought it was time for him to go; and it goes for the chairman, Sir Philip Carter, who refused to listen to those who wanted Howard out. At one stage there was even a radio announcement that Mike England would be coming in as manager but, throughout all of the uncertainty and speculation, Sir Philip remained steadfast.

For the club, that FA Cup tie at Stoke is the one that mattered most. I know a lot of people focus on the Milk Cup quarter-final tie at Oxford United later that month but without the victory at the Victoria Ground, Oxford doesn't happen. It's as simple as that. The FA Cup run changed the whole mood of the club. It gave us a stake in a season that had been getting away from us, and allowed us to dream a bit.

I'm not going to say that with one win we were all of a sudden visualising running around Wembley with the Cup. But we knew that we had shown the kind of character and togetherness that can take you a long way. Everything was transforming before our eyes. From lacking in confidence in ourselves and in one another, we were able to look at each other in the dressing room and on the pitch in the belief that we had something about us.

Not that we were flying – it would still be some time before we really started to hit our stride – but mentally at least the penny had dropped. That was key to us coming through the next round against Gillingham, when Steve Bruce hit the bar with a header late on in the first game at Goodison, and Tony Cascarino missed a one-on-one late on in extra-time in the replay. Howard always thanked Tony for saving his job whenever he saw him after that but he wasn't the first striker to fluff his lines when confronted by Neville Southall – and he wouldn't be the last.

Even those scares helped us psychologically. I wouldn't say that we felt invincible but there was a growing feeling that we could survive whatever was being thrown at us by opponents, a sense that grew still further after we beat Gillingham 3-0 in the second replay at Priestfield.

I was better placed than most to understand how the team was feeling because I probably embodied it more than anyone. Having had so many injuries, being back playing had given me a new lease of life and I felt ready to take on all-comers. We beat Shrewsbury Town 3-0 in the next round and the match report in *The Times* will always stick in my mind because it perfectly captured the mood I was in. 'Watching Peter Reid on Saturday was like trying to follow an ex-convict on his first few hours out of jail', David Powell wrote. 'Determined to make up for lost opportunity, Reid could not stay still for a minute. A moment's inattention and you were likely to miss a piece of devilish improvisation.'

What the team was doing was having a positive impact on me and, for the first time since I'd joined Everton, I was able to consistently have a positive impact on the team. As a player you need to feel valued and you need to believe that you are contributing. That was happening on both fronts but I still needed a bit of luck, like Bruce's header smashing against the crossbar and like Kevin Brock picking Adrian Heath out with a back-pass, which allowed Inchy to score a late equaliser that kept us in the Milk Cup at Oxford. Events that had been conspiring against us were now going in our favour and the defeats that had damaged us earlier in the season were happening less regularly.

Something had changed and it wasn't the training, it wasn't the players and it wasn't the tactics. It was our confidence. That was the key element that transformed promising young players into good ones who could hold their own at the highest level. We didn't become more talented all of a sudden or switch players around to find a winning formation, it was a natural development that happened because the manager allowed it to in the face of enormous pressure on himself.

Sometimes you have to go through difficult periods if you want to get to where you want to be. There are some clubs who can maybe take success for granted and the expectation is that they will find a way to win when others wouldn't. But it had been 14 years since Everton had won a trophy and that suggests that because the club hadn't been geared to winning for so long, we had to make it happen. Those bad times that we had, especially over that Christmas period, shaped us and hardened us as individuals and as a group. Maybe if results had been okay the outcome of the process would have been different, which is why whenever any team I played in or managed after that had a tough time I always remained positive because I'd been at a club where a difficult period had been the springboard for huge success.

Even when we did suffer a setback during that period of growth, the manager was finding ways of turning them in our favour. When we lost 2-1 at Sunderland I'd had a right tussle with Paul Bracewell in the middle of the park. I nearly got sent off and Howard ended up dragging me off but he had spotted something that day that none of the rest of us had. He had seen that Brace was exactly the kind of player we needed to help take us to the next level. The team was still evolving and improving and after we won the FA Cup final later that year, the manager went out and signed him.

At the time, I wasn't sure. It wasn't that I doubted his quality because I'd seen at first hand just what a good player he was. My worry was that he seemed very similar to Kevin Richardson but he would come into the team and help us to become champions, even if he is not celebrated anywhere near as much as he should be outside of Everton. People just don't realise how good he was but Howard recognised it, he saw it before anyone else had and he spotted it in a game that we lost.

For Merseyside football and the people who followed it, that was a magnificent time. It had to be as well, because the region was under attack from a Tory government that, at one stage, considered putting it into "managed decline." Unemployment was spiralling out of control, cuts were being made to vital services and the only industry thriving was poverty. As a player you can be divorced from reality at some clubs but at Everton – and at Liverpool for that matter – how could we be when we were confronted by it all the time?

In my case, I knew countless people who were struggling to make ends meet but I also knew I had a responsibility to try and put smiles on faces whenever I could, and that meant being part of a winning team. There was a sense of defiance on the terraces and that spread to the dressing room. The feeling was that, through football, the two clubs and its supporters could stick two fingers up to the Tory government and to the rest of the country.

Predictably, it pissed down at Wembley on the day of the Milk Cup final. On our big day, London was doing its worst to Merseyside. We had expected that and it wasn't going to dampen our spirits, not when the 35,000 ticket allocation that had been given to each club had proven nowhere near enough to satisfy demand, and Blues and Reds were doing everything in their power to be at Wembley.

As equally inevitable as the rain, the game itself was tense and tight. There was far too much at stake for it to be anything else. You can't relax in any final but, when you're playing in the first one between two clubs from the same city and it's being watched by some of the most passionate fans in world football, nothing is going to be easy because no-one can allow it to be.

Even the build-up was testing, especially for those of us who were local lads. The clamour for tickets was huge, and so was the media attention. In that case, a lot of the journalists focused on the fact that I'd been a Liverpool supporter as a kid, which was no big deal, but then they started flagging up that I'm from a family with divided loyalties and interest grew.

One of the papers asked me to pose for a picture, with me wearing an Everton scarf and my dad wearing a Liverpool one, to capture the mood of the city. It was a good idea from a media perspective and I agreed to it to try and help the journalist out, and also to have a bit of fun, but my dad was very reluctant to get involved. This was the man who'd brought me up to be a Liverpudlian, who'd taken me to my first game at Anfield and who had made me a stool to stand on in The Kop so I could see. Although he wouldn't have changed any of that, he didn't want to make himself the centre of attention because of it. He did it in the end, but by then there was no question where his loyalties lay. Like me, he was an Evertonian and no matter what had gone before there was only one team that he wanted to win at Wembley – and it wasn't the one in red.

Whatever the sense of togetherness that the occasion created and no matter how many times the supporters sang "Merseyside" in unison, this wasn't a game to lose, even if so much of what surrounded it made your heart feel like it could burst with emotion. This was Everton versus Liverpool and there was a trophy at stake. I pictured various scenarios before kick-off and the one I kept going back to involved Ratters lifting the cup and us celebrating on the pitch afterwards. The one I kept putting to the back of my mind was Liverpool winning the Milk Cup for the fourth year in a row, this time at our expense.

As it happened, neither eventuality came to pass as the game ended in a draw and both teams did a lap of honour together, as well as posing alongside one another for one of the most iconic football pictures ever taken. Everywhere you looked there were symbols of solidarity and civic pride, the kind which I don't believe any other city with two great rivals would ever produce.

We should have had a penalty, though. That's the one thing I look back on with regret about that entire day. Even now, when I replay the images in my mind I still can't believe it wasn't given. The chain of events was quite straightforward. Adrian Heath beat Bruce Grobbelaar to a loose ball and prodded it towards the Liverpool goal, only for Alan Hansen's outstretched arm to stop it from crossing the line. We all looked at Alan Robinson, the referee, but he gave nothing. I slaughtered him but it was a waste of time, he wasn't going to change his mind.

In fairness, we'd got away with one in the semi-final against Aston Villa when the ball hit Kevin Richardson on the hand. Does it even itself out? Maybe it does sometimes but there is no worse place for it to happen than at Wembley and I think anyone who saw it, except Mr Robinson and maybe the most one-eyed Liverpudlian, would agree that Hansen's was a particularly blatant one. It wasn't quite Maradona against England because there was no jump, no punch and it wasn't a premeditated attempt to cheat.

But whether it was just instinct, he turned into Michael Jordan on the goal-line and got away with it. I would have loved to have seen him analyse that incident on *Match Of The Day*.

If he had, and done so impartially, he would have had to admit that Liverpool had got away with one. That's the way it goes sometimes and, in fairness to them, they made the most of their good fortune by winning the replay at Maine Road a few days later. Again, there was nothing in the game but Graeme Souness, a great player whose brilliance is sometimes overlooked because of the focus on his toughness, settled it in Liverpool's favour with a goal that ensured the Milk Cup went back to Anfield rather than crossing Stanley Park to take up residence at Goodison.

Souey actually miscontrolled a Phil Neal pass outside our penalty area but his football brain was so good that he was able to turn and hit it instantly with his left foot, and that's how he did Neville. There was still almost 70 minutes remaining but we couldn't get back on level terms. We gave it absolutely everything but Liverpool held out. It was small margins that went in their favour, and both teams knew it. I'd argue with anyone that we took more from that final than Liverpool did.

At that stage, they were better placed than we were to get results in games of that magnitude and there was no shame in that because this was only Everton's second major final since 1970. They were the established superpower, who would go on to win a fourth European Cup a little over two months later – but we were the coming force. Even though we lost, everything about the final, from the way we competed despite being much younger – in terms of both experience and age – to the closeness of the outcome underlined that this was another step along the path.

The whole mood of the club was changing. From setting the team up with a view to seeing how the opposition would play and then adapting accordingly, Howard was now sending us into more games with the attitude that they should worry about us more than we should worry about them. By the time we played Liverpool in the FA Charity Shield at the start of the 1984/85 season, this transformation in our mindset was complete. They were European champions, the team that had just won the treble, but neither Howard nor anyone in the team saw any reason for us to do anything out of the ordinary to stop them. We knew – and this is arrogance in a good sense – that if we performed as we knew we could, they would be the ones who would have to come up with ways of stopping us, and not vice versa.

Liverpool were a great side, I would never argue otherwise, but the time had come for us to start believing in ourselves. We knew that if we did so then anything would be possible. A dressing room which had been bereft of belief at the start of January was bubbling over with it just seven months later. Howard was coming of age and so, too, were the players.

I've been asked on countless occasions how it was possible to go from one extreme to another in such a short space of time and the only conclusion I can come to is that many things came together at once – some by accident, but many more by design. The end result was a team who knew exactly what it was about. But the main catalyst for change was a 24-hour period in the previous November when Howard made a couple of decisions that might not have seemed significant at the time, but which turned out to be two of the best in the club's history.

His first move was to promote Colin Harvey from reserve-team manager to first-team coach. The second was perceived to be a huge gamble as Andy Gray, a striker with dodgy knees whose best days were widely believed to be behind him, was signed from Wolves for £250,000. The impact of both was massive.

They brought know-how, enthusiasm, experience, confidence and desire. While Colin's influence was strongest on the training ground whereas Andy's was most keenly felt in the dressing room, the effect of their presence was immediate.

Visibly, the level of training lifted straight away. If you weren't at it, Colin quickly let you know about it. That made the tempo higher and the need to be sharper greater, with passes being zipped in to feet with the expectation being that you would be switched on enough to deal with that approach. Kevin Ratcliffe said that even games of head tennis became so competitive that they were like World Cup finals and he's spot on. A winning mentality was being bred, and we were all getting caught up in it.

Andy's charisma ensured he was at the heart of it all. We all knew he had issues with his knees but he had no problem with his mouth. Whenever there was banter you could bet your life that he'd be in the midst of it all, and that lifted the whole dressing room environment. John Bailey had always mixed it in there because he's such a naturally funny fella but Andy brought something different, which added to what we already had. The only way I can describe it is as a raucous magnetism. He would slaughter anyone and everyone, usually but not always with a smile on his face, and no matter what kind of character you were you couldn't help but respond. Even some of the younger lads, who'd previously been a bit shy and reserved, found themselves getting more involved.

Bails was undoubtedly one of our biggest characters. He was like something out of a sitcom, only the lines he came out with could never have been written. There was this time when he walked in and told us all that he'd had an agent on offering him the chance to go and play in South Africa, and Howard had told him he might let him go. He was all excited, telling us all about the money he was going to earn – £5,000 up front and around £500 per week – and the lifestyle he was going to be enjoying, which basically revolved around having barbecues and going to the beach when he wasn't playing.

Just as he was in full flow, mapping out this wonderful vision of how great his new life was going to be, Jim Arnold, who we all accused of reading the *Daily Telegraph*, burst his bubble – or at least he thought he had. "What about Apartheid?" Jim shouted, acknowledging that there was more to South Africa at that time than burgers, beer and beaches – but his attempt to bring some reality to Bails' dreams backfired. "No problem," Bails said. "I'm getting one with three bedrooms right on the beach." You can't argue with logic like that.

It even reached a point when the banter became so competitive that we had an A-team and a B-team in the dressing room. The likes of Kevin Ratcliffe and Graeme Sharp were on the latter, while myself and Adrian Heath were A. Neville had to be on the A-team, even though he didn't drink because we were all scared to tell him otherwise. It was absolutely ruthless and you couldn't get away with anything but I would say that, in the course of my life, that dressing room is one of the happiest places that I've ever been. Andy's arrival was the catalyst for that but the way the lads responded was magnificent, and the togetherness that was fostered was key to the success that we enjoyed. Football might change and people might come up with new words to describe old methods, but the one thing that stays the same is that, if you have a good dressing room, you have a chance of doing well. At Everton, we had one of the very best.

For it to be like that, though, there had to be quality. If there isn't, and you're not holding your own in games at the very least, then it isn't long before the jokes and the laughs run short. In our case, the closing of the gap between natural talent and what was being produced on the pitch was personified by Trevor Steven. He'd been bought as a central midfielder but didn't flourish there so the manager tried him out on the right wing, and he was a revelation. Trevor's transformation was one of the big droplets in the pond and Kevin Sheedy's development, from a player with a great left foot to one who knew how – and when – to use it to maximum effect was another. Kevin Ratcliffe had been a left-back but when Mark Higgins got injured he moved into central defence and made the position his own alongside Derek Mountfield, another young defender.

A couple of weeks or so after the Milk Cup final replay, Sharpy was left out of the FA Cup semi-final line-up. Howard wanted to go with Andy and Inchy up front, and that was one of those moments when you realised just how good the team – and the squad – was becoming. Things were evolving in front of our eyes. At the age of 27, I was one of the older players in the group along with Andy, which goes to show just how young that squad was. For very little outlay, Howard had put together a group of players that was ripe for development, and he was finding different ways to bring the very best out of all of us.

How he isn't more lauded than he is for what he did defies logic. This was one of the greatest feats of team building that English football has ever known and it was achieved against a backdrop of real pressure because Howard could so easily have lost his job in the first month of 1984.

Despite our improvement and the rapid progress that had been made, when the draw for the semi-final of the FA Cup took place we knew that we weren't favourites to reach the final. Southampton were the team who most neutrals were expecting to go on and lift the trophy so we wanted to avoid them at that stage. Ideally, we were hoping to get Plymouth Argyle, who were in the Third Division, or even Watford, who completed the last four. So who did we get paired with? Southampton.

We played them in a league game at Goodison not long before the semi and Lawrie McMenemy rested four of his best players, – Reuben Agboola, Steve Williams, Mark Dennis and my old Bolton team-mate, Frank Worthington – which wasn't the done thing at the time, and it caused a bit of a stink. It was obvious that they had one eye on the semi-final that day but we won 1-0 and by the time we got to Highbury we had lost only three of our previous 25 matches, a run that allowed us to go into the game with growing confidence.

As should be the case in a game that decides who will reach a cup final at Wembley, this one was as close as it was hard-fought and it could have gone either way. Neville made three or four brilliant saves, the best of them coming from Danny Wallace, and Peter Shilton was in brilliant form for them, although Mick Mills had to help him out by clearing off his own goal-line after Inchy had beaten the Southampton goalkeeper.

There was something about that day, though, that gave us a feeling that no matter how good a season Southampton were enjoying [they would finish as runners-up in the league], we were the ones who would be making it to Wembley. It started on the way to the ground when we saw the supporters. The Southampton fans were turning up in luxury Pullman coaches, whereas ours were in the back of trucks, hanging off the back of lorries and travelling 10 or 12 to a car. When I saw the lengths that people were going to in order to support us, I knew we couldn't lose.

The road to Wembley had started with Howard opening the window at Stoke and telling us to win it for the fans but there would be no need for him to do that this time. What we were seeing with our own eyes made us realise what we had to do, and who we would be doing it for. Once inside the stadium, we realised it was full of Evertonians. This was our day. It had to be.

The only fly in the ointment had been Howard's decision to drop Sharpy. Like Andy King at Stoke, he was devastated and after the game he said he was going to ask for a move. Obviously it was his disappointment talking and Andy Gray pulled him on the team bus and said: "Hey, you'll probably get the winner in the final. That's how football is. Get your arse in gear."

Late in extra-time we got a free-kick on the right-hand side and because Sheeds had got injured in the Milk Cup final I took it. I was trying to think of how to play it and then I decided just to stick it in the area because I knew we had Andy, Derek and Kevin, who could all win a header if the ball was put into their area. I whipped it in, Derek got a great little flick-on and Inchy finished it on the move.

What followed will live with me forever because I've never seen a stadium like it. The supporters invaded the pitch after the goal and it was absolute bedlam. Brian Moore was a brilliant commentator, one of the very best, and his commentary that day captured the mood. "In a way you can understand their jubilation," he said, and he was absolutely spot on.

We can't go condoning people getting on to pitches but anyone who knew anything about Everton's history building up to that point would know that this was an explosion of joy and relief. There was no malice. Lads just couldn't contain themselves and I got that. It was pure emotion. It was about being in the shadow of another club and emerging from it, it was about reaching an FA Cup final for the first time since 1968 and it was about Everton Football Club putting itself back on the map. Who could begrudge the supporters getting carried away about all that? I know I couldn't, even if I couldn't get into the players' lounge afterwards because there were so many of our fans in the tunnel area. It was absolute euphoria. Take your best glass of red wine, take a sip and the feeling was a million times better than that. That's the only way I can explain how it felt. It was just amazing.

A team which had started 1984 in 16th place in Division One, and whose poor form had prompted demonstrations against both the manager and the chairman, was on the verge of something big. The upturn in form and fortune was staggering, having lost only five of the 35 games we played from New Year's Eve to before the FA Cup final. But for the transformation to be given the catalyst we needed to go to the next level, we knew we had to win the trophy.

We had already been to one final and fallen just short so, amidst the excitement, there was an awareness that we couldn't allow that to happen again. The difference this time was that we would be favourites because we were facing Watford but when I looked at their attack, I knew they had the quality to cause problems for most teams. They had Nigel Callaghan, Mo Johnston and George Reilly, who was always a handful for any defender because of his physical approach, and they had a way of playing under Graham Taylor, a manager and a person who I had utmost respect for, that suited them to a tee.

On top of that, they had John Barnes, a phenomenally talented winger who would go on to become one of my closest friends in football once we finished our playing careers. There were doubts about Barnesy's consistency then but looking at the side that Watford would put out at Wembley he was their biggest threat. But without being disrespectful, we knew that we could get at them and we also knew that we had the individual ability – and the collective organisation – to keep their attacking players quiet.

We stayed at The Bellhouse Hotel in Gerrards Cross the night before the final and I roomed with Adrian Heath, although he probably still hasn't forgiven me for waking him up at two o'clock in the morning to turn the television off. In those days, you would share out different jobs in the room and it was done on a territorial basis, so if the kettle was on your side you had to make the tea, and so on.

I always liked to watch television until fairly late because it would help me to relax and that night Inchy was fast asleep, snoring away, but the TV remote was on his side of the room so I gave him a nudge and told him to turn the television off. He wasn't best pleased. "You're fucking winding me up," he said, but I wasn't. Rules are rules.

To make matters worse, we got woken up early by comedian – and Evertonian – Freddie Starr playing football outside the hotel. Freddie was wearing an old fashioned Everton kit so it was a surreal sight to wake up to on the day of such a big game, but that was the way the FA Cup final was back then. There was a real sense of occasion and that added to the feeling that we were involved in something really big, even if some of us weren't best pleased at being deprived of some of our beauty sleep to switch off the TV for someone else.

As had been the case at Stoke in the third round and at the semi-final against Southampton, we were inspired by our supporters in a way that no team-talk ever could. The journey from the hotel to the stadium is something that will always live with me. Everywhere I looked I could see blue and white. These were people who were desperate for a trophy, having gone 14 years without winning anything at a time Liverpool seemed to be winning everything. How could you not be desperate to win it for them?

Forget your own personal desire, as big as that was for all of us, it was nothing compared to the longing to do it for the supporters. We had the TV cameras on the team bus with us, which was normal back then but there was no chance of the attention becoming a distraction. As soon as we saw the fans we knew we had to get the job done for them.

Barnesy had an early chance but scuffed it, but I was never in any doubt that we would win and I didn't like feeling like that on the pitch. I liked to feel tense and under pressure, to have that fear of failure hanging over me because that is what made me perform. I didn't want to feel comfortable because I knew that could lead to complacency. No matter how good you might think you are, that can undermine any team. But there wasn't a moment, from boarding the team bus to the final whistle being blown, when I felt that we wouldn't win. It wasn't about fate, it was about an absolute belief in the team Everton had become.

I'd looked around the dressing room beforehand and seen a group of players who knew exactly what they were about. I'd listened to the manager tell us that we'd been here once and come away with nothing and that we couldn't allow that to happen again. I'd also heard him talk about the supporters and the sights that we had seen on the way in. This wasn't a time for tactical talk, it was a moment to recognise the opportunity that was in front of us and to realise who we were representing. But, most of all, it was a day when we all knew that we belonged on the stage that we were on. It wasn't arrogance: there was an air of confidence and a sense that we were ready to achieve.

It did feel unnatural to me because I'm a fierce competitor and I like to have an edge, but the other lads felt exactly the same way and, looking back, I realise that this was a key stage in our development. You can't manufacture tension, it's either there or it isn't, and in this case there was very little because we knew as a group that we were ready to go to the next level. As much as we respected Watford, there was nothing in the build-up to that day that would have made us feel nervous. We knew we were good. We just had to go out and prove it.

The game wasn't a classic, and it's probably best remembered for Andy Gray's controversial goal that tested the boundaries of what kind of pressure is acceptable to put on a goalkeeper. We were 1-0 up when that incident happened, with Sharpy making good on Andy's prediction that he would score in the final with a well-taken finish on the turn. Although we weren't under any real pressure, we wanted another goal to make the game safe.

The moment we had been waiting for came early in the second half when Trevor Steven beat Neil Price for the umpteenth time and sent a searching cross to the back post. It was the kind of ball Andy thrived on and he attacked it but Steve Sherwood, the Watford goalkeeper, looked favourite to get there. As Sherwood stretched up, his hands made contact with the ball but Andy got there almost simultaneously and nodded it over the line.

I looked at John Hunting, the referee, and for a split second I thought he might not give it. My mind was cast back to Nat Lofthouse putting Harry Gregg into the back of the net in the 1958 FA Cup final, a goal that I'd seen numerous times. But this was a different era, one in which goalkeepers were more protected so I wouldn't have been surprised if the decision had gone against Andy – but it didn't. The referee signalled a goal and we were all but home and dry.

When he blew his whistle to end the game I headed for Howard. The look on his face gave away not only what it meant to him but also what it meant to Everton. If I live long enough to see a happier expression I'll be a lucky man. Everywhere you looked, people were ecstatic, none more so than Bails, arguably our best player on the day, who donned a pair of massive glasses and a comedy hat to lead the celebrations. This was the defining moment for myself and for the team and, although we went on to enjoy even more success, I can't think of a time when I was more content than I was as we ran around Wembley with the Cup.

You received a lot of complimentary tickets in those days and it was seen as a pay-day for the players but, let's put it this way, I didn't have a pay-day because I had a lot of friends and family who were desperate to be at the game. I was just delighted that so many of them were able to share such a wonderful moment with me. We also ended up paying for a reception at the Royal Lancaster for our families because the club couldn't afford to get them all into their one at The Bellhouse but, after a bit of arm twisting, they allowed us to take the FA Cup in and it was getting thrown about the room well into the small hours.

There was a fair bit of alcohol taken and I ended up losing my medal in the lift but, thankfully, Adrian Heath's dad found it and brought it to my room. Again, there was euphoria but there was also an equally intoxicating feeling that this had to be the start of a journey for Everton Football Club, not the end of one. There was a fierce determination to go on. What we had achieved was great but it wasn't enough and we all knew that we had to kick on – and we believed that we could.

Howard spoke for all of us when he talked to the media the following day. "What I really want Everton to be is the best," he said. "What I really want to win is the championship. The FA Cup is tremendous for the fans and the players. But, for me, it is just a start. It gives us a major trophy. It puts us at Wembley against Liverpool again in the Charity Shield. Most of all, it puts us into Europe, where we should always be."

This was a new Everton. Our ambition was limitless – and so was our belief – and the only disappointment was that my Uncle Jimmy, my mum's brother, hadn't made it to the final because he had been involved in a car accident on the way down. He was a huge Evertonian so I made sure I spoke to him on the phone afterwards and he just kept on repeating the same word over and over again. Whatever I said he would respond with, "magnificent", and I knew that he was speaking for every Everton supporter. That's what it meant to them. It was a truly great moment. A few days later I went to hospital to see him and handed him my medal. He didn't say anything but his eyes gave the game away. He had the look of someone who'd just become a father for the first time.

To win it after all those years, and so soon after there had been protests against the manager, made it even sweeter. People talk about comebacks in football, and the focus is usually on one-off games but we'd come back from the dead and turned ourselves into the first Everton side to parade the FA Cup through the streets of Liverpool since 1966. Not only that, we'd been to Wembley twice, turned our form around and finished a respectable seventh in the league – emerging as a team that most neutrals believed had the potential to get even better. I didn't just believe we would improve – I knew it.

As usual, I was prepared to put my money where my mouth was, too. Ahead of the 1984/85 season I gave an interview to a national newspaper journalist, who asked me what my expectations were for the campaign. "If we can maintain the form we have been showing in the last few months we can really go on to great things," I said. For once, I'd called it just right.

# 7. EVERTON'S GREATEST TEAM

*'The only pressure I felt came from the fear of getting beat. I knew enough about myself to know that I couldn't handle that prospect. It was like playing on the playground but in front of 50,000 people. I didn't like being defeated on the playground so what's the difference?'*

TO prepare myself for Everton's long-awaited return to European competition after a five-year absence I had a low-key summer. The highlight was a family holiday in Cornwall where I looked forward to playing abroad, while my dad struggled to come to terms with anything foreign.

I made him try an olive and he looked at it like it was from outer space before having a bite and immediately spitting it out. He almost spewed up. I was in bulk but he wasn't happy and he let me know about it for days afterwards. His son might have been on the verge of sampling everything that is great about the continent but he was a hairy-arsed fella from Huyton. He wasn't about to give that hard-earned image up for the sake of an olive.

Like my dad, Howard was keeping things simple and English, signing Paul Bracewell from Sunderland, a move which raised a few eyebrows because central midfield didn't seem an obvious area we needed to strengthen. A few months earlier, I would have felt threatened by Brace's arrival, especially if it had happened during the period when I was struggling to get into the team. But I was sure of my place and the question was where the new man would fit in, although that turned out to be the wrong way of looking at things.

The reality was that this was the first major sign of Everton being able to build from a position of strength. Howard had brought someone in who would not only add to what we already had, he would actually improve us as well. Again, the manager was one step ahead and it didn't take long for his foresight to have the desired impact.

The first indication that something special was happening came in a pre-season friendly against Olympiakos in Athens. As ever, the performance on the pitch was preceded by a performance off it, with me welcoming Brace into the fold in customary style. The gaffer told us that we could have a bevvy but when the other lads went out into town for a night out, Brace and myself decided to take it easy and stay at the hotel.

Things didn't quite turn out as planned, though, and while the rest of the team got back handy, having had a few drinks, we carried on into the early hours and got smashed. At least Brace knew straight away what it was to be an Everton player, which was fine in itself, but we had a game to play later that day. It was only a friendly and there was no need for us to be under any real pressure but, equally, we wanted to maintain the high standards that had helped us turn the previous season into such a success.

We won 3-0, but it was the style in which we played that

was most impressive. What sticks in the mind most was Alan Harper's performance. He was playing next to me in midfield and he was like West German legend Gunter Netzer, dictating play with his passing, and the Greeks couldn't get near us. We walked off to a standing ovation and that was when it struck me that not only were we maintaining our standards – we were improving on them. On and off the pitch, Everton had become a club that was ready to go from strength to strength.

The problem was that no matter how good Everton had become, we still had to show we could be masters in our own city before we could conquer the rest of the country, never mind Europe. If we'd been based in London or Manchester that wouldn't have been a foreboding challenge but our home city was Liverpool. The team which carried that name was not just the best in England, they were also the reigning European champions.

In English football, there was no taller order but we were ready to knock them off their perch before Sir Alex Ferguson had even thought of doing it. We had shown we could go toe-to-toe with Liverpool and we also believed that while we had got stronger, they had been weakened by the departure of Graeme Souness to Sampdoria. The 1984 FA Charity Shield at Wembley gave us a chance to strike an early psychological blow – and we took it.

Usually, I don't read too much into pre-season results but there was a bit more at stake for both sides in this one. Not only was it another local derby, but it was a clash between two of the teams who were expected to challenge for the title. It wasn't a classic but we edged it 1-0, with Bruce Grobbelaar scoring an own goal after Alan Hansen had blocked Sharpy's shot on the line. The last time he had been in that situation against us, Hansen had used his hand to stop us from scoring and got away with it, but this time the luck was with us and, more importantly, so was the momentum. It might only have been a friendly but there was no one wearing blue at Wembley who thought it was meaningless. We knew that it mattered – and so did Liverpool.

Having struck an early psychological blow we were ready to hit the ground running – or so it seemed. Our first league game went wrong in a big way as we lost 4-1 at home to Tottenham but although the result was bad, our performance wasn't. They played a 4-5-1 system and even though we went 1-0 up through Adrian Heath's first-half penalty, they did us playing on the break.

It was one of those games in which you walk off wondering what's just gone on because you know you haven't played that badly – and they haven't played that well – but the result suggests otherwise. It affected us, though, giving the confidence that we'd built up a little knock. We lost our next game two days later when West Brom defeated us 2-1 at The Hawthorns, even though we'd played quite well.

Little doubts suddenly started to creep in, and people outside the club were asking whether our form in the second half of the previous season had been a flash in the pan. Inside the dressing room we knew it hadn't but we also knew that we couldn't waste much more time before showing our quality, which was why it was such a relief to win at Chelsea next up. It was only 1-0 and we were still short of our best but we were on the board, and that was what mattered most.

The key to that victory was the gaffer's calmness. There was more attention on that game than usual because it was being screened live on television on a Friday night. Most of the focus was on us but Howard kept things really simple, giving us one clear instruction: "Keep a clean sheet." That was all he said to us and that appeal – to get back to basics – was exactly what we needed. There was no need to be clever or to look for a complicated formula, we just had to be as disciplined as we could and do our jobs. He got the performance he had demanded. It was ugly and it won't live long in the memory for anyone except those who know how vital it was, but we got the three points and the catalyst that we were looking for.

From there, our form improved steadily – if not spectacularly – and as we headed into mid-October we found ourselves in eighth, five points behind leaders Tottenham, but with a game in hand. We were well placed but then we faced an acid test, back-to-back league games that had the potential to define our season, for better or worse: Liverpool at Anfield, where Everton hadn't won for 14 years, followed by Manchester United at Goodison Park.

In hindsight, the results we earned in those fixtures make sense, particularly given what followed, but at the time there was little expectation we could win both. Without Souness, Liverpool were struggling but the Anfield factor was huge and most neutrals – and even the most fatalistic Evertonians – believed that they would find their form against us because that was what they seemed to do. It didn't matter what anyone else thought, though, and it didn't matter what Liverpool had done in the past. We had a quiet confidence that we could get the job done.

The previous weekend we'd beaten Aston Villa 2-1 to move us up to sixth and had played really well, so we knew that form was on our side as Liverpool hadn't even scored in their previous three league games. I wouldn't say we had nothing to fear because they were still a great side with some brilliant players. But they were more vulnerable than they had been and we had a belief that we had the necessary qualities to exploit their weaknesses. There was also an insatiable desire to put one over on them and, being a local lad who'd crossed enemy lines, I was probably feeling it more than most.

In my role as a TV pundit I covered a recent Merseyside derby at Anfield and I still felt the same feelings that I'd had as a player, but I couldn't get on the park and show my passion. All I could do was look at my successors in blue shirts to see if they were feeling the same way that I was. Unfortunately, watching them line up I didn't think they looked up for it. That might not be fair, although the fact that they lost badly suggests otherwise, but that was the impression that I got.

When I went there as a player the feeling I got was similar to the euphoria of having taken a drug. I couldn't wait to get out there and get at them. They could have locked the dressing room door and I would have smashed my way through it. That is the feeling that you have to have as an Everton player at Anfield and we had it that day.

In terms of energy and getting in behind them, we took it to them and Sharpy scored the goal of a lifetime, a dipping volley over Bruce Grobbelaar from over 25 yards out that prompted delirious Evertonians to dance on the Anfield pitch. That was *the* one. That was the goal that shook the football world, the result that tilted Merseyside on its axis and underlined Everton's status as the coming force, while Liverpool looked up at us from 17th place. It felt like a power shift was taking place – and it was. To be part of something like that is special and without being big-headed, I was playing a pivotal role.

On the Monday after the derby, someone passed me the *Daily Telegraph* and showed me the match report, which said: 'Reid, the dominant figure in a game played with ferocious intensity, had the intelligence and application which exploited Liverpool's haphazard approach in midfield.' I'm not as convinced about the intelligence bit as the journalist was but I had the desire, and it was growing all the time. As we began to become accustomed to being showered with praise, we all knew that the one who deserved the most was Howard. Seeing a manager come into his own is an incredible thing. During that period he was seeing things that no one else would have thought of.

One of the best examples came before the derby when he had a load of Adidas Tangos delivered to our Bellefield training ground. Like a lot of clubs, we trained and played with Mitre balls then but Liverpool, despite still having a kit deal with Umbro, used Tangos. Howard's attention to detail was such that he wanted us to train with the same type of ball before we played with it in a game. His planning and preparation paid off when Sharpy struck to leave Liverpool feeling like they'd been 'Tango'd'.

United were next up and if the victory over Liverpool was huge in terms of its symbolism, the significance of this win was to be found in the standard that we set because, and this is in no way an exaggeration, our performance was the best that I was involved in as a professional footballer. As a player, you have days when six or seven play well and it's more than enough to get a result. But to have all 11 on it on the same day is something that very rarely happens.

United had a really strong side under Ron Atkinson and in a different era they would have been regarded as more than just a good cup team, but we made them look like novices. That isn't disrespecting them because we would have made any opponent look the same. We were fantastic, winning 5-0 with Kevin Sheedy getting two of the goals, with the other three shared between Adrian Heath, Gary Stevens and Sharpy – and we could have had even more. Within the space of seven days we had rocked the two superpowers of English football and, in doing so, we'd stated our intention to get to the pinnacle.

As a player, you know when a team is doing well and when

it isn't. With results like those I didn't need anyone to tell me that we were flying. But someone did, someone whose opinion mattered more than most because of what he'd achieved, and it made me realise that the idea something special was building at Everton was starting to take hold.

I was in the dressing room getting changed when Joe Mercer came in and I can still hear the words he spoke because they had such a profound effect on me and the other lads. "I've seen Brazil play in blue today," he said, and you could have heard a pin drop. This was a man who had been a legendary player with Everton and Arsenal, and who had taken Manchester City to the league title as manager, a member of English football's aristocracy. But here he was, stood in front of us in our jockstraps and shinpads, telling us we'd just put in a performance that reminded him of the greatest team there's ever been. He didn't stop there, either, because shortly after he went out and told the media that it was the finest display by an Everton side that he could remember. How could we not take confidence from that?

I couldn't wait to get into the players' lounge afterwards and I'd arranged with Bryan Robson beforehand that we'd have a bevvy, no matter what happened, because that was the done thing. I'd known him for a few years by then, having first played against him for Bolton when he was with West Brom. They had beaten us and two things stuck in my mind from that game – Robbo's curly perm, and just how good a footballer he was.

We had a bit of banter on the pitch and hit it off so Len Cantello, who had joined us from West Brom, organised a night out down there in a pub called The Four In Hand. We went in at midday and got out at midnight. It was quite a session and, from then on, I would see Robbo socially more often than I saw him on the pitch because the two of us had our fair share of injuries.

He remains great company and is undoubtedly up there as one of the best players – and drinkers – that I have known. If there was a league table of drinkers, Robbo would be up there with Terry McDermott. Without giving away state secrets, those two would finish joint-top, although if brandy was involved Sam Allardyce would take some beating. The big thing with all of those lads who enjoyed a bevvy was that they all got up the next day and did their jobs, and did them incredibly well. We played hard but we did enjoy the social side – and we still do.

I used to go to the Quarry Green social club in Kirkby with Robbo and Terry and there was one Sunday session in particular that went down in infamy. We had already had a good go when last orders came, but there was no chance that we wanted to finish. So all three of us went to the bar and, between us, we ordered 50 pints. It's a sight that will live with me forever. Three men, already full up on ale, with 50 pints in front of us. Looking back, I would say it was too much but knowing Robbo and Terry, they would probably say it wasn't quite enough.

Anyway, I got in the Goodison players' lounge after the 5-0 victory and I had the drinks lined up when Robbo popped his head in. He said he couldn't stop because Big Ron had just read the riot act in the United dressing room so he'd see me on Tuesday instead. I hadn't forgotten that we were playing United again three days later in the third round of the Milk Cup but, as soon as he said that, I realised that we would be running the gauntlet at Old Trafford, given the hammering that we'd just handed out. Big clubs don't take kindly to getting a beating like that and there aren't many clubs bigger than United, so we knew what lay in store.

It was like going into the Colosseum. They were baying for us on and off the pitch and the game was brutal, but we stood up to them and won 2-1. That was another test passed. We had already shown that we could play, and now we had proven that we could battle and find a way to win. We never went on to win the Milk Cup. Grimsby Town knocked us out in the next round in a game in which their goalkeeper, Nigel Batch, had the game of his life to leave me devastated. But I've always thought that our win at Old Trafford has been overlooked when our journey from the lower reaches of Division One to the very top is analysed. You don't become the best by playing fantastic football every week, there are times when you have to dig in and show that – mentally and physically – you can cope with all kinds of different challenges.

Over two games against United we had shown our silk and our steel. It was a potent mix, exactly the kind that Howard had in mind when he became manager and stated his intention to "play as attractively" as possible by bringing in players who could "excite and win things." By autumn 1984, that statement was starting to seem more like a prediction that would come true, rather than an ambition that every new manager shares.

Personally, I'd shown that I could hold my own against some of the best players in the country. Liverpool might have lost Souness but they still had the likes of Ronnie Whelan, Jan Molby and John Wark in midfield, all of them really tough competitors, and on top of that they had Dalglish dropping deep. For their part, United had Robson – one of England's greatest-ever midfielders – Remi Moses and Gordon Strachan. These were high-quality affairs and if you came out of them with your honour intact you were doing well, so I took no little confidence from the knowledge that I'd thrived. The bigger the game, the more I enjoyed it, that's just the way it was.

People talked about pressure beforehand and asked how we would deal with these household names but the only pressure I felt came from the fear of getting beat. By then, I knew enough about myself to know that I really couldn't handle that prospect. It was like playing on the playground but in front of 50,000 people, and I didn't like being defeated on the playground so what's the difference?

As a team – and as individuals – we had passed our acid test with flying colours, coming through with a confidence that was starting to border on arrogance. Handling that kind of belief can be difficult because it can be very easy to slip into complacency, but it's also something that you have to deal with if you want to be the best. Liverpool had done it, as personified by Souness, who walked on to every pitch in the country as if he owned the place – and now we were doing it.

Everton's mental outlook was being transformed. From being a club which was in danger of accepting also-ran status, we were now one who saw every other team as a stepping stone to our success: whether the opponent was Liverpool or United no longer mattered. We were in the midst of a 10-match winning streak so it would have been absurd had we harboured any doubts. The only questions were how far our run of form would take us, and whether we had the nous to go all the way because it had been so long since Everton had been in this position. There were no question marks hanging over our desire, though, as Howard constantly discovered whenever he tried to give any of us a rest.

The game has changed now – in some ways for the better and in some for the worse – but in those days you just played. You didn't have sports scientists telling you about being in the red zone and in danger of getting injured, and you didn't have journalists writing articles about the importance of rest and the need for a winter break. You just got your boots on, went out and had a go. Howard was a bit ahead of his time in that he recognised when we were showing signs of fatigue, but realising it and doing something about it were two different things.

There were a few occasions when he told me that he was thinking of leaving me out so that I could get a bit of a blow or allow a knock to settle, and I just looked at him like he was mad. It was the same for the other lads, too. I'm not saying that rest isn't beneficial because I know that at the right time it is. But when you're part of a team that's playing well, that you've fought so hard to get into to become successful individually and collectively, the thought of giving your place up to have a breather goes against everything that you're about.

The physical demands were huge but we were embracing them, which is why I laughed when I read an interview with Mesut Ozil in the 2016/17 season in which he talked of the demands of playing in the Premier League. He was going on about his legs being black and blue, but the physicality that he was talking about is nothing compared to the physicality that we encountered. I'm delighted that skilful players – of which he is one – are more protected now and that is right but there is still room for a tackle, as long as it's done the right way. That side of the game is definitely being lost if a player like Ozil is complaining about how physical it is, when whole matches can pass by without a big challenge being made.

I don't think I was ever 100 per cent fit playing in a football match after doing my first big knee injury, but I just took my anti-inflammatories and got on with it. There was no point moaning about the discomfort or using it as an excuse. I either accepted a bit of pain and dealt with it as best I could, or else I'd allow it to beat me. If my knee was sore before training I'd take my tablets then and I'd almost always take them before games. The one thing I didn't want to happen was for my knee to blow up during a match, as that would either have limited my impact on it or forced me to go off. I had a bursa at the back of my right knee that used to pop up every other game so I had to deal with that, or else I wouldn't have been able to play.

I know in modern medicine they like to do things a little differently and use those drugs more sparingly but, for me, they were an absolute necessity and normal for players of my generation. The only time I didn't take them was during the summer when we didn't have games. It was just something that I had to get on with; it wasn't a hardship. There were times when I had to have cortisone jabs to be able to go out and play but all of this stuff was part and parcel of playing football at the highest level. If I had to go back and do it all again I would. All of the needles, all of the tablets, all of the pain and all of the discomfort were all worth it.

At the same time as we were making waves at home, we were also embarking on an adventure abroad. Our success in the previous season's FA Cup had ensured that we qualified for the European Cup Winners' Cup. At first, it didn't seem particularly continental as we were drawn against University College Dublin which, for most of the Everton players and supporters, felt more like a domestic tie because Liverpool has always had the feel of an Irish city more than an English one. When you go into European competition you have visions of playing at the Nou Camp or the San Siro, places like that. We got a trip to Tolka Park to face a team of students!

Years later I read a brilliant interview with the late Dermot Morgan, who played Father Ted in the television series of the same name, and he was asked why he liked to go to UCD games. He said it was because he liked to avoid crowds, which is a great line but on the night we played them it was packed, and the atmosphere was fantastic. It was UCD's European debut and they'd qualified for the competition – like us – by winning their domestic cup, having beaten Shamrock Rovers, which underlined that they had something about them.

The previous season, Tottenham had beaten another Irish side, Drogheda United, 14-0 on aggregate en route to winning the UEFA Cup. The expectation was that we might do something similar, especially as Howard had made no secret of the fact that he would be fielding a strong line-up, regardless of the perception that we could play a weakened side and still go through comfortably. As it turned out, it was a good job that he did because UCD were right up for it.

We were the better side from start to finish and I lost count of the number of shots that we had. It was probably the only game I've ever played in that was literally attack against defence. We couldn't score, though, and the students somehow managed to hang on as they secured a goalless draw, which remains one of the most famous results in their history.

They could have had an even more famous one in the second leg, too, because they came within inches of knocking us out. Sharpy had given us the lead in the first half but that was the only time over 180 minutes of football that we managed to break them down. In the last minute, a player called Joe Hanrahan, who later joined Man United, slid in at the back post and hit the outside of the upright. It had been one of the most one-sided ties that I had ever played in but we were that close to going out to a team of part-timers.

It was too early to start thinking that our name might be on the trophy. We'd had too much of a scare to think that positively. But when you survive that kind of scare, as happened on our FA Cup run earlier that year, the experience does add to your resilience, even if you would much rather have gone through without being given the fright of your life.

We didn't have too many experiences like that during the 1984/85 season, though. In the vast majority of our games we were the ones in control, and we weren't having to rely on the vagaries of fortune going in our favour to get results. There were setbacks along the way – before Christmas we lost league games at Norwich and at home to Chelsea – but the way we responded was incredible. The next time we tasted defeat was at the end of the season when we already had the championship in the bag. That unbeaten run lasted from December 22 until May 11 and the longer it went on, the more certain it became that we would win the league title.

It seems almost blasé saying it now, but there wasn't a time during that spell when I feared that we might fall short. There was one night when I went out to a bar called Benny's with Arthur Albiston, the Manchester United defender, and he pointed out that we had a tough run-in, highlighting the difficult away games that we had in comparison with the easier home fixtures that Tottenham had. I took in what he was saying, because it wasn't without foundation, but I just thought: 'Well, we'll just have to win the aways.'

It didn't even enter my head that we might come unstuck because I knew what we had in our dressing room, and I knew that we had more than enough to get ourselves over the line. As it was, it was two of those tricky away games that turned out to be the making of us as champions as we recorded a famous victory against Spurs at White Hart Lane, before getting an equally hard-earned win at Sheffield Wednesday.

The game at Spurs went down in Everton folklore, mainly because of the unbelievable save that big Neville made to prevent

Mark Falco from scoring a late equaliser, and rightly so, as it confirmed our status as champions elect. We knew that this was the fixture that could determine our destiny: lose it and we would run the risk of losing momentum and handing the initiative to Tottenham; draw and we would remain in control; win and we would be taking a crucial step to the title.

Andy Gray was at his best at times like this and he underlined the size of the occasion beforehand when he told a TV interviewer that this was "probably Everton's most important league game since they clinched the title in 1970." He was right, but maybe the word "probably" wasn't needed. This *was* Everton's biggest league game for 15 years, it was enormous.

Andy also said something else that was, if anything, even more pertinent. Asked if we would settle for a draw, he replied: "Only wins satisfy this team" and although he admitted afterwards that we would have all taken a point, he was capturing the attitude that had fuelled our challenge, one that was totally in keeping with Everton's Latin motto, 'Nil Satis Nisi Optimum', only the best is good enough. If we wanted to set the standard for others, first we had to set it for ourselves. This was a night for doing that but we knew everything – from our ambition to our ability – was going to be tested.

The tempo was fierce, as it should be when so much is at stake, and that suited us as our intensity and knack of winning the ball high up the pitch – Gegenpressing anyone? – allowed us to take a 2-0 lead, with Andy and Trevor Steven getting the goals. At that stage, it looked like we would knock our biggest title rivals out of the race with the minimum of fuss but Graham Roberts got a goal back and Tottenham started to believe again.

It was a great finish. The ball fell to him after a short corner routine and I said to myself, "Go on, hit it." Roberts did just that and he smashed it into the top corner. Talk about being careful for what you wish for. Had they got another, they might have knocked us out of our stride but the great thing about that team was that, at any given moment, any single individual would stand up and be counted when – and where – it mattered most.

That night it was Neville, for me then the best goalkeeper in the world. Even now, when I watch highlights of the game it still takes my breath away when the big fella somehow palms Falco's header over the bar from point-blank range. Falco did everything right, he met the cross perfectly and the ball was flying into the roof of the net. At best, a good keeper might expect to get a touch but still be unable to keep a header like that out, but Neville was a great keeper and he kept it out. Astonishing. We couldn't blow it after an incident like that – and we didn't. As soon as the final whistle was blown we knew we were going to be champions.

We still had to go to Hillsborough, though, and that turned out to be another game where we needed Neville to bail us out. He made some brilliant saves out of a sheer desire not to be beaten and we defended for our lives at times, but we dug in, and Andy's first-half goal got us another vital three points. They were the games that saw us through.

Character played a huge part but so did talent. I've always felt that the ability of the players in that team has been underrated outside of Goodison Park. Pat van den Hauwe probably personified that. Everyone focused on how physical he was and, to be fair, his "Psycho" nickname didn't help on that front but he was a magnificent footballer. He could tackle but he was also a tremendous athlete and he was brilliant in the air. He did go on benders and he did go missing and not turn up for training but, as a player, he was top drawer.

Then you have Derek Mountfield, who only ever got one

England Under-21 cap, but we knew his value to us and he scored 14 goals for us, 10 of them in the league, in 1984/85, even though he was a centre-back. It was great for Derek to play in a team that had such brilliant delivery from wide areas, with Sheeds and Trevor on either flank. His willingness to attack every ball turned their crosses into goals and chances on so many occasions that he became a major attacking weapon for us.

That was what that Everton team was about – every one of us making the most of the talent that we had, for ourselves and for each other. Then you bring the so-called squad players like Kevin Richardson and Alan Harper into the equation, although I would never have described them as such. They were so much more valuable than that, and you have a group of players which any manager in the country would have given his eye teeth for. That was the reason why we went into our home game against Queens Park Rangers on Bank Holiday Monday, May 6, knowing that victory would allow us to clinch the title.

It was party time. I don't mean that disrespectfully to QPR, who were a good side, but we were going to beat them no matter what. It was all about us and what we did on the day but in one way it wasn't about us, it was about the supporters who had waited for Everton to become champions of England once again, and who might have been starting to fear that it might not happen.

They were hanging off the Littlewoods clock, straddling the railings, clambering on to roofs of houses around the ground, anything that would allow them to see Everton's coronation. It was a full house and the gates were locked a couple of hours before kick-off, which might seem totally normal to fans who have grown up in the modern era, when Premier League stadiums are invariably full and tickets are scarce. But in the mid-1980s, even the biggest clubs were often below capacity.

Our average attendance that season was around 32,000, a respectable but not spectacular figure considering the quality of football that we were playing. But when you put that number into the context of the socio-economic situation it becomes incredible that so many people were attending football matches so regularly, regardless of how good we might have been.

This was a period in which unemployment in Liverpool exceeded 20 per cent, when young people had to "get on their bike", as Norman Tebbit so disgracefully put it, if they wanted to find work, and when poverty had become so endemic that you could feel it. Merseyside wasn't just struggling, it was on its knees. So to have tens of thousands of people scrimp and save, just so they can watch you play football at a time like that, is humbling.

I'm very politically aware and my respect for our fans is matched only by my disdain for those who made their lives so difficult out of sheer political dogma. They were desperate times and two things kept Liverpool going: football and humour. Without those elements, the people who wanted to drive the city into the ground – some of whom still do – might have succeeded.

The city was decimated, which is why I always say that Alan Bleasdale's *Boys From The Blackstuff* wasn't just a brilliant drama, it was a real-life portrayal of how people were living their lives. It might have been a drama but it was utterly factual. People didn't have the money to go to watch football and that was despite admission prices being relatively cheap. Every single person who came through the gates of Goodison that season played their part in Everton winning the league title in a way that went well beyond the call of duty.

That was why the "win it for them" message that Howard regularly delivered was so powerful. I could remember as a kid being at St George's Hall when Shankly told the Liverpool players that they were privileged to play for their supporters but now the shoe was on the other foot, and I understood implicitly how lucky I was to be playing for our fans. That feeling really hit home on that Bank Holiday Monday.

Howard had told us the day before that it was going to be manic but nothing really prepared us for those sights. The risk when the atmosphere is like that is that you might get consumed by it and it either saps your energy, or makes you too excited. This was when Howard's experience and intuition came to the fore. This wasn't the time for inspirational speeches or grand tactical plans. He just said to us, "Go out there and let those supporters see you play like champions" – and we did. We still had five league games to go after that but we were determined to get it done, and Derek and Sharpy got the goals that meant we couldn't be caught.

That team was efficient in big games and against QPR we got the job done with the minimum of fuss. This was the behaviour of a big club and a team which wasn't just prepared for success, it was ready to go on to bigger and better things. Everton weren't just champions of England, we were treble-hunters looking to establish a dynasty.

On top of that, we had taken Liverpool's crown and you can't under-estimate the importance of that on Merseyside. They had been the dominant force and it hurt Evertonians, so to change that was massive, but something that stayed with me was the way that Joe Fagan, the Liverpool manager, reacted.

I've got no doubt that behind the scenes, Liverpool were gutted because they didn't get to achieve as much success as they did by being good losers or because they were content with being second best. The rivalry between the two clubs was incredibly intense and it was underlined by a couple of confrontations I had with Ronnie Moran after derby matches later in the decade.

After Liverpool had won one I went down the tunnel and there was Mr Liverpool himself waiting for me. "Hard luck, son, you've played well though." I knew what he was up to so I told him to fuck off. The following season, we beat them so I raced off the pitch looking for him, but this time he wasn't in the tunnel area so I marched straight into the boot room. "Unlucky Ronnie," I said, repeating his sentiments from after the previous encounter. "You played well, though." Suffice to say, he responded with a Scouse blast of Anglo Saxon and sent me on my way.

Those two incidents sum up the rivalry between Everton and Liverpool. There is always a respect, sometimes it is grudging but it's always there, and at times we can be confrontational, but it is all underpinned by a desire to get one over on the other. Which is why an interview that Fagan gave to the *Liverpool Echo* after we'd taken his club's title struck a chord with me.

'I want to congratulate Howard Kendall, his players and his coaching staff on winning what is really the biggest championship of the lot,' he stated. 'They won it fair and square and they were the best team over the whole season, there's no doubt about that. I am especially delighted for Howard because he's such a nice chap and has come back well after a very sticky time. He took a lot of criticism and now he's entitled to a lot of credit.'

Everything that Fagan said was right but for him to come out and say it was a big thing and I had so much respect for him, stepping outside of the rivalry to give credit where it was due. I knew full well that he and Liverpool would be doing everything in their power to strike back, but he would have been equally well aware that Everton would be hell bent on not conceding an inch because our rivalry demanded nothing else.

Not long after, though, a tearful Fagan was pictured on the front of the *Echo* as he was led from an aeroplane while being comforted by Roy Evans. His pain following the Heysel Stadium disaster was as clear as it was heartfelt and he would never manage Liverpool again, but the implications extended well beyond Anfield and impacted on Everton and all other English clubs.

That is why I always look back on May 1985 with mixed feelings. It was a month of immense joy for Everton but it was also a time of great despair. Even now, more than three decades on, I can still feel the contrasting emotions that were stirred. We were champions of England but we would not get the opportunity to prove ourselves in European competition, and that still hurts. How could it not?

# 8. MAY '85

*'The punishment applied to us, even though we had been guilty of nothing. It was like banning the entire Canadian athletics team because Ben Johnson had been caught cheating but we had no choice but to accept our fate, even though it was clearly unfair'*

THERE are only 31 days in May but as far as Everton were concerned, in 1985, it was a month with enough highs and lows to last a lifetime. After being crowned champions on the 6th, we had a European Cup Winners' Cup final on the 15th and an FA Cup final on the 18th.

We had seven league games in all, including a Merseyside derby against Liverpool, while our great rivals had a European Cup final of their own on the 29th. A period like that is always going to be eventful, especially with all of it affecting two clubs from one city. While I look back on much of what occurred with a mixture of pride and fondness, I was also left with profound feelings of regret and disappointment that lingers to this day.

What happened on the pitch takes care of itself. We won one final in the most glorious of circumstances, lifting Everton's first-ever

European trophy on an unforgettable night in Rotterdam, and lost another disappointingly as Manchester United prevented us from winning the treble on a day when we never really got going.

What happened off the pitch, though, ensured that our setback at Wembley was put in perspective on a number of levels as 39 football fans, mainly followers of Juventus, were killed when trouble broke out prior to Liverpool's European Cup final against the Italian champions. English clubs, including Everton, were banned from continental competition as a result. So a month which began with us triumphantly looking forward to taking our place among Europe's elite for the first time since 1970 ended with our path being blocked through no fault of our own.

It was the sense of anticipation that made it worse. That spring had been a wonderful time to be an Evertonian. The big games were coming thick and fast – and we were winning all of them. Semi-finals in the FA Cup and Cup Winners' Cup, came and went without our hopes of becoming only the second English club to win a treble being damaged. We were *the* team, and this was *our* time. No more spells in the shadows, no more hoping that our rivals might fall short against someone else because we'd been unable to stop them. We were the standard setters – and everyone knew it.

The only questions about us, after being crowned champions, was how many trophies we would add to our haul, and how good a position we would be in to challenge for the European Cup the following season. We answered the first, with mixed results, but we never got to answer the second.

Not that what went against us can detract from what we achieved. Having survived that scare against UCD, the Cup Winners' Cup became a competition we thrived in, and one in which we established ourselves as a coming force in Europe.

Inter Bratislava and Fortuna Sittard were both dispatched comfortably, 4-0 and 5-0 on aggregate respectively, as we grew in confidence and belief. Then came the big one, Bayern Munich in the semi-final. They were favourites and rightly so, considering their heritage, but while we respected their ability and reputation as one of the giants of the game, we did not fear them.

They probably hoped that the mere sight of their name would be sufficient to make us take a backward step, but if they were banking on us having some sort of inferiority complex they were to be proved mistaken.

The tone was set before the draw had even been made when *Kicker*, the German sports magazine, carried a story after Bayern had beaten AS Roma at the quarter-final stage. 'Bayern triumph in Rome and now they want Everton' the headline stated. What Bayern wanted, Bayern got, but they were given more than they had bargained for – much more.

Everyone remembers the second leg at home and rightly so, because it was arguably the greatest night that Goodison Park had ever experienced. But in order to be in a position to make that occasion unforgettable we had to produce something special, albeit in a more resolute, less spectacular way, out in Munich. We also had to do without Andy and Sheeds, who were both injured.

Bayern had some great players including Lothar Matthaus, Soren Lerby, Michael Rummenigge and Dieter Hoeness so they were favourites. It's at times like that when you need your manager to make the difference and Howard did that; tactically, he got everything spot on.

We played a 4-5-1 with Sharpy up front on his own and Trevor Steven playing off him. The idea was for us to be difficult to break down so that we could keep things tight and quieten the 67,000 crowd at the Olympic Stadium. It worked a treat and if Jose

Mourinho did something similar nowadays it would be hailed as a tactical masterclass but aside from the local paper, the *Liverpool Echo*, who described our performance as 'a shrewd exhibition of patience and controlled football', not too many other plaudits came our way. Not that we needed any praise from outside. The goalless draw that our performance earned was more than enough to please us.

We hadn't been able to get an away goal that would have made life easier for us but, by dropping off and sitting deep, we had been able to get the result that we had been looking for. Most importantly, we knew that if we turned it on at Goodison we had enough quality to eliminate a very good side, especially with the backing of our fans, and we left West Germany the following morning fairly confident.

Just to illustrate how happy we were about getting a draw, in the hours after the game I was in my hotel room with Brace, who I was sharing with, and Andy turned up with a crate of German beer that he insisted we have a couple of bottles of. I wasn't going to argue and we spent some time just enjoying the moment in the knowledge that we were one home win away from becoming the first Everton team to reach a major European final.

The price of our success, if you can call it that, was that the big games were coming thick and fast. Three days after holding out in Munich, we had another semi-final, this time against Luton Town at Villa Park in the FA Cup. The good thing was that, by then, we were used to dealing with the kind of schedule that modern managers moan about as soon as they have to play more than once a week. The quick turnaround meant that there wasn't enough time for nerves to set in for us to contemplate the enormity of chasing a treble. We were leggy, though, there was no getting away from that. The effort that we had put in against

Bayern worked against us and Luton, who had a very good team, were the better side.

When you don't have energy you need know-how and having gone 20 matches unbeaten going into that one, we knew how to cope mentally, even when we were below par physically.

Luton tested us to the full and David Pleat had obviously told them beforehand that the best way of getting through would be if they took the game to a tired team and they did that in the early stages, especially with Emeka Nwajiobi having three good chances to score, one of which forced Gary Stevens to clear off the line.

All we could do was try to hang on in there in the hope that when their fire died down, our extra quality would begin to show. But even that target became more difficult when Ricky Hill gave Luton the lead with eight minutes of the first half remaining. It was a good goal, although maybe if I'd been a bit sharper I might have been able to block his shot but they deserved to lead, even if I wasn't all that impressed by their supporters behind the goal waving straw boaters above their heads to celebrate as if they were at the Henley regatta.

We were knackered but as the game wore on we were the ones who grew stronger, which tells you everything you need to know about our heart and desire. It would have been easy for us to accept our fate, to let our heavy legs dictate our response and our minds to decide to focus on winning the league and the Cup Winners' Cup, but we did the opposite. From somewhere deep inside we managed to summon up the energy to go back at Luton but although Brace hit the post with one effort, we were indebted to Neville yet again when he made a magnificent save to prevent Hill from scoring a second. Had that gone in we probably wouldn't have been able to recover but we never gave up, even when the clock seemed to tick quicker towards the 90-minute mark than it does normally.

With around five minutes remaining we won a free-kick on the edge of their box. I can still hear the supporters' reaction now as they chanted, "Sheedy, Sheedy, Sheedy" in the knowledge that his brilliance from dead-ball situations would give us a shot at salvation. In the previous round, at home to Ipswich, Sheeds had memorably scored twice from a dead-ball situation. The first was ruled out by the referee because he had taken it too quickly. In the aftermath I was standing next to him and said to Sheeds: "What are we going to do?" and he just looked at me and said: "What are *we* going to do? Fucking leave it to me."

He told me he was going to stick it in the other corner and I've gone, "fuck off", but he was as good as his word, dinking it past Paul Cooper, who was a really good goalkeeper. Just having the nerve to attempt that is impressive enough but to have the talent to execute it is remarkable. People go on about having bollocks on a pitch and more often than not they refer to putting tackles in but to do something like that takes massive bollocks. That mix of audacity and ability sums Sheeds up. He was a special player. Of course, in the semi-final, Sheeds drove it past the wall and inside Les Sealey's left-hand post and bedlam broke out.

It was a devastating blow for Luton, who had been so close to knocking us out and it was a shot in the arm for us. All of a sudden, we were the ones making the running and Gary Stevens came close to winning it in the last minute but, as the game went into extra-time, we knew that the dynamic had shifted in our favour. I thought I was going to be the match-winner when I had a dig but Sealey pulled off a great save. It was Derek Mountfield who turned out to be the Everton hero when he got on the end of another Sheedy free-kick in front of the Holte End.

Howard admitted afterwards that he'd feared we were beaten before Sheeds equalised and he spoke for us all in that respect but he also highlighted our refusal to be beaten, the quality that had allowed us to emerge unscathed from difficult games in Munich and Birmingham in the space of three days. The funny thing was that although Everton were the ones going for the treble, a lot of focus had been on the other semi between Liverpool and Man United at Goodison. That probably irked our supporters a bit but I didn't care who got through because I knew that, regardless of the media attention, whoever we got, we were better than both.

Another all-Merseyside final would have been nice but, as it was, United got through after a replay at Maine Road. We'd already turned them over a couple of times that season so they didn't hold any fears for us. The only question was whether we'd meet them in the FA Cup final at Wembley on May 18 having already played in a European final just three days earlier? The only team that could prevent that from happening was Bayern but we were on a roll and would take some stopping.

For every Evertonian of a certain vintage, the night of April 24, 1985 was an "I was there" moment. I was definitely there, battling away in the middle of the park as if my life depended on it, even though there are times when it seems too surreal, too magical to have happened. Ken Rogers in the *Echo* said the game was 'a full-blooded, no-holds-barred affair that bubbled like a volcano at times' and I can certainly vouch for the blood because I ended up getting six stitches in a calf wound that turned my sock crimson red. I never felt a thing, though. Adrenaline does that. It makes you feel no pain, even when you should be in agony and it gives you an ability to perform above the norm.

Usually it comes from within, but on that occasion it was caused by the Goodison crowd, which whipped every single

Everton player into a frenzy that meant we would not be denied, come what may. It wasn't to Bayern's taste and their manager, Udo Lattek, told Howard that the game that we played "was not football," but I'd been brought up to see football as a game that had to be won at all costs. If that meant going the extra mile in a physical sense then so be it. His complaint is still music to my ears anyway. I might even have it engraved on my gravestone when I die: "Here lies Peter Reid. He might not have played football against Bayern Munich but he was on the winning side."

Not that Lattek's criticism stands up to scrutiny. We played that night. We played as if it was the last game any of us would ever compete in. We played as if we wanted it more than anything else in the world. Bayern wanted it, too, and I've got a scar on my calf to prove it, they just didn't want it as much as us. There was a European final at stake, what were we supposed to do, let the chance pass us by because the opposition manager wouldn't like it if we got stuck in? If I'd ever heard Howard come out with something like that I would have been devastated because what it really means is your own team fell short when it mattered. That's the reality. If Bayern had won he wouldn't have cared if we'd spent 90 minutes playing like a Sunday League outfit. They lost, though, and losers make excuses; it's just that his wasn't a very good one.

If he was honest he would have admitted that the atmosphere inspired us, and intimidated them. I could sense it was going to be like that on the way to the game because we had been at St George's Hall beforehand, which we'd done for all of our home European games that season, and the route to Goodison was mobbed with people. As we got closer to the ground the team bus struggled to get through because there were so many people on the streets and this was an hour-and-a-half before kick-off.

When we got inside, Adrian Heath, who had cruelly been ruled out for the season after picking up a serious injury in December, was asked to go and do a TV interview. I followed him out, just to get a feel for things. I went up the steps and popped my head out and the stadium was already packed. I still had my suit and best shoes on but if I'd been told to play there and then I would have done because the adrenaline was already kicking in.

Handling all of that emotion was going to be crucial because the risk was that, if we went behind, the positive feelings we were experiencing could quickly become negative. An away goal had to be avoided no matter what, not that we weren't capable of scoring twice. We just didn't need any additional tension, particularly against a top-class side like Bayern.

They had ambitions of their own, though, and took the lead after 37 minutes when Hoeness scored after Neville had saved well from Ludwig Kogl. The silence when the ball hit the back of the net was eerie but it was typical of us – and the run that we'd been on – that we were left having to do it the hard way. It seemed that for 18 months leading up to that night we had needed to fight for everything we had achieved; nothing had come easy or been handed to us on a plate.

At least we were in a situation that we had become accustomed to, even if it was one that we had been determined to avoid. It was the first goal that we had conceded in Europe that season but it was a hugely significant one because it meant the tie could not go to extra-time, and left us facing the prospect of either out-scoring Bayern or going out.

To make matters worse, I was struggling a bit because I'd gone in for a tackle, and just about managed to nick the ball away when this kid came in and smashed me. It was a beauty and I knew straight away that he'd done a bit of damage. He stood over me, looking down at me like he was Muhammad Ali towering over Sonny Liston, but the physical damage that he'd inflicted on me wasn't enough for him. He wanted more than blood. "You English pig," he shouted, before walking away as I was clocking who the player was, just in case the chance came for me to give him a bit back.

I saw that it was Hans Pflugler and decided there and then that this wouldn't be the last time that we had a confrontation, even though the gash that he'd opened up on my calf wasn't going to make it easy for me to complete the match, never mind exact a bit of revenge on my West German friend. With blood pouring out of the wound I was forced to go to the sidelines to get a wet sponge that I stuffed down my sock, before racing back on to the pitch. There was no way I was going off in this one. I was having Pflugler and Everton were having Bayern; it was that simple.

We'd had opportunities to score before and after Kogl's goal but, through a combination of brilliant defending and a bit of luck, they kept us out and we went in at the half-time interval knowing that the next time we emerged from the tunnel we would have just 45 minutes to come back. As was becoming his trait at such moments of high tension, Howard kept things simple, telling us that if we kept playing the fans on the Gwladys Street would suck the ball into the goal at the end we would be kicking into in the second half.

While all this was going on our club doctor, Ian Irving, was stitching my calf and I was looking at the damage while listening to Howard, instructing us to get the ball into the box whenever we could, to put their defence under pressure. However, all I was thinking about was this blond geezer who'd put a hole in my leg. My mood wasn't made any better by the fact that they were winning but I think even if we'd been two or three goals ahead

I would still have wanted to enjoy a reunion with him. That wasn't my priority – winning the game was – but it was definitely prominent in my thoughts at that point.

The second half was fast and frenetic, exactly as Howard had hoped it would be, but the Swedish referee, Erik Fredriksson, was being quite sensible and letting the game flow as much as he could, without giving fouls and handing out bookings every few minutes. That suited us and it suited me, in particular, because it took me back to when I was a kid in Huyton, when every street game turned into a battle, with no quarter being sought and certainly none being given.

Shortly after the re-start, Sharpy equalised from Gary Stevens' long throw and Goodison erupted. Honestly, it felt like the noise hurt my ears more than Pflugler's challenge had hurt my calf. It was as if a thunderclap had gone off overhead and for a split second it scrambled my senses. The outpouring of euphoria was that great but the reality was that, as things stood, we were still going out on away goals unless we got another. There aren't many more tense situations than when you need a goal, but you also know that if you commit too much to attack you risk a hammer blow at the other end.

With the crowd roaring us on, we managed to strike a balance as we took control of the game, dominating possession in the knowledge that another opportunity would come our way if we also kept things tight defensively. We had to remain patient but when the second goal arrived, with 15 minutes left, it felt like the roof had come off as Andy took advantage of goalkeeper Jean-Marie Pfaff's failure to deal with another Stevens long throw. Pandemonium. The Everton supporters thought we were through but the game was still on a knife edge and, anyway, I still had a score to settle.

I knew my chance would come and when it did, I took it. I saw Pflugler coming at me out of the corner of my eye and I smashed him. As he was rolling about in pain I stood over him, ready to unleash some verbal vengeance on top of the physical retribution. "Have some of that, you Nazi bastard," I said. It wasn't politically correct and I'm definitely not nationalistic, but he'd called me out and I was giving some back. It felt good, too. This was law of the jungle stuff and I was putting my aggressor in his place.

As the adrenaline and the machismo both went into overdrive I went to walk away, only for my victim's voice to stop me in my tracks. "I'm Danish," he said, and I went cold. I'd got Soren Lerby instead. It was a case of mistaken identity and poor Soren, who's now a good friend, had been on the receiving end. Not only had Pflugler got away with it, I was left nursing a guilty conscience to go with my bloody calf. We still had a game to win though so this was no time to start feeling sorry for myself.

For a team accused of not playing football, the third goal wasn't too shabby. Sheeds used superb skill to keep possession under pressure on the left before knocking the ball forward to Andy. The big fella showed his awareness by picking Trevor Steven out with a clever pass, which Tricky finished brilliantly. For the third time that night, Goodison erupted. That was it. There were only five minutes remaining and we were not going to let this slip.

The stadium rocked and those of us on the pitch couldn't hear ourselves think but a confrontation between the two benches caught my attention, and it was only afterwards that I discovered what Lattek had said to Howard. I also found out that he'd said Andy Gray should take up rugby, which wasn't a bad shout to be fair, and it showed just how much we had got under their skin.

Not that we gave a shit about what they were saying. The Champagne flowed in the dressing room afterwards and the lads decided to carry on the celebrations at a club called The Continental in Liverpool city centre. I was definitely up for that but I was in the treatment room because my leg had swelled up. John Clinkard, our physio who was vital for my career and was the spitting image of Magnum PI, told me the only place I was going to was Lourdes, a private hospital in the south of the city. "I'm fucking not," I responded, but then Doc Irving came in and backed Clinks up.

I was standing my ground because there was no way I was missing a party after reaching our first European final. That was until Howard arrived and sided with the medical professionals and, the next thing I knew, I was in an ambulance on my way to hospital, while the other lads were heading into town for the mother of all parties.

So there I was in Lourdes with my foot up, getting the blood drained from my calf while everyone else was in the 'Conti' having the time of their lives. I was gutted because I couldn't share the moment with them, but any disappointment was insignificant in comparison to the feeling of incredible pride that came from being involved in one of the best games of my career and, most importantly, winning it. The adrenaline had long since subsided but I was still high and it would be quite a few days before I came back down to earth.

I missed the next game, a 3-0 defeat of Norwich City at Goodison, but I was back for the crucial fixtures away to Sheffield Wednesday and at home to QPR, when we produced back-to-back victories to sew up the league title. It was after those matches that Howard started to rotate the team a little bit. When we faced Nottingham Forest at the City Ground, the start of a seven-day period which also included the Cup Winners' Cup and the FA Cup finals, he rang the changes just to be on the safe side. I was one of the players who missed out and although I would rather have played, I couldn't really moan about the manager's decision because he was making sure I'd be in the best condition possible for two of the biggest games of my life.

I liked playing against Brian Clough's teams, though. I liked the way they played football and I liked the way he managed. The season before we'd played them at the City Ground and, as usual, my dad needed tickets. I went outside to see him beforehand and said I had four for him but he told me he needed six. I was about to head back into the ground to see what I could sort out when I heard a familiar voice.

"Young man," Mr Clough said. "Is that your father, young man?" I told him that it was and he told me to bring him in. The next thing I knew, he was walking down the corridor with my dad with his arm around his shoulder, as if they were two old pals who'd just met up for the first time in years. I followed behind to see where they were going but I was wearing my boots and the studs kept slipping on the wooden floor so it wasn't easy.

They went in through some double doors and I didn't know what was on the other side so I popped my head in to see what was going on. There was Mr Clough at the bar of what was obviously the boardroom and he was ordering drinks. "Young lady, could you please give this gentleman a large scotch, his son is a rather good player and I like him a lot."

After that, he took my dad to the directors' box and he watched the game from there as Cloughie's guest. I took a shine to him for the way he looked after my dad but this time around, his mood was very different.

I was sat on the away bench with Sharpy, Inchy and Andy Gray. We heard footsteps approaching and we all looked to see who it was but I think we all knew before we saw him, because he even walked with authority. I was about to exchange pleasantries and tell him that he didn't need to worry about my dad this year because he was sorted for tickets, but I never got the chance.

Sharpy had been involved in a challenge that had ended up with Gary Mills breaking his leg in a game earlier in the season so there was a bit of bad feeling and Cloughie wasn't about to let bygones be bygones. "I wanted you out there today, young man," he said to Sharpy, and he replied: "Fuck off, I've got two cup finals coming up."

The other three of us sat there waiting for an eruption, ready to back Sharpy up when it came but Clough's response disarmed us. "And all the very best in them," he said. That was just the way he was; unpredictable, passionate and partisan but a football man to the core. We lost 1-0 that day, our first defeat that calendar year, but it didn't matter. Our focus was where it mattered – on Rotterdam and Wembley.

Rapid Vienna were our opponents in the Cup Winners' Cup final and the build-up went like a dream. We flew to Holland and the atmosphere in and around the city was magical. The team was full of confidence and, the day before the game, Howard asked us if we wanted to train on the pitch, in keeping with our usual European routine, or else go for a walk near our hotel. We opted for the latter and it caused a furore with the media and, at the pre-match press conference, Howard was asked if we were taking our opponents seriously enough.

The manager came out with a quip about us knowing that we hadn't needed to see the pitch because we knew it would have goalposts, lines, 18-yard boxes, penalty spots and so on; it was a good response because we hadn't intended to show any disrespect, we were just in a positive frame of mind about ourselves and adapted our preparations accordingly.

If we felt good about ourselves, the Everton supporters probably felt even better and we were getting reports about how many of them were travelling over from Merseyside and the fun that they were having in Rotterdam. They were having a great time and we got to witness some of the festivities when we went for a walk on the day of the game. There is the famous story about the Evertonians playing football with the Dutch police and that captured the mood.

There was a carnival atmosphere and, as players, we enjoyed sampling it from a distance but we also had a fierce determination to get the job done. There was no point in the fans having a great day only for it to be ruined by an anti-climax of a night. We had to win.

I was confident that we would because I'd seen Rapid play. They had faced Celtic in the second round and lost the second leg 3-0 after winning the first 3-1 but, because there'd been some sort of crowd trouble at Celtic Park, UEFA ordered the second leg to be replayed at a neutral venue. It was a ridiculous decision but the game took place at Old Trafford so I went along to watch it with Sharpy and Andy.

I was hoping that natural justice would prevail and Celtic, a club that I've always admired, would get through. But Rapid won 3-0 and we couldn't believe it. It was a great result for the Austrians but having seen them in action we fancied our chances. It wasn't about being blasé, but we never felt we would get beat. They had some good players – Hans Krankl was their big name – but we were stronger and just had to prove it when it mattered.

Rapid had been banging on about how they were going to take the game to us but it never happened, and we were the dominant side from the off. Andy thought he had given us the lead in the first half but his goal was wrongly ruled out for offside. It was just a case of us remaining patient because it was only a matter of time before the breakthrough came.

I know people have said that the longer the game went on the more they feared we would be hit by a sucker punch but I never felt that way and, at half-time, Howard told us that if we kept moving the ball quickly and shutting down early the goal would come. That was exactly how events transpired, too, with Andy opening the scoring after Sheeds had shut them down on the left and Sharpy had moved the ball on quickly. The manager's instructions had been followed to wonderful perfection.

I'm never complacent out on the pitch but the game felt like it was only going one way after we took the lead – and that sense grew still further when Trevor Steven scored at the back post from Sheeds' corner. My confidence didn't diminish even after Krankl had pulled one back. If anything, his goal gave us the little jolt we needed and we put the result beyond doubt almost immediately as Sheeds scored from outside the box to secure Everton's first European trophy.

We were flying back the same night and we enjoyed some Champagne on the bus on the way to the airport and on the plane, but we couldn't have the kind of party that our achievement deserved because we had another massive game in less than three days' time. There's an urban myth about the team going to Chinatown in Liverpool after we got back in the early hours of the morning but, as far as I'm concerned, it never happened or, if it did, I know I wasn't there even though a great pal of mine, Derek Hatton, is adamant I was. I've gone into Chinatown with Derek many a time and had some wonderful nights there with him but, on this occasion, I was picked up at Speke Airport having had a few.

The manager had given us Thursday off to allow us to recover but one of the last things he said to us in the dressing room in Rotterdam was that we had another game on Saturday, and that it just happens to be a final. He told us to enjoy the night and to enjoy being winners but the strongest message from Howard was that there was another job that needed to be done. Point taken.

The problem is that, even if your pre-match preparation is right and you eat and drink all the right things, there's not much you can do to counteract the emotional energy that you've invested, not just on a wonderful night in Holland, but in the days, weeks and months leading up to it. You've committed everything to climbing the mountain but, having reached the top, you realise that, in 48 hours or so, you'll have to go back down and start climbing again. Not only that but there'll be someone else, in this case Man United, trying to hold you back so they can get to the summit before you.

Not that this was a negative, it just wasn't easy. By having five days to prepare for such a massive game, United had a bit of an advantage on us – but we wouldn't have swapped places with them for anything. We were the champions of England, the newly-crowned winners of the Cup Winners' Cup and this was a position that we had longed to be in. If being one of the very best teams around meant coping with fatigue and having games come thick and fast, then so be it. My attitude was the same as ever – bring it on.

I got home at around 4am on the Thursday and spent most of the day relaxing and even on Friday, the day before the final, it wasn't particularly intense. We had some games of head tennis that were pretty competitive but they were enjoyable as well, and a lot of the work we were doing in training was built around getting rid of the stiffness that had built up in us. There were loads of supporters outside Bellefield and at one point a kissogram turned up, which pretty much summed up the atmosphere. But even if it was a bit more light-hearted than usual, that was a positive thing. You can't be mentally wired for every minute of every day at a time like that.

We knew what we had to do, we knew how we would go about it and none of that would have changed in any way if we had prepared any differently. Our preparations were exactly right in terms of the challenge we were facing and the run of games that we were in, but in those situations it's only when you get out on the pitch that you discover how you really feel. So while we were confident, we weren't kidding ourselves that this would be anything other than a major test. Ron Atkinson had put together a strong United side that had proved itself a force to be reckoned with in cup competitions, even if they hadn't been able to end a lengthening wait to win the league.

The outcome of the final might suggest otherwise but I have always maintained that we played well on the day, and were the better side – but you don't always get what you deserve. We'd discovered that in a much less important way during the build-up when their Cup final song, *We All Follow Man United*, charted four places higher than ours, at number 10, even though *Here We Go* was a much better and more memorable record, despite our questionable voices. We had recorded the song in London and had enjoyed a few drinks when down there, just to lubricate our vocal chords obviously, but my abiding memory was of performing it on *Wogan*.

We battered the ale on the way to the studio and when we got there one of the producers took one look at the state we were in and told us we couldn't go on, unless we stopped drinking. We did as we were told but then Andy Gray stepped forward as shop steward and said, "I'm not having this," telling the producers that we wouldn't be going on unless they gave us another bevvy, so they let us have another drink.

The worst thing about the experience was that we didn't know the words; there was only Paul Bracewell who knew them all. He was like George Michael in Wham while the rest of us mumbled along behind him like a load of Andrew Ridgeleys. It's embarrassing when you watch it back but in many ways that song captured football at the time and it definitely encapsulated the camaraderie and team spirit that we had at Everton. Just don't ask me to sing it, not without Brace anyway.

Even though United had got the better of us on the chart front, at their end of the M62 they knew that the team they were taking on had improved immeasurably over the course of 18 months, and the *Manchester Evening News* underlined that in their FA Cup final special pull-out with a little dig that we picked up on. 'Twelve months ago, as excited Everton fans queued for FA Cup final tickets before their Wembley date with Watford, one of them asked another, "How long have you been waiting?" "Fourteen years," came the reply.'

I was tempted to scrawl on the bottom that United's wait to become champions had gone on even longer but I decided to see it as a back-handed compliment. Anyway, I knew that what was written was irrelevant, it was what happened on the pitch that mattered.

United had also been boosted a couple of days before the final when Robbo scored a hat-trick in a practice match as he proved his fitness following a hamstring injury.

United had 11 full internationals in their team and the bookies had them as slight favourites but we made the early running, and I came close to breaking the deadlock when my shot struck Gary Bailey's post via a slight deflection off John Gidman.

We traded a couple of chances but, in the main, goalscoring opportunities were few and far between on a really hot day. Andy and Sharpy both admitted to feeling tired early on and extra-time started to feel inevitable long before it actually happened.

When the extra 30 minutes did arrive we had a numerical advantage as I became the answer to a pub quiz question that asks: "Which player was fouled by the first player to be sent off in an FA Cup final?" I wish that player wasn't me. I was on my way through on goal when Kevin Moran, who I knew well from nights out in Benny's, caught me and sent me sprawling. In the modern game a challenge like that would be a red card but, in 1985, things were nowhere near as clear-cut.

To this day I don't think Kevin deserved to be sent off. Peter Willis, the referee, was slaughtered for his decision, with some even claiming that he wanted to make a name for himself in his last game as an official. I don't know about that but I do know that the decision didn't do us any favours. Ron Atkinson pulled off a tactical masterstroke by dropping Frank Stapleton back into central defence and the game went from being quite open, if a bit unadventurous, to the kind where the team with 10 men has to close all the spaces they can and keep things tight.

United did that and they also had a sense of grievance, which can be a powerful weapon on the football pitch. We thought that we had them but, on this occasion, we were wrong. On a day when the game was always going to be settled by a single goal, it was United who got it. It was an exceptional finish by Norman Whiteside, a player who, if he'd been blessed with a yard more pace, could have been world-class because he had everything else, but we could have prevented it.

At times like that, when there is little between the two teams and there is so much at stake, small margins make all the difference. If Pat van den Hauwe had been able to close Norman down a fraction earlier, or shown him on to his right side, maybe he wouldn't have been able to get his shot off. Not that there is any blame attached to Pat, he had performed brilliantly for us all season and Norman's curled finish was exquisite regardless. But in that instance the small margins went in United's favour, rather than ours, and that was enough for them to win the Cup.

I was devastated. When you've enjoyed the sweet taste of success, defeat is even harder to swallow. When the final whistle was blown I was disconsolate, even though I knew we had given it everything we had. We had come so, so close to winning the treble and suddenly it was gone. The only consolation was that we all knew that we had become a special team, one that was ready to challenge the best sides in Europe, even if United at Wembley had been a step too far towards the end of a gruelling but glorious campaign.

We were ready to compete in the European Cup and the only question was whether Europe's best sides were ready for us, particularly given the way some of our vanquished opponents were talking about us. Hans Krankl captured the general mood, admitting that it had been "a long time since Rapid played against anyone of their class", and describing us as "possibly the best side in the whole of Europe."

Udo Lattek, who'd finally got over the setback of his Bayern Munich side losing to us in the semi-final, went even further with his comments. "Britain has always produced teams of great stamina," he said. "This, together with skill, has made Liverpool so dominant. But in Mr Kendall's team we may be seeing another dimension of this forceful, unrelenting football. It's no surprise that they seem capable of winning all the competitions they are in because they are super-fit and almost super-human in their search for success. They work so aggressively and hungrily for each other, they seem ready to chew up anybody who stands in their way. Perhaps this is a new trend to be set by the new power from the city of Liverpool."

A new power from the city of Liverpool. That sounded as good as it seemed right, but the chance remained that Liverpool could join us as qualifiers for the European Cup because they were ending an otherwise disappointing season with a final in that competition against Juventus. That prospect didn't bother me. I wanted to test myself against the best and it didn't matter whether that meant crossing Stanley Park or the English Channel.

In the event, I got to do neither as the month of May ended in the worst way imaginable. What should have been a memorable European Cup final between Liverpool and Juventus became a tragedy when clashes between supporters before kick-off led to the deaths of 39 people, the overwhelming majority of them supporters of the Italian club. I was in Mexico at the time, having travelled out there to join up with the England squad the day after the Cup final, and my focus was mainly on looking to pick up my first international cap.

Like all of the players out there, we were all interested in the European Cup final, which was taking place at the Heysel Stadium in Brussels. The problem was that we couldn't watch the game because it wasn't on television anywhere near our hotel, the Camino Real in Mexico City, and it wasn't as if anyone had mobile phones so we could be sent updates by text or anything. As big as the European Cup was to us, we were in a part of the world where it wasn't the be-all and end-all.

It wasn't until CNN turned up at the hotel chasing English reaction to the unfolding disaster in Belgium that we discovered that something was badly wrong. My first instinct, like everyone else, had been to hope that everyone would be alright but as we got more information it soon became clear that wasn't the case. As soon as someone mentioned fatalities the football match became irrelevant but obviously UEFA, in their wisdom, decided that it should still take place and Juventus won 1-0.

All of these years later, I still struggle to come to terms with the idea that players had to kick a ball around a field while bodies were being removed from the terraces. But the authorities decided that was the best way of averting further trouble and a match took place, with the winners lifting a trophy at the scene of a horrific tragedy.

Being more than 5,000 miles away from home, I did feel detached from events but we wouldn't have been able to avoid them even if we had wanted to because the Italy squad were in Mexico City at the same time as we were. It was 12 months before the World Cup finals and quite a few countries had travelled out there just to test everything out, but it's hard to imagine there could have been a worse time for the England and Italy squads to be in the same place.

Someone came up with the idea of both teams attending a requiem Mass in honour of those who had died. Although we were happy to attend because it was the least that we could do, as high-profile representatives of English football we felt uncomfortable going and on the way I was wondering whether I would be able to look some of their players and officials in the eye.

Mercifully, they all had dark shades on, which removed that problem, but it was a solemn occasion. I don't think anyone inside that church felt good about themselves but it was important the two countries showed solidarity at that time, and it was also right that we paid our respects. A trip that was supposed to be a positive experience had turned into a test of our diplomatic skills and everything we had travelled to Mexico for – the football, the climate and the facilities especially – felt almost irrelevant.

It soon became clear that there was an appetite for English clubs to be banned from European club competition, and a lot of it was politically driven. Margaret Thatcher, the Tory Prime Minister, was determined to make an example of supporters of a game she neither understood nor cared for.

At the time, she was basically at war with the working classes, having taken on the miners and other trade unions, and there was no love lost between the people of Liverpool and herself. That meant she was never going to fight ours – or football's – corner after Heysel.

There were no attempts to find an alternative punishment, despite Liverpool's decision to withdraw from European competition. She wanted us all to suffer because that suited both her dogma and the class warfare that she was waging. Within two days of the disaster, Bert Millichip of The Football Association stood outside 10 Downing Street and announced that all English clubs were being withdrawn following Thatcher's intervention.

Another two days passed and UEFA, having been given free rein by the British government and The FA, confirmed their own ban for "an indefinite period", with Liverpool set to serve a further three years on top. It would be five years before English clubs returned and, by then, Everton had lost their way, and I was heading towards the end of my career.

The ban was a hammer blow and I can't pretend I wasn't gutted because I had waited so long for a chance to play in the European Cup. It had been taken away from me through no fault of my own but I also had a sense of perspective about it all. Whatever my own disappointment, and however strong Everton's justified sense of grievance, it was as nothing compared to the grief that the families of the 39 victims were experiencing. Their loved ones had gone to a football match in the hope of having one of the greatest nights of their lives. Instead, their lives had come to a premature and tragic end.

From a football point of view, and I accept that this isn't particularly significant in the grand scheme of things, Everton weren't going into the European Cup just to make up the numbers. As English champions and Cup Winners' Cup holders we were going to be one of the stronger teams in the competition. We knew that the way we were set up – with a tight defence and a side that was well-organised and disciplined in general – made us a genuine contender. But the punishment applied to us, even though we had been guilty of nothing. It was like banning the entire Canadian athletics team because Ben Johnson had been caught cheating but we had no choice but to accept our fate, even though it was clearly unfair.

What I still can't fathom, even after all these years, is why the final was held at the Heysel Stadium in the first place. Why was a decaying ground, that was basically an athletics venue with inadequate segregation, selected to host such a prestigious game, particularly one that had the potential for crowd trouble? The stadium was unfit for purpose, especially considering the size and nationality of the two clubs involved. It was that simple.

UEFA have got to be held responsible for that decision. I am not shifting the blame in that respect but they had a duty to select a stadium that was fit for a European Cup final, and they failed in that basic requirement.

They were even warned beforehand by Peter Robinson, Liverpool's chief executive, that the presence of a neutral area in the middle of the Liverpool end could be a recipe for disaster if Juventus supporters managed to get tickets in that section. He also asked for the sale of alcohol to be stopped early on the day of the game because of his concern that something could go wrong but, despite being given assurances by the Belgian FA that this would happen, it didn't.

None of which exonerates those fans who charged across the terrace in pursuit of their Juventus counterparts and, in doing so, contributed to a malevolent chain of events that led to people losing their lives. The so-called English disease was running rampant again, literally in this case, and the consequences were catastrophic. But Liverpool Football Club itself cannot be held responsible for what happened.

As tragic as these events were, they were out of their control. No matter how strong our rivalry was with them, there was no one at Everton who blamed anyone at Liverpool, either on the playing side or the administration side. An independent inquiry in Belgium later determined that Liverpool were in no way to blame for what happened.

It was a huge, huge disappointment, though, there is no way of getting away from that. At one point, I spoke to Howard about it and also to PFA chief executive Gordon Taylor, asking them if the ban was against the Treaty of Rome because it infringed our human rights, but I was told that UEFA competitions are invitation-only – and that invitation had been withdrawn. It was a big blow for everyone and, looking back, it was a bigger blow than I realised at the time.

When the ban was announced, part of me was convinced that it would end much earlier than five years and that, when it did, Everton would be ready to take their place in the European Cup. In hindsight, that was false hope but that was the way a lot of us saw it. The fact that our chance of competing against Europe's elite disappeared altogether is something that I still regret. I wouldn't be human if I didn't feel that, as an individual and as a football club, we have been hard done by and I would be a liar to say anything else but, again, it is about perspective. Much worse things happened to me in my career.

I can remember crying myself to sleep because I thought I wouldn't play again so, however big this setback was, it has to be put in its proper context. And the biggest athing of all is that 39 men, women and children lost their lives. However hard done by I might feel about the punishment, I know that it is a sporting disappointment and nothing more.

# 9. MISSING THE BUS

*'The result devastated me, and later that evening I told Howard I wouldn't be taking part in the tour of the city the following day. He told me I would be fined but I couldn't have cared less, and I didn't get the plane home'*

HOWARD KENDALL was in charge for another couple of seasons and we won the league title again two years later, but the ban did lasting damage to Everton. The biggest setback, for me, was that the young players who had been developing, and who were fulfilling their potential, were denied the opportunity to go to another level by playing on the biggest stage of all.

Gary Lineker came and went in the space of 12 months as he took the opportunity to go and play in Europe with Barcelona, while Gary Stevens and Trevor Steven joined Graeme Souness at big-spending Glasgow Rangers, and also got to test themselves in continental competition.

In Howard's case, our run in Europe had given him a taste for experiencing different styles of football and he ended up going to Athletic Bilbao after Barcelona had shown an interest in him, only for Terry Venables to decide that he was staying at the Nou Camp. Would all of those things have happened had we not been banned from Europe? I doubt it.

Links might well have still gone to Barcelona because of the size of the club and the financial rewards that were on offer but top players weren't leaving the best English clubs to play in Scotland before the ban, the reverse usually happened up to that point, so I have to imagine that Tricky and Gary would have remained with us. So a great side, arguably the best in Everton's history, was broken up far too soon and the momentum that we had built ended up being lost.

As a club, though, we have to accept that we didn't make the most of the admittedly poor hand that we'd been dealt. At the time the ban was introduced, we were the best team in the country but by the time it ended Everton had fallen off the pace. Part of the reason was that, in the second half of the decade, the decisions made by the club were not proving as successful as they had been in the first. The absence of European football was a significant factor in our decline but it wasn't the only one.

What shouldn't be forgotten is that the season after Heysel we still had a great side, one which could – and, perhaps, should – have enjoyed one of the greatest seasons in Everton's history. The 1985/86 campaign has gone down in history as the year that Liverpool won the league and FA Cup double in Kenny Dalglish's first season as player-manager and I can't dispute what is in the record books, and nor can I claim that Liverpool did not deserve their success. But what I can say is that we had both trophies in our grasp, only to let them slip.

While you don't get anything in football for hard luck stories, besides runners-up medals that you don't really want, it could so easily have been Everton who paraded both trophies around the streets of Liverpool, rather than our great rivals. Ultimately, a lot of things fell into place for them just as they went awry for us, and that proved to be the difference.

As we ended the season empty-handed it is looked back on with immense disappointment, by myself as much as anyone, but it shouldn't detract from how well we performed at times and how magnificently we responded to being denied our place among Europe's elite. This might sound egotistical, although it isn't intended to be, but maybe if I'd been able to play more things might have turned out differently. I had a problem with my Achilles during pre-season and my injury problems never really went away, meaning I was only able to start 15 league games. Given the role I had played in the previous season that was never going to help our cause.

The dynamic of the team and the dressing room changed, too, because Howard had sold Andy Gray and replaced him with Links. Andy had been a huge figure for us on and off the pitch and he was one of the catalysts for the success we had enjoyed. I was gutted when he left – particularly as he had become a really good friend in the short time he had been with us – and so were the fans, who protested against his sale.

Losing Andy was a blow but because we were replacing him with Links, who was emerging as one of the best goalscorers in the country, it was also another sign that Everton were growing and becoming more ambitious, and that Howard was developing that ruthless streak that the very best managers have. These days clubs would keep Andy as a squad player and use his experience at the right times but, in that era, that wasn't really the done thing. So as players we had to cope with a change in personnel, prompting a change of style.

We went from having an aggressive target man who liked the ball to feet and wanted crosses to attack, to a lightning-fast forward who wanted the ball played in behind for him to run on to. It took a little bit of getting used to and we lost our first game of the season, at Leicester City, but then they had a point to prove, having seen Links join us and it wasn't too long before we started to hit our stride. However, Man United had flown out of the blocks, setting a pace that no one could live with as they won their first 10 league games.

Obviously, that wasn't ideal but there was no panic at Everton. We knew there was still a long way to go and we also had the confidence of champions, which allowed us to remain calm while others were getting over-excited. One of the tabloids actually declared the title race over after United had chalked up their 10th win with a headline which stated: 'It's All Yours, Ron!' This, even though there were still 32 league games remaining, while another compared them to the great Real Madrid sides.

I know the newspapers like to sensationalise things but making the call that early left them at risk of looking daft, particularly with Liverpool, West Ham United and ourselves showing signs of making it a real contest. Not that I had been able to make much of an impact. Having picked up three England caps the previous summer, I made my Wembley debut for my country on September 11, 1985, with a Romania side featuring Gheorghe Hagi providing the opposition. I'd been a doubt because I'd had a slight groin strain during the build-up and I'd had to pull out of training two days earlier but the England physio, Fred Street, worked his magic and I was passed fit.

It was a massive occasion for me; I'm not particularly national-istic and, like a lot of people from Liverpool, I'm not usually one for singing the national anthem. But the pride I felt – standing on the pitch at Wembley wearing the Three Lions on my chest while *God Save The Queen* was belted out – is something that will live with me forever. This was the completion of a journey that began with me being a hopeful from Huyton. Most importantly of all, Sir Bobby Robson had picked me ahead of Ray Wilkins, a player who I had a lot of admiration for. Again, I thought of Jimmy Headridge and what he'd done for me, but I also thought of my mum and dad and all the sacrifices that they had made to allow me to fulfil my potential.

When I received a cap in recognition of my first England game at Wembley it was an incredibly proud moment but I would love to have been given a few more, so that I could present them to all those who had helped me along the way. Being selected to face Romania was recognition of all of our efforts but things didn't really go to plan. In the second half of a tight 1-1 draw, I received the ball and went to check inside on to my right foot – and my Achilles went. I knew it was bad straight away but I'd waited so long for a chance to establish myself on the England scene that there was no way I was going off. I gritted my teeth and got on with it, but it wasn't easy.

I saw a specialist a couple of days later and he injected the tendon, put me on crutches and told me to do nothing for a week. I was hoping that would be sufficient time to recover but the injury dragged on and, while I was out, England qualified for the World Cup finals in Mexico the following summer thanks to a 5-0 win over Turkey at Wembley. It was hard missing out on something like that but the fact I had a World Cup place to fight for, and Everton had a league title to aim at, kept me going.

That was until late-October when I broke down during training and was sent to see a specialist, who decided that I needed to undergo an operation which involved the sheath of my Achilles being stripped off because it was full of adhesions. It felt like I'd wasted six weeks and I ended up going under the knife at the end of the month, with the only consolation being that I missed the dreaded Screen Sport Super Cup which English football's authorities, in their wisdom, had brought in to try to make up for the absence of European competition. It was like replacing a vintage wine with a can of coke. Everton recognised that it was a poor substitute for playing in the European Cup and treated it accordingly, using it to blood young players, while the supporters stayed away in their thousands.

During that period I was on the sidelines along with Derek Mountfield, who had also picked up an injury, leaving Howard having to pick Pat van den Hauwe in central defence and a fit-again Inchy in my midfield role, even though he had asked for a transfer, having become frustrated at losing his place in attack to Links. That was the story of the season for me and Everton in many ways. Injuries caused so much disruption that it became difficult to match the standards we had set in 1984/85.

From having a settled side and a clearly defined way of playing, we suddenly had a team that was changing seemingly from one game to the next, at the same time as trying to incorporate a different kind of striker. The good thing was that Links was top drawer and the runs he made, and the way he finished, did make it easier for us, even though he seemed to train even less than I did – and I was injured most of the time!

He had that self-confidence that top players have and even when he went through a bit of a sticky spell early on in his Everton career I asked him if it was driving him mad, and if the pressure of the £800,000 fee was getting to him. He just looked at me, and said: "I'm getting chances, they'll go in." I loved that attitude and he was as good as his word. People might have looked at him and his angelic good looks, or heard him speak in that softly-spoken way, and got the wrong impression. As several right-wing politicians are now finding out when he takes to Twitter, Links has an inner steel that gives him an edge that a lot of people don't have.

He's naturally laid back – as highlighted by his routine the day before matches, which basically involved having a long, hot bath – but he isn't shy about coming forward when he feels it's right. That trait, almost as much as his prolific goalscoring, helped him to become a key member of the team fairly quickly. We had to adapt to him rather than him adapting to us and that was what happened but, in the main, I wasn't part of that process, as my injury problems kept me out until the start of February.

Thankfully, the team coped well enough without me. When I came back into the side we were second-top, just two points behind leaders Manchester United, who had begun to run out of steam after their whirlwind start. I'd played a few reserve games to build my fitness up but it was still a surprise when I got the nod to make my first-team comeback.

The first I heard about it was when I picked up a newspaper the day before we played Spurs at home and read a back-page headline, saying, 'Reid To The Rescue.' The boss hadn't given me any indication that he thought I was ready and, if he had, I definitely wouldn't have gone out with Barbara and Louise on the Thursday night and had a couple of bottles of wine because I never did that so close to a first-team fixture.

It was my first game in five months and Howard obviously didn't want me to get worked up about it. He had waited until the day before to let me know but, because he had a good relationship with the press, he'd let them in on the secret before telling me. It was only something minor but in terms of showing how shrewd

Howard was, as a man-manager and as a media operator, that is as good an example as any. The press lads got their story, the fans got a bit of good news and I got to play. Everyone was happy.

The supporters showed me how much I'd been missed by giving me a wonderful ovation, which meant a lot to me after being missing for so long, but it was an awful day for football, with a swirling wind affecting the game. Tottenham's tactical plan was built around getting plenty of bodies behind the ball, which made life difficult for us. I struggled and I knew at half-time that I was four or five games away from getting back to my level but I knew I had to get through the 90 minutes, even though I was getting more tired and was struggling in situations that normally wouldn't give me any problems.

Howard could see that and he was about to take me off when I scored with eight minutes remaining. I didn't actually see the shot go in. There were bodies in front of me and the ball came back off the underside of the crossbar but the referee gave it, and Links assured me that it had crossed the line, which was more than good enough for me.

I don't know whether it was the euphoria or the fatigue but whatever it was, I almost cost us two points shortly after when I put John Chiedozie in with a back-pass that put us bang in trouble. Thankfully, Neville came out and forced him wide and the chance was gone. I knew I owed the big fella one because he'd bailed me out, as he kept on reminding me for days afterwards and rightly so, as his intervention had allowed us to go top of the league. United would lose at West Ham the following day.

A 4-0 win over Manchester City meant that we went into our next game, the Merseyside derby, knowing that a second successive victory at Anfield would take us eight points clear of Liverpool. It was the kind of advantage that would make us

**England Blues:** Posing with Trevor Steven, Gary Lineker and Gary Stevens ahead of the 1986 World Cup finals in Mexico

**Worth The Wait:** The crucial 3–0 victory over Poland (above left) marked my first involvement in Mexico, before I joined the celebrations following one of Gary Lineker's two goals in the second-round victory over Paraguay (above right)

**Moment Of Destiny:** England's starting XI pictured ahead of the iconic 1986 World Cup quarter-final against Diego Maradona's Argentina. Back row (left to right): Peter Shilton, Glenn Hoddle, Gary Stevens, Terry Fenwick, Gary Lineker, Terry Butcher. Front row (l to r): Steve Hodge, Kenny Sansom, Trevor Steven, me, Peter Beardsley

**What Happened Next?** I'm close by as Maradona takes possession in Argentina's half. Nine seconds later he'd scored one of the greatest goals of any World Cup finals

**Dye For The Cause:** (Clockwise from top left) My 'new' look during the FA Cup fifth-round tie at Wimbledon, February 1987; in the thick of the derby action with old rival Steve McMahon, two months later; with Michael and Kevin Ratcliffe; being chaired off by fans after securing the league title at Norwich City, May 1987

**Champions:** The 1986/87 squad show off the First Division trophies with me (front, fourth left) sharing a joke with Graeme Sharp – perhaps at Mick Harford's expense? Back row, left to right: Kevin Sheedy, Trevor Steven, Ian Snodin, Neville Southall, Dave Watson, Bobby Mimms, Wayne Clarke, Neil Pointon, Derek Mountfield, Paul Power. Front (l to r): Pat van den Hauwe, Alan Harper, Adrian Heath, me, Graeme, Kevin Ratcliffe, Gary Stevens, Neil Adams

**Derby Daze:** This is how it feels to lose an Anfield derby – showing my disgust following defeat at our big rivals in November 1987

**Singing For England:** Helping record *All The Way*, England's Euro '88 song which peaked at No.64. I was gutted that I didn't appear during the tournament – winning my final cap a couple of weeks before – and Bobby Robson's side bowed out after losing all three games

**Joining The Staff:** (Left to right) Colin Harvey (manager), me (player-coach), Terry Darracott (assistant), Graham Smith (youth-team coach) and Mike Lyons (first-team coach) ahead of the 1988/89 season, my last with Everton

**Grin Times:** Sharing a word with old skipper Kevin Ratcliffe after returning to Goodison for the first time with QPR, a chastening 4-1 defeat in April 1989

**On The Move:** Taking on Jan Molby during my final game for QPR, a memorable 3-2 defeat of Liverpool at Loftus Road, November 1989

**Team Spirit:** In familiar pose, now reunited with Howard Kendall at Manchester City. This 2-1 defeat to Charlton in February 1990 called for drastic measures...

**What Could Have Been?** Two players who caused me some regrets – the decision to sell Colin Hendry and a potential Newcastle team-mate in Paul Gascoigne, in action on the opening day of the 1990/91 season at White Hart Lane, which Tottenham won 3-1

**12th Man:** Sharing a word with Manchester City team-mate Gary Megson

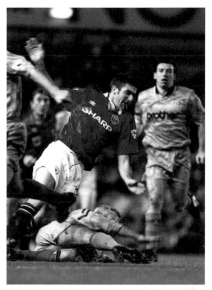

**Can't You Wait?:** I wasn't too happy when Sir Alex Ferguson moved for Eric Cantona ahead of the Manchester derby, the Frenchman's debut in December 1992

**Big Money:** With Terry Phelan after signing the left-back from Wimbledon in 1992

**Villa Earner:** Taking on former Everton team-mate Kevin Richardson in my penultimate game for City in April 1993 – not as lucrative an experience as it was the season before...

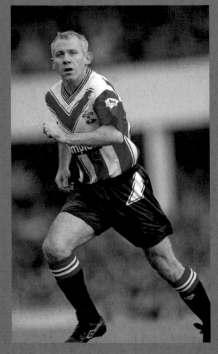

**Final Hurrah:** I enjoyed a running battle with our Shaun in my final professional match as a player, Bury v Rochdale, Gigg Lane, August 1995 (copyright Harry McGuire); (below) with Louise, Mum and Dad

**New Saint:** In action during a 3-1 Southampton victory over Chelsea in December 1993, one of eight appearances I made following my dismissal by Manchester City earlier in the 1993/94 season

favourites to reclaim our title, even though United were only three points behind us, while Chelsea and West Ham were also still in the race.

For once, the derby was a pretty straightforward affair. We won fairly comfortably on a day that will always be remembered for Bruce Grobbelaar allowing a shot from Kevin Ratcliffe to go through his body, before Links made the game safe with a typically well-timed run and finish. It was only the third time in 16 years that Everton had won at Anfield and, on the two previous occasions, the club had gone on to win the league title, so things were looking good for us.

To celebrate, I went to The Quiet Man with my family and Derek Hatton joined us. I got a bit of stick from the Reds in there but it was my own mum who stopped me in my tracks just as I was getting into full flow. My dad had cornered me and we were talking about how well things were going and how far we had come, having spent so long in Liverpool's shadow, when I realised that my mum was staring at us.

"Don't forget," she said, "I was the Evertonian when you two were both Liverpudlians," and that was that. How could we forget? Even if we tried to she was always going to remind us. I knew that I'd made a mistake early in my life but all I could do was try to make up for it. Being part of an Everton team which had found a way to record back-to-back wins at Anfield wasn't a bad way of making amends.

Everything was looking good. We were flying in the league, progressing in the Cup and all the talk was about how we had a chance to do the double. After what happened the previous season I was taking nothing for granted and there wasn't any conversation about what we might achieve in the dressing room, but there was a quiet confidence. In Links, we had the league's most prolific goalscorer, we had a group of players who had gone the course and distance and we had a manager who was one of the very best around. We knew Liverpool were a threat and also recognised that the other contenders were not going to disappear easily, although United ended up doing that, having been crowned champions by the press in the autumn. Having got ourselves into such a strong position it was all about us.

The one thing you can't account for is injuries to key players and we'd already had enough bad luck on that front so the hope was that fortune would be kinder to us, as the business end of the season approached. As it was, Lady Luck didn't just desert us, she did so after leaving us lame having struck down both Neville and myself. I'd already had enough problems to last me a lifetime in that one campaign and, even after winning the derby, I picked up a knee ligament injury in a challenge with my old sparring partner, Steve McMahon.

Those kind of war wounds are the type you expect to pick up if you are a combative midfielder but that didn't make my latest knock any easier to take. As ever, the Liverpool supporters had regaled me with, "He's fat, he's shit, he's never fucking fit" and at least one of those claims was proving to be accurate, but there was nothing I could do other than get my head down and work my way back to fitness all over again.

Unfortunately, as soon as I returned we lost the player who we could least afford to. Neville had been crucial to everything we had achieved and having him in goal was massive, because his brilliance gave us the confidence that the opposition would have to do something special to beat him. With him in the side, you could even afford to make mistakes and he would bail you out, as he'd done for me when I put Chiedozie in on goal. At that time there wasn't a better goalkeeper anywhere in the world. So when I heard that he'd got injured playing for Wales in a friendly against the Republic of Ireland in Dublin, I hoped it wouldn't be a major problem.

I was at a testimonial dinner for Paul Jones, my old Bolton team-mate, when the news came through but there wasn't much detail, initially, other than that he'd been carried off after falling awkwardly following a challenge with John Aldridge. That didn't sound good but I went into training the next day praying that the news would be better than I feared. As it turned out, it was worse – much worse.

Howard told us that the injury involved a dislocation of his ankle and, on top of that, there was ligament damage. It was so severe that Neville's right leg was put in plaster and Everton had arranged for Sir John Moores' private jet to be sent over to bring him back. There was talk that the injury was caused by the game taking place on a rugby pitch at Lansdowne Road and there's probably something in that, because Neville did it landing in a pot hole rather than from any contact. But when Howard phoned Mike England, the Wales manager, he said it was the kind of incident that could have happened anywhere, even on the training ground at Bellefield. "No, it couldn't have happened at Everton," Howard said. "He has Wednesdays off here."

Unfortunately, Neville would have a lot more days off from then on as he focused on his recovery. Losing him was a hammer blow. The previous season he had deservedly won the Football Writers' Player of the Year award so it wasn't just us at Everton who recognised how important he was. Everyone knew it, including our title rivals, who will have been boosted by news that his absence would be long-term.

Liverpool, in particular, really kicked on and after losing to us they went on a long unbeaten run, which raised the prospect of us going head-to-head for the title. There were even complaints about "a Mersey monopoly" in some quarters, which I found ironic considering there were no similar objections about the region being treated unfairly by a Tory government which did not care for it. Clearly high unemployment and endemic poverty was fine in their minds, but winning a lot of matches could not be tolerated. That probably spurred both clubs on, though.

Not that I wanted to see Liverpool up there with us – I wanted them to disappear. They were that itch that we couldn't scratch and the gap was closing. Before Neville got injured we drew at home to Chelsea and, in the league game straight after, we lost 2-1 at Luton on that horrific plastic pitch. It was a surface I hated and I picked up another injury, this time a calf strain, after playing on it a few weeks earlier in the Cup. I was watching more games than I was playing and the only consolation was that, unlike Neville's, my injuries were not long-term, even if they were frustratingly recurrent.

My latest comeback came in a 1-0 win over Newcastle United that allowed us to keep our noses ahead of Liverpool but the following weekend they beat Manchester City at Anfield while we could only draw at Man United, which meant our great rivals went top on goal difference. It was clear that Liverpool were not going to go away and neither were West Ham or Chelsea, but we were determined not to give our title up.

In the FA Cup, Sheffield Wednesday were barring our path to a third consecutive final but, ahead of the semi at Villa Park, we received some good news when a story broke confirming that Terry Venables would be staying at Barcelona for another season. They had been looking at Howard as a possible replacement and we didn't want to lose him. El Tel's decision did us a big favour and the timing could not have been better.

Not that the same could be said of Doc Irving's deployment of a stink bomb on the team bus on our way down to the Midlands. The lads took it well, though, stripping him off and throwing his shirt and shoes out of the coach window. The stench clearly didn't affect us too much as we went on to beat Wednesday as our third FA Cup semi-final in succession went to extra-time.

Again, it was a hard game, not that I was expecting anything else with Neville, Sheeds and Links all out injured. The lads who came into the side, especially Bobby Mimms in goal and Inchy up front, did really well. We even suffered another blow in the first half when Trevor went off with a groin strain but Alan Harper replaced him and went on to score the opener early in the second half, which summed up how we were making the most of what we had. Carl Shutt equalised soon after, though, and the game went into extra-time.

Before that got underway both teams had a break on the pitch, with the Wednesday players having glucose and vitamin drinks while Graham Smith, our youth coach, brought a pot of tea out for us! Our refuelling might have been more quaint but it did the trick, and Sharpy scored the winner with a superb volley.

This time, Champagne and lager came out instead of PG Tips as we celebrated in the dressing room, and then we found out that we would be facing Liverpool in the final. Everything was going well but the stakes were getting higher and it increasingly looked like the title would be coming back to Merseyside, as well as the FA Cup. The only question was whether the two major honours would be shared out between us, or if one of the two clubs would win both and the other none.

Thankfully, the games for club and country were coming thick and fast so there was no time to dwell on the thought that we might end up with nothing, and they could end up with everything. We were winning regularly anyway so confidence remained high. On a personal level, I was also continuing to stake my claim for a World Cup place with a strong performance as a second-half substitute in a 2-1 win over Scotland whetting my appetite still further.

If my career taught me anything, though, it is that just as things seem to be going really well, disaster can strike – and vice versa. Just as I was finding my form, without being 100 per cent fit, injury struck again. As if the two points we dropped in a goalless draw at Nottingham Forest were not painful enough, I left the City Ground on crutches having been caught by Colin Walsh.

It was only an ankle tap but I was in agony and, with only a couple of weeks to go before the FA Cup final, the papers were speculating that I would miss that and the World Cup. I was more hopeful and a scan revealed that there was no ligament damage but I was still cutting it fine if I wanted to get back before the end of the season. I knew that the next game, against Oxford United at the Manor Ground, was out of the question.

While all of this was going on there was also speculation about my future. I had been having talks about a new contract and it was a bit trickier than I'd hoped. At one stage the boss told me he had tried to sign Gary Mabbutt and Spurs had asked for me in some sort of swap deal. There were also rumours that Bordeaux were interested but I wanted to stay. I was flattered by the interest from elsewhere but Everton were my club and even the thought of earning a bit more at a London side couldn't sway me. But I also recognised that this contract would almost certainly be my last chance to be financially secure so it was an important one.

Then Cologne got involved when a Belgian lawyer contacted Howard to tell him that the West Germans were trying to sign me and the boss referred him to my solicitor, Zack Harazi. Even that knowledge didn't turn my head. Everton had a reputation in the game for not being the best payers but things had improved on that front.

Zack spoke to the Belgian but there was nothing concrete about Cologne's interest and I cooled on the idea when he asked me to sign a letter, giving him the authority to act on my behalf. That simplified everything and my resolve to stay strengthened. I was hoping that when I put pen-to-paper I would be committing my future to the reigning champions, but that ambition suffered a significant blow at Oxford.

I had bad vibes even before kick-off and it wasn't because I wasn't playing, as I'm a terrible watcher. It was the worst I'd ever felt before a game. I couldn't relax because I had a bad feeling about what was going to happen; it wasn't really a premonition but it didn't feel right. I asked the boss if there was a chance of a bit of 'team spirit' – that was our name for whisky. We would sometimes have a gulp before we went out and, on this occasion, he gave me a scotch and lemonade. I knew I would be powerless to effect the game so even that didn't help.

When I looked around the dressing room I got a feeling that most of the lads were feeling the same as I was on a night when we needed them to be full of confidence. It was so quiet, maybe it was apprehension or tension, but whatever it was it showed in our performance. Links famously missed a few chances that he would normally have taken, having worn a different pair of boots, but that was only part of the story. We weren't on our game, even though we were playing at a ground that had come to be seen as a lucky venue for Everton because of what had happened there a couple of years earlier. This time around the result transformed our fortunes for the worse as Les Phillips scored a late winner.

Just to compound things, Liverpool defeated Leicester,

meaning that if they won at Chelsea the following Saturday they would take our title. Of all the scenarios you can have there can't be many worse. It's bad enough knowing that you've blown your own chances, and I knew that we had, even though Liverpool still had a tough away game to come. But to leave the door ajar for your local rivals to sneak through is horrendous.

Just to darken my mood, I did something that I've always regretted. As I was coming out of the ground a young lad asked me for my autograph and I ignored him – and his dad had a go at me. He was right and I was wrong. I was absolutely devastated but that's no excuse. When players finish their careers they often talk about things they wish they had done differently and that's definitely one of mine. However bad I was feeling, I should have stopped for the lad because if football is about anything it is about kids going to the game.

In fairness to Liverpool, they got the job done at Stamford Bridge on a horrible day when we battered Southampton 6-1. Every goal we scored seemed to be met by a groan rather than a cheer because everyone at Goodison knew that our efforts would be futile. All of which left us knowing that we would have to beat them at Wembley or else we would end up empty-handed, despite having played some brilliant football that season.

We discovered in advance of the final that there was a plan for both teams to fly back from London on the same plane before touring the city together. In the head of someone who didn't understand the Merseyside rivalry that was no doubt a great idea, particularly as the two sets of fans were always going to mingle well at Wembley as they had done previously. But for a professional sportsman, who knows what victory and defeat feels like, it is hard to think of anything worse.

As soon as I heard about the plan I knew that I wouldn't be on the plane or the bus if we lost. I just couldn't handle something like that. In no way was this disrespectful to Liverpool. Just as Joe Fagan had done 12 months earlier, I congratulated them on winning the title when I bumped into Alan Hansen and a number of their players at a race meeting at Haydock a couple of days after they won at Chelsea. It wasn't easy for me to do that because I was hurting but I knew it was the right thing to do. At least I was going to be fit for Wembley and I would be in a position to make a difference, something that had been beyond me too many times for my liking during that season.

Not all of my preparations were ideal, though, as a couple of days before the game my car was stolen from outside my house. That wasn't a major issue and the main thing was that I was going to be fit for what would be one of the biggest games of my career but, like any player, I didn't like disruption. Regardless of that, I would have walked to London if needs be because this was another chance to show that we were better than Liverpool.

We were confident of doing that. The game was tight but we were the better side, and Links put us 1-0 up in the first half after I put him in with a long ball in behind Hansen and Mark Lawrenson, after Kenny Dalglish had lost possession in midfield. That was the beauty of Links. He had a gift for timing runs and defenders were often powerless to stop him because he was so rapid. Not for the first time that season, a goal from him had given us a platform to go on and win, and Liverpool knew that they were in trouble.

I could pick up on the tension in their ranks and it came to the boil in the second half when Grobbelaar and Jim Beglin had a spat on the pitch. As a player, there aren't many better sights than that because it shows that the opposition is rattled, but on this occasion it might actually have been exactly what they needed because it cleared the air and, shortly afterwards, they equalised. Rushie – who else? – scored it after Gary Stevens had tried to play a pass up the line to me, only for Ronnie Whelan to cut it out and Liverpool punished us.

Gary has always been blamed for what followed but that is incredibly harsh. Yes, he lost possession and, yes, it was an avoidable mistake but that Everton team was built around bailing each other out when we failed as individuals. On this occasion, we weren't able to do it.

We responded well, initially, and I thought we should have had a penalty when Steve Nicol impeded Sharpy before Grobbelaar made an unbelievable save to keep out his header. But Craig Johnston put Liverpool in front just after the hour and Howard decided to go for broke, taking Gary off and replacing him with Inchy. That just resulted in us losing our shape, especially with Brace being moved to left-back.

Rushy finished the game, after clipping me on the halfway line and sending me sprawling. That was it. The double had been blown. All I could do was try to drown my sorrows but even that didn't work because, as I was stood at the bar, McMahon turned up and asked me if I wanted a double. That didn't go down well. There's a time to take the piss and that wasn't it.

The result devastated me, and later that evening I told Howard I wouldn't be taking part in the tour of the city the following day. He told me I would be fined but I couldn't have cared less, and I didn't get the plane home. A story emerged that I'd stayed in London to try to finalise a move to Cologne but that was already dead in the water by then.

The reality was that I'd got a lift back to Bolton from Mike Morris, a good friend who's now an agent. I told him: "Pick me up at the team hotel," and he started to question whether that was a good idea, so I responded: "Just fucking be there and get me up that motorway to the Red Lion." When I got home I spent some time with Louise before going to the ale house. I was having pints of Guinness and then the landlord, a big Red from Kirkby, came in and I had to put up with him gloating.

My absence from the parade became a big talking point in the media and Zack, my solicitor, had to release a statement saying that I was "very, very upset," adding that "the result probably got to him more than others." I then got involved, using the theft of my car as an excuse but I knew I wasn't kidding anyone.

As loyal as ever, my mum gave an interview to the press defending me and, knowing me better than anyone, she called it just right. "It was a complete misunderstanding," she said. "He was so upset, completely gutted by the Wembley defeat, that he simply couldn't face up to the tour of the city. He loves the supporters and he desperately wanted to win the Cup for them. He would have been facing all those fans, in his eyes, as a failure. He is a winner and that's why he's such a good player."

I couldn't argue with any of that because I just couldn't handle the thought of Liverpool parading the FA Cup and league championship that we'd lost but, publicly at least, Howard needed to keep up appearances. He told the media that none of the arguments that had been put forward on my behalf were good enough. He never did fine me, though. He called me and gave me a bollocking, which he had to do, but that was as far as the issue went.

The day after I should have been on a tour of the city I got the shuttle to Gatwick to take a flight to Colorado, to join up with the England World Cup squad. But when I got to the airport there were reporters everywhere. I don't think there's ever been so much fuss about someone missing a bus.

A season that had promised so much ended with rancour and regret. I could make excuses, and the loss of Neville and myself, the Football Writers' and PFA Players' Player of the Year from the previous season, would be a valid one. I could try and put it in the context of how far Everton had come, that only being the second best team in the country was such a huge let down. I could argue that the best team hadn't won because for at least two thirds of the season we were better than Liverpool, and some of their players have been realistic enough to admit that.

But when it comes down to it, they got over the line first and we didn't. They were the ones who found a way to win when it mattered, and they were the ones who took the honours because of that. I don't begrudge them that success; it hurt me then and it still hurts me a little bit now when I look at how close we came, but it would be dishonest of me, especially given the type of player that I was, if I claimed that winners didn't actually deserve to win.

It was nip and tuck and if we'd won at Oxford we would have claimed the title, and taken that confidence into the FA Cup final. If things had gone our way I would have been on that open-top bus tour of the city but they didn't, so I wasn't, and I'm not sorry that I missed it. I'd be lying if I said I was.

I didn't hate them for beating us and I made sure I congratulated all of their players after we lost at Wembley, but I did hate myself for not being able to change the way the season ended. Maybe if I'd got rid of the ball a split second earlier at the City Ground I wouldn't have got caught by Colin Walsh, and things would have turned out differently – but I didn't. That was a turning point and it went against me and Everton.

# 10. MEXICAN SUMMER

*'When the national anthems kicked in I was ready to fight everyone. It wasn't about jingoism, politics, the nationality of the opposition or even the Malvinas; Argentina were standing in front of me and a place in the semi-final of the World Cup'*

EVERYWHERE I went in the summer of 1986, Colin Walsh came with me. Not literally, but his presence was there all the same. All it took was for someone to touch the spot where he'd caught me and it would feel like I was being stabbed with a knife, or smashed with a hammer.

The response depended on where the contact was and how heavy, but either way it was agony for me. It turned out that when he did me, the nerves had been left exposed and came alive, but it took a long time before that diagnosis was made. That kind of injury was so rare that the medical professionals didn't tend to look out for it, which left me at the mercy of anyone who left a bit in on a tackle.

The slightest touch and I would be up in the air like Yosemite Sam in the cartoons and I couldn't do anything about it. At one stage I thought it must be a break or a stress fracture because it wouldn't go away. Although I like to think that I've got a high pain threshold, the fact that this was such a sharp and acute discomfort bothered me, and it worried the medical staff at Everton and England.

Not that it was of any concern to my opponents, as I'd discovered during the FA Cup final when Ronnie Whelan caught me. I was in agony straight away and I made my feelings clear but Ronnie, who was a lot more cynical than he looked, just smiled at me and said: "Well, you shouldn't be in the papers all the time going on about fitness tests and how you've been struggling." Point taken.

I wish I could ignore it but it was impossible. I'd had big injuries previously but this was different because it was so mysterious. I was taking painkillers and wearing strappings at the top of my ankle and the front of my shin, but even those measures couldn't help me whenever there was any kind of impact. That made me a doubt for the FA Cup final and it also prompted concerns that I wouldn't be fit to go to the World Cup with England.

It was entirely logical that people wondered whether I would make it to Mexico and I couldn't really complain when stories started appearing in the press questioning my fitness, and whether it might be better if someone else took my place. But I wasn't going to give that up unless I absolutely had to and I knew that I could handle pain, especially if doing so meant I would be able to play on what I consider to be the biggest stage in football. I'd already had Europe taken away from me, I wasn't about to let the World Cup follow suit.

The problem was that even if I got into the squad I knew that I was unlikely to get into the team, initially at least, because Bobby Robson had his first XI. Winning a starting place was going to be a big ask. Peter Shilton was in goal and in defence you had my club team-mate Gary Stevens, Terry Butcher, Terry Fenwick and Kenny Sansom. I thought the preferred midfield was a bit unbalanced because it was Chris Waddle, Bryan Robson, Ray Wilkins and Glenn Hoddle, with Mark Hateley and Gary Lineker up front.

There was a lot of quality in that side but it lacked natural width. While you might get away with that in qualifiers and friendlies, it will be found out in competitive games at the highest level. I didn't want that to happen because I wanted England to do as well as we could but I knew I would remain a squad player unless a weakness or two got exposed. That's football. When you're on the periphery you need an opportunity to open up or else you'll remain there and if that means one of your mates misses out, so be it. That's how ruthless it is, and how ruthless it has to be.

Brace didn't even make it because he was injured and that was a massive blow to him because he was in his prime and would have been a real asset to England, but his absence reminded me of the need to make the most of my chance. That was what was foremost in my mind when I flew out to join up with the squad with the other Everton lads, after we'd been given permission to travel to Colorado later due to our involvement in the Cup final.

We stayed at a hotel called The Broadmoor, which prompted a few predictably unsavoury jokes, but it was a beautiful place and we trained at a nearby US air force academy, which had fantastic facilities. The reason why The FA had chosen Colorado was that it was 8,000 feet up and we were going to need to become acclimatised and used to playing at altitude because those were the conditions we would be facing in Mexico.

With us being late arrivals we were playing catch-up and I didn't want to fall behind so we were doing things like going into the steam room to do sit-ups and press-ups, which medical science would frown upon in the modern age, but we just wanted to get ourselves into peak condition as quickly as we could to maximise our chances of challenging for a place. Bobby had actually told us to take it easy for a few days and to find our level gradually but when there's a World Cup on the horizon you're not going to allow nature to take its course, you're going to try to force the issue, which was why we were going to such extreme lengths to get up to speed.

No matter how hard I tried, though, I knew I was facing an uphill battle to get into the side, a feeling that was only reinforced when the squad numbers were confirmed. I was given number 16, which didn't surprise me, but I knew the plan was for the team to be one to 11. 'Sweet 16 and you're not getting picked,' I thought, but I knew that it was up to me to do everything I could to ensure that my number did come up before we came home.

Other players might have taken the hint when the team tracksuits were handed out and there wasn't one for me. I can only imagine how Roy Keane would have reacted, for example, but when it happened to me I took it in my stride. Bobby made me feel a lot better by letting me wear his until Umbro flew another one out for me. Not that what I was wearing was my biggest problem, with my ankle nagging away. There were occasions during the build-up when I was restricted to short passing routines while the others were doing shooting practice.

I'm not a worrier but when I was told that the temperature in Monterrey, where we would be playing our first game of Mexico '86, would probably be higher than the 105 degrees that I had been enduring in the steam room, I did start to become concerned. Firstly, I doubted whether it was possible to play in that heat and secondly, I knew that those conditions would find me out if I carried on having issues with my fitness.

I wasn't the only one with problems, though, because Robbo was really struggling with his shoulder, which kept on popping out. It happened during a warm-up game against Mexico but Fred Street managed to put it back into place without the press discovering that our captain – and best player – was in a bit of trouble. On top of that, he strained a hamstring during a training session and that was kept under wraps, too, but the signs were becoming ominous that Robbo might not be in the best physical condition for what was such a major tournament.

At least things were starting to look up for me and I began to feel a lot better about my fitness after doing a 600-yard run. Our pulse rates were checked as soon as we crossed the finishing line and then at 15-second intervals afterwards. Mine went from 160 to 120, 112 and then back to 98, which is my normal level, within a minute. That was promising and that night I allowed myself a couple of glasses of wine, the first alcohol that had passed my lips since I'd been out there.

I could have done with a drink a couple of days later when training at the academy was interrupted because a mercury drum burst, and the facility had to be evacuated. A load of fellas wearing protective suits came rushing in and military vehicles were bombing around so we had to get out of the way. At first, it looked like we might not be able to go back in, which would have been a nightmare for Peter Beardsley because his false teeth were in the dressing room and we were due to fly to Canada the following day. But we eventually got the all-clear after an hour. That was good news for us and even better for the people of Canada, who were saved from the prospect of being confronted by a toothless Beardsley while we were there.

They were even treated to the rare sight of me playing as I got a 10-minute run-out towards the end of a 1-0 win against their national team. It was only a brief cameo and Canada didn't really test us enough for us to get out of first gear, but it was important for me to get some minutes under my belt without feeling any pain. I managed that but unfortunately Links went off after falling heavily and injuring his arm. At first, the worry was that he'd suffered a break but it turned out to be just a severe sprain, which was a massive relief because we couldn't afford to lose our main goalscorer at that stage.

We were due to travel to Monterrey via Los Angeles at 5am the following day but I went out for a few beers with Robbo and Ray Wilkins after the game, a decision I came to regret when our flight was caught up in severe storms. Although I slept through some of it I was awake for the worst part and I found out the hard way that turbulence is much, much worse when you're feeling worse for wear. The giveaway that I wasn't at my best came when it went dark and I still had my sunglasses on.

I've never been so relieved to be back on land and after we got to Monterrey airport we had to travel to our base in Saltillo, a journey which took us through mountain roads. We had a police escort and the security was incredible, with armoured cars everywhere we looked. We had three men armed with tommy guns on our coach. I was sat at the back with 'Butch' Wilkins and I asked one of them, a bloke called Rufus, if I could look at his gun. He took the ammunition out before giving it to me and as soon as I got my hands on it I shouted Gary Bailey, and it gave him the fright of his life when he turned around and saw me pointing a gun in his direction.

Not surprisingly, Bobby gave us a warning not long afterwards that the news media would be watching our every move, looking for a story that would make headlines back home. We knew most of the football writers and, in the main, they realised that we had a job to do and left us to it, but the news reporters would look for any angle to create a story so we had to be on our guard. There would be no more pointing of guns at Gary or anyone else. This was the start of the serious business and we didn't want any distractions, especially as it was going to be difficult enough training and playing in the kind of searing heat that made even gentle exercise more taxing than any of us had been used to.

In those conditions, all you can do is train, rest, eat and drink. Days were long and hard and we couldn't even have the luxury of training in the morning because our fixtures were later in the day and that meant we had to train of an afternoon, or else we wouldn't have stood a chance of being prepared. On top of that, it was a three-hour round-trip from hotel to training ground so everything was more arduous than we had expected. Our only comfort was The FA providing us with our own chef which meant we could have bacon, eggs, baked beans and corn flakes to order, even though we were in the heart of Mexico. At times like that, little things can make a big difference.

My ankle was still bugging me and with only a week to go before our first group game against Portugal I started to worry about it, even though Bobby was doing his best to stop me from fretting. As good as the manager was being about it, I couldn't help myself and with every passing day my concern grew stronger. It was like there was a clock ticking in my head and it was going faster while the healing process, if you could call it that, was slowing up. I knew I wasn't in Bobby's first-choice midfield because he was always going to go with Glenn on the right and Robbo and Ray in the middle if they were fit but unless I could prove my fitness, I wouldn't even be in a position to challenge their places.

Just as there was a danger I might start feeling a bit sorry for myself something much more serious happened that gave me a sense of perspective. Doc Vernon Edwards had been working with England since the days of Sir Alf Ramsey and he was a hugely respected figure, so it shocked all of us when he suffered a heart attack on the bench while we were playing a warm-up game against Monterrey. I'd actually been sitting next to him and I thought he looked terrible but I had no idea how serious it was until Fred Street got him out of the way, and an ambulance was called. He was taken to hospital and his condition stabilised fairly quickly but it was a worrying time for everyone and Doc Edwards would eventually be forced to step down from his duties, which was a big loss to everyone.

While I'd been worried about how he had looked, others had been keeping an eye on me and they didn't think I was in peak condition, either. It was during a conversation with a journalist from the Press Association that I found this out, as he told me that a Mexican had pointed at me and asked if I used to be a player! I know I'm not blessed with Peter Pan genes like Roger Hunt but that was a bit much, even if the state of my ankle was making me wonder if my England career was about to move into the past tense before it had really got going.

It was only a couple of days before the Portugal game that the pain started to ease, but by then it was too late for Bobby. When he named the team I found out that I wasn't even on the bench. I wasn't surprised and I wasn't in a position to complain but it still hurts, when a team gets announced and your name isn't even mentioned. All I could do was back the other lads and hope we got off to a good start because there's nothing worse than having a non-playing sulk in a squad, but I have to admit I was gutted when the players were getting changed before the game.

They felt worse than me after the final whistle, though, because Portugal beat us 1-0 despite us being the better side. At the end the England fans turned on the players a bit. They were chanting, "You don't know what you're doing" to Bobby and singing, "We want our money back" and you couldn't blame them. They had travelled a long way and shown incredible commitment to the cause, and all they got in return was a disappointing defeat.

What they didn't know was how much of a physical struggle it had been for the lads playing in those conditions. Some had come back into the dressing room gasping for air at half-time and had to use oxygen tanks. Although I would never use something like that as an excuse, it does underline that even though we lost there was no lack of effort or desire; it just hadn't been our day.

The game also confirmed my own feeling that the team was unbalanced, particularly with Glenn out wide, and speaking to a few of the lads afterwards they agreed with me that we needed a change of shape if we were to get the best out of the players at our disposal. Those views also came out in a team meeting the following day but nothing was resolved, and I had another setback during a training session for the players who hadn't been involved in the opening game, when I went over on my ankle.

Whatever I did, Colin was there, nagging away at me and reminding me of the damage he'd done a couple of months earlier. I needed something to lift my spirits and it came when I bumped into Bobby Charlton at ITV's base and he told me he thought that I should be in the team. You get used to people backing you – and sometimes not – in football, but when someone who has achieved as much as he has says he would have you in the team it means an awful lot.

Unfortunately, the Bobby who mattered most wasn't as convinced and he named an unchanged team for our second game against Morocco. But the way football is means you always have to be ready because things can change in the blink of an eye.

It was during that game that Robbo's shoulder popped out again and Ray got sent off for throwing the ball at the referee. All of a sudden, our established central midfield pairing had been lost.

At half-time there was a discussion about how we should approach the second half, considering we were a man down, and there were a few shouts that we should stick with two up top. But I went to Don Howe and told him we had to get four men in midfield because Morocco had been dominating possession and that was what we went with. The lads got behind the ball and they couldn't play through us; we also looked more balanced and although a goalless draw wasn't the result we had gone into the game looking for, it was a good one in the circumstances.

It also meant that if we won our final group game, against Poland, we would qualify for the knockout stages. Bobby had some massive decisions to make about the team, which meant it was up to me to convince him that I was ready to play a leading role. My hopes grew when Ray was harshly banned for two matches and I became confident of playing when I featured in the probable starting line-up during training.

I thought the formation still needed a tweak and the boss seemed reluctant to put Trevor Steven in as a right midfielder to allow us to play with a four. His hand was forced when Waddle went over on his ankle and he was left with no choice but to pick Tricky alongside Glenn, Steve Hodge and myself.

It was in a team meeting on the morning of the game that the starting line-up was confirmed and, as soon as Bobby told us we would be playing 4-4-2 with Beardsley playing off Links, I knew that we'd win. The only thing I would have changed is I would have found a place for John Barnes because he was a fantastic footballer. It doesn't make sense that he wasn't involved until he came on as a substitute against Argentina in the quarter-finals.

It wasn't the moment to think about individuals and what might have been done differently, though; it was time to focus. I got a note from the BBC's Kevin Cosgrove that carried a message that was simple but effective: "Go stuff the bastards." We had nothing against Poland but they were standing between us and a place in the next round so, for one day, they were the enemy.

The good thing was that, unlike Morocco and Portugal, Poland were going to be almost as uncomfortable with the conditions as we were. It was only when I went out on to the pitch for the warm-up that I realised how hot it was. It hit me as soon as I stepped out of the tunnel and my first thought was, 'I haven't played for a month and my first game back is in a furnace.' It did cross my mind that I might not last the 90 minutes but just as I was thinking that, I saw a couple of familiar faces in the crowd.

Jimmy Coyle, who'd played football with me as an apprentice at Everton, and my old school-mate, Richie Harrison, had travelled over to support me and they'd brought a flag with them bearing the name of my dad's local, The Quiet Man, which lifted me as soon as I spotted it. Afterwards I was delighted that they had been there, not just because it helped me, but also because they saw England win – and win well.

It's easy to forget but after the first two group games Links had been getting stick. He hadn't been at his sharpest but the team hadn't been playing to his strengths, either, so it was unfair that he was the focus for much of the criticism. Everything came right for him against the Poles, though. The delivery from wide was perfect for him and the service from behind was also good and Links took full advantage, scoring a hat-trick that underlined his status as one of the most feared goal-poachers at the tournament.

With him as a spearhead the rest of us just had to make sure we did our jobs and we did that, although there were a few occasions when I had a few words with Glenn because I thought he was guilty of hitting long balls when we should have been looking to keep possession. But that was a minor issue on an otherwise brilliant day, and I could feel a sense of togetherness growing.

At one point when we were 3-0 up I shouted, "Come on lads, get into them," because I didn't want our standards to drop. Zbigniew Boniek, who was a fantastic player, gestured at me as if to say there was no need for that because the game was done. He probably had a point but Terry Fenwick had seen the exchange and hollered at me: "Fucking kick him if he gets anywhere near you." I just cracked up. Terry wasn't being serious but, like me, he didn't want to give the opposition any feeling of comfort.

Not that any of us were able to relax in that heat and when I went off at the end, with the job done, Viv Anderson threw a towel over me but it didn't cool me down. I thought he'd put it in hot water instead of cold, and was about to give him an earful when I realised that it was my body temperature that had made the towel heat up as soon as it touched my skin.

I was exhausted but I'd come through with no ill-effects and we had survived a serious pressure test, which meant we would face Paraguay in Mexico City in the next round. The only negative was related to club rather than country as speculation surfaced that Barcelona were interested in Links. Sometimes you can take rumours with a pinch of salt because you know agents and clubs plant stories in the media for various reasons, but I spoke to Gary about it and he told me that his agent, Jon Holmes, had travelled to Spain to open talks, and that a deal could be close.

I know there is an argument that, as a team, Everton had not benefited from Links as much as he had from us but he scored 30 league goals in his first season with us and was only going to get better. Prolific strikers are hard to come by in any era and when you have one you don't want to lose him. But out in Mexico I was just happy he was back scoring goals for England, even if I knew his form would make it more likely that he would leave Everton.

When we arrived in Mexico City we were taken to the Valle de Mexico, which was to be our base, and at first we didn't realise what a dump it was. We gathered in one of the reception rooms to watch the latter stages of Scotland v Uruguay and there was a bit of a split in the camp because there were those who were shouting, "Get the Jocks out" and then there was the likes of me, who had friends and team-mates in their squad, and who wanted them to do well as a result. As it was, they could only draw 0-0 and went out, but at least while the game was on Scotland had helped England because they had distracted us from our surroundings.

It was during the night that we found out the hard way that whoever it was at The FA who was responsible for booking our hotels had made a mistake. Like a lot of the lads, I had grown up in a working-class area and had been used to not having the best of everything. The one thing that you can't do without when you're away at a major tournament is sleep, and this place was like staying at the side of a motorway. All through the night I was kept awake by trucks and cars driving past and there was no double glazing, so there was no escape from the noise.

I gave up trying to sleep at around 6am and went downstairs, thinking it might just have been my room that was affected but when I got down, most of the players were already there because they'd been having similar problems. In fairness, The FA had done a brilliant job in arranging our training facilities at the nearby Reforma Club. It was a perfect venue and I doubt many of the countries at that World Cup were as fortunate as us in that respect, but we needed every advantage if we were going to progress and our hotel was undoubtedly a disadvantage.

When we got back after training I refused to go to my room because it was like a prison cell and things got worse when we realised how bad the food was, a problem that came to light when Gary Bailey discovered a ladybird in his soup. Unlike my dad, I'm game for trying most things but I draw the line at insects. That was the final straw.

We got together and the decision was taken that we would move and we ended up going to the Holiday Inn, the same hotel that the Italians were staying in. Needless to say, I was delighted. Not only did it have double glazing in all rooms, it was in a quiet location and the place was spotless. I had a wander around and came across the dining room as it was being set up for the Italy players to have their lunch and there was a bottle of wine on every table. We couldn't do that. Whereas their culture is to have a little sip of wine with a meal, ours is to finish the bottle, so we had to make do with good old agua.

It was a good job that I was sober because it was while we were there that I learned that Barcelona had agreed a £2.8m fee with Everton for Links. It was a blow but I couldn't allow it to affect me and, besides, it wasn't as if I could do anything about it. The money was good for the club and the move was perfect for Links, so all I could do was hope things worked out well for him and us.

At that stage, it was more important that I focused my attention on a former Barcelona player rather than a future one as Diego Maradona had emerged as the individual that we would need to stop if we managed to get through. Argentina beat Uruguay 1-0 the night before our game against Paraguay and although they hadn't been brilliant, Maradona had given his marker the run around. He looked every inch the top player that his reputation suggested he was.

The following morning I received a telex from Derek Hatton

wishing me luck on behalf of Liverpool city council which was a lovely gesture, especially considering I'm a Knowsley lad. That reminded me that we were all carrying the hopes of a nation with us. When you're so far away from home, with the company only of your team-mates, it can be easy to become detached so it was good to get a message like that. Some see it as a pressure, but just as had been the case when Howard opened the window of the away dressing room at the Victoria Ground, I always thought it was important to realise who you are playing for and to be inspired by them, even if they were thousands of miles away.

I'm not usually superstitious but I decided to wear the exact same t-shirt, shorts and tracksuit for the Paraguay game as I wore before we played Poland. It was probably Links' fault. He had his lucky boots on when he scored a hat-trick against the Poles and he hadn't worn them when Everton blew the title at Oxford, so I was taking no chances.

The one change that was out of our control concerned the defence, with Alvin Martin coming in at centre-back because Terry Fenwick was serving a ban, but that didn't make any difference to the way we approached the game and we were confident of getting through. Paraguay started well and had a couple of early chances but Shilts did well to deny them and we settled down after Links scored the opener. The result was never really in doubt from that moment.

While we were comfortable in the game, I was struggling physically after Colin made yet another appearance. The game was only 10 minutes old when I played a pass with my left foot and got clattered on my right. I'm not saying it was deliberate but it was some coincidence that I was caught on the exact spot where I'd been having so much trouble.

The pain hit me right away but all I could hear in my mind was my dad's voice telling me not to let them know that I was hurt. That was easier said than done but I got on with it until half-time when I went in and told Fred that I was sore. He put some ice spray on my ankle and told me to give it 10 minutes but I was struggling, and I knew I was going to have to go off.

Just before I did, Beardsley scored our second so as soon as the ball hit the net I signalled to the bench that I couldn't go on and Bobby replaced me with Tottenham's Gary Stevens. I watched the rest of the game from the sidelines with ice packs melting on my leg. I was up celebrating when Links got his second though to guarantee that we would be going through. It was a great feeling to be part of an England team that had reached the quarter-final of a World Cup, even though I hadn't been able to complete the 90 minutes. While the other lads basked in the glow of qualification I was whisked off to hospital for an x-ray.

The doctors saw a fracture straight away but it was the one that I'd suffered playing for Bolton against Barnsley years earlier and they couldn't pick up any other significant damage. I had mixed feelings because I knew something was wrong and it worried me that, whatever the problem was, it wasn't being identified by the medical professionals. But the main thing was that I wouldn't be prevented from playing against Argentina.

Maradona's name was the one on everyone's lips. That didn't surprise me because I'd seen him play against England and Scotland in the early 1980s. My abiding memory was of how easily he had gone past Alan Hansen, who wasn't only one of the best defenders around at the time, he was also very quick.

That left a lasting impression and every time someone mentioned him, which seemed to happen every two minutes in the days leading up to the game, the vision of him leaving Hansen for dead kept on coming into my head. We knew all about him and what he could do and no matter how hard we tried, we couldn't avoid him.

There were massive billboards all over Mexico and Hugo Sanchez was on a lot of them, but Maradona's face was on most of the others. Even if we wanted to forget about him, we couldn't. We also weren't allowed to ignore the diplomatic tensions that existed between Great Britain and Argentina. The Falklands War had happened just a few years earlier and there were those who saw a football match as an extension of that conflict.

After the Paraguay game I was limping down the tunnel back towards the dressing room when a South American reporter approached me. "What about Argentina and the Malvinas?" he asked me. He caught me off guard and, given my feelings towards Thatcher, I could have said anything but I managed to contain myself, telling him that England and Argentina are football teams and politics was nothing to do with us. The reporter didn't get the answer he'd been looking for but his question gave me an insight into the issues that were going to dominate the build-up.

We dealt with it well but there was an edge that couldn't be ignored and it came to the fore in the dressing room half-an-hour before kick-off, when Bobby gave his team talk. "It's not so long back that our country won a war against Argentina," he told us. "So we better win this game." So much for my idea that politics and football shouldn't mix! "But relax," he added. "It's just a game of football, so relax. I've had a telegram from Margaret Thatcher wishing us luck and another from the Queen, but relax."

During that talk he used the word 'relax' more than Frankie Goes To Hollywood and every time he did, the tension ratcheted up a bit further. He knew what he was doing. He wanted us bang at it and he wanted us to take out all of the nervous energy that was building up on our opponents. Like us, he knew that the

Argentinians would be much more intense about the political situation than we were.

The game was at the Azteca Stadium in Mexico City but the FIFA officials wouldn't allow us to train there the day before because there'd been a torrential downpour the previous night so we headed to the nearby Atlantic Stadium, only to discover that the gates were locked. We sat on the coach, wondering if we would even get a proper session in before the biggest game of our careers, but the local police came to our rescue when they found someone who picked the locks. Even then we couldn't access the dressing rooms so we had to climb to the top of the ground, walk down the steps and get changed at the side of the pitch.

It wasn't the most professional setup I've ever encountered but it was vital for me that we got into the stadium because I needed to prove my fitness. Fred didn't take it easy on me, and rightly so, because he needed to be able to tell the manager whether or not I was ready to play but I came through. I was still feeling pain – Colin wasn't about to ease off on me altogether – but the discomfort wasn't inhibiting me and I went to bed that night with my head buzzing about what the following day would bring.

There are certain days in your life that you are able to recall with an unusual level of detail because they were so important, or so dramatic and, for me, June 22, 1986 is definitely one of those. If I close my eyes I can still picture the colourful scenes that greeted us on the way to the stadium, with England and Argentina fans everywhere we looked, and I can hear the Beatles and Rolling Stones songs that Gary Bailey played on his ghetto blaster. I can even remember the faces of some of the security men who accompanied us, all moustached and tanned like extras in a Sergio Leone movie.

The pre-match scene in the dressing room also comes back

strong with Shilts doing his exercises, Kenny Sansom and Ray Wilkins taking the piss out of one another, Links relaxing on a bench as if he was just winding down for a kip and Robbo on another bench, looking disappointed because he wouldn't be involved. I was gutted for him. He was one of my big mates and I knew how much it would hurt him not to play because I had suffered so many injuries myself. But I also knew that I had to be ruthless because the minutes before a massive game are too important to be wasted on thinking about anyone else. I just focused on what I was going to do.

I was well in the zone when I left the dressing room to go and warm up but as I walked up the tunnel a familiar voice broke my concentration. It belonged to referee George Courtney, who had been selected to officiate in Mexico, and I had a quick chat with him, which helped to relax me a little bit. It was a good job I'd bumped into him because when the national anthems kicked in I was ready to fight everyone.

It wasn't about jingoism, politics, the nationality of the opposition or even the Malvinas; Argentina were standing in front of me and a place in the semi-final of the World Cup. If you don't feel 10 feet tall and ready to take on all-comers at a time like that you're going to struggle to perform.

That's how vivid my memories are. Unfortunately, the strongest recollection of all was the sense of anguish that engulfed me when we lost. After Maradona had done his best and worst, we responded well, particularly after John Barnes came on and put in a sensational performance, which confirmed my feeling that he should have been involved long before then. Argentina couldn't handle him because he was going at defenders and getting crosses in. We scored from one of his deliveries when Links got on the end of it, and the positive spin-off of him being under-used by Bobby was that he was fresh enough to keep going at their defence over and over again.

The next time he got to the byline, he whipped another brilliant ball into the box and we were all up off the bench, ready to celebrate a goal. I'd gone off by then because my ankle had flared up again and my ice pack went all over the place as I got over-excited about the equaliser that was about to happen, but Links didn't score. Even now, when I watch it, I'm expecting the net to bulge, that's how inviting the cross was but a defender got in between Links and the dropping ball and it somehow doesn't go in. That was our last chance; we were out.

I was numb and I can't remember anything about the walk from the bench to the tunnel, but I can recall what happened as I got closer to the dressing room area because it went off in a big way. They were all singing Argentina songs, which I didn't want to hear just then but I knew that this was their soundtrack of victory, and we had to put up with it. If the boot had been on the other foot I would have been leading the singing so I couldn't really complain about them revelling in what was a massive win.

Terry Butcher had other ideas, though, and obviously something that had happened on the pitch had provoked him and he went for one of their players. All hell broke loose, it was absolute mayhem. Punches were thrown but it became a melee so quickly, and there were so many people involved, that it ended up being a mass bout of grappling because nobody could get any leverage to throw any digs. The security guards waded in and brought it all to a halt but I just wanted to get into the dressing room.

When I did I sat in a scene of sheer desolation. Looking back now I do take pride from having been involved in such an iconic game but, at the time, all I felt was pain and this time Colin wasn't the main cause – it was Diego.

# 11. ANOTHER TITLE LEADS TO THE END

*'What pained me most was that I was having to
walk away from a club that I didn't just love,
I was absolutely besotted with it'*

I STARTED the 1986/87 season the way I had ended the previous one, with Colin nagging away. The hope was that a period of rest after the World Cup would sort the problem out, particularly as nothing major was showing up on the examinations I'd had. But whenever there was contact with the bottom of my shin and the top of my ankle I'd be in agony.

It was also doing me mentally so, out of desperation, I went for a bone scan and although it wasn't clear, the suggestion was that I might have suffered a stress fracture in that game at Nottingham Forest three months earlier. The doctors were taken aback because I'd played at a World Cup in the meantime but no matter how much it confounded medical science, I knew that a combination of desire and adrenaline had got me through.

Nevertheless, my leg was put in a plaster cast, which meant that

I would miss the start of the season, but at least I had a diagnosis and it wouldn't be too long before I was fit enough to come back, fit and ready to play my part in Everton's bid to reclaim the league title. That was what I thought but, as my early career had demonstrated, things don't always go to plan as far as injuries and myself are concerned. Just when I thought I was ready to return, I suffered another setback that made me even more demoralised.

I managed to get through one 'A' team match and half of a mini-derby against Liverpool when I realised the injury hadn't gone away so I went to see John Clinkard, who must have been sick of the sight of me by then. I know I'd had enough of seeing him, even though I liked him a lot and had a lot to thank him for, for getting me out on the pitch and in the best possible condition, even when I had been really struggling.

He sent me to Bon Secours, a hospital in Beaconsfield, and it was there that a surgeon called Mr Williams finally got to the root cause of the problem. He opened my shin up, had a good look around and his diagnosis was that when I got the initial smash against Forest, the contact had chipped a bit of my shin bone and exposed a nerve. In effect, I was playing with a live wire in my leg and any time anyone went near it I was getting a shock. I'd never heard of it and neither had Clinks, but at least now we knew why I was reacting whenever I was touched.

Back on the all-too-familiar routine of treatment, rest and recovery, it would not be until January 31, 1987 that I was able to play again, with a fourth round FA Cup tie at Bradford City marking my return. When I did come back, Everton were riding high towards the top of the table, just two points behind league-leaders Arsenal but with a game in hand. I was taking my place in a team that would go on to win the title, an achievement that I believe is one of the greatest in the club's history, mainly because this success was built around a manager getting more from a group of players than perhaps should have been possible.

It was different in 1985 because that was a special team in which several brilliant players came into their prime at the same time. Two years later, a few of us had been affected by injuries, others had left and some who came in were either stop-gaps, signings for the future or not yet at the same level as the ones they were replacing. When we could get our strongest team out we were still a very good side but that didn't happen often enough, and Howard was usually left to make do and mend.

The good thing was he did so brilliantly. Other managers might have become frustrated and used the injuries as an excuse but he went the other way, getting as much out of all of us as he could. The signings who stood out for different reasons were Paul Power, Dave Watson and Ian Snodin, who had made the best decision of his life by rejecting an approach from Kenny Dalglish and joining Everton instead.

Everyone contributed towards the success. Wayne Clarke scored important goals towards the end of the campaign, with a number of others, including Sheeds, Inchy, Tricky and Sharpy, all chipping in as we coped with Links's departure to Barcelona by sharing the goals around again. This was a team in the purest sense because we were better than the sum of our individual parts. No wonder several clubs, including some abroad, were keeping an eye on Howard.

Just by finding a way to deal with life after Links highlighted what an undeniably brilliant manager he was. There has been a bit of revisionism about what Gary brought in the short time he was at Everton and a lot of people question whether the team suffered because it was built too much around him as an individual. I can see that argument but, it's straightforward – if we had kept things tighter at times we would have won more games because we had one of world football's best goalscorers up front.

Yes, we had to adjust the way we played to suit him and yes, we didn't win anything with Links in the team. Yet if you go around every club in the country at the start of the season and tell them that they can have a forward who'll score 30 league goals, every single one of them would bite your hand off. There was less aggression up front than there had been with Andy but unless we'd signed Mike Tyson that was always going to be the case. He brought more pace and we had the additional option of being able to play the ball over the top if teams squeezed us.

There were times when some of us had to give him verbal volleys and there was one occasion when I got into him and told him he had to get hold of the ball and not just run in behind all the time, but he bought into it and as the season went on everyone adapted. We had to change when he came and we had to change again when he left but the core of the team remained the same, which definitely helped us.

Bringing Power in from Manchester City for a small fee was an absolute masterstroke. Pat van den Hauwe was missing quite a lot of games and Paul brought experience and quality to the left-hand side of the team, just when we needed it. Kevin Langley and Neil Adams came in as well, with Clarkey signing later in the season. But, early on, the supporters were fearing the worst because we had lost a genuine superstar, and hadn't brought anyone of that level in to replace him.

I understood their fears and I'd be lying if I said I knew we would end up as champions again, but what gave me most faith was that the success we had enjoyed was due to Howard's ability to make clever signings, and allow a team to develop. So while Spurs had Clive Allen seemingly scoring every week and Rushie was doing a similar job for Liverpool in his final season before joining Juventus, Everton went down a different route – and it paid dividends. We still had a very good squad and, in some ways, it was underrated; but Howard, Colin and Mick Heaton had to work incredibly hard and be unbelievably resourceful to allow us to get the results that we did.

It was only later, when I became a manager myself, that I realised just how responsible he was for what we achieved. You get managers and coaches who want to be at the forefront when things go well, and who want to tell the world how they've inverted the triangle and reinvented football. But those three just got on with their jobs, and that's probably one of the reasons why they're not celebrated anywhere near as much as they should be. The players who worked under them know how special they were, though, even if the rest of the football world would rather blow smoke up the arses of managers who spend hundreds of millions creating a team that gets everyone behind the ball, and then expect to be hailed as master tacticians.

One of Howard's greatest strengths was his man-management skills. I'd discovered that on my first day at the club, when I couldn't train properly because I was hungover, and I benefited from it throughout my time at Everton. I would respond to him and he knew it. So when he pulled me to one side not long after I'd come back from injury, and told me that I wasn't doing enough, I took his criticism on board.

It wasn't that I'd been kidding myself, thinking that I was playing well when everyone could see that I wasn't. I knew I'd been hopeless because I was lacking strength, energy and rhythm. I wasn't sharp and I was getting caught in possession, I was weak and it was a real problem for me. In terms of my form, it was one of the most testing periods of my Everton career. There were games where, if anything, I tried too hard because I was so desperate to get back to my best.

Things came to a head – in more than one sense – when Wimbledon beat us 3-1 in the FA Cup. They basically battered us out of the competition and I literally couldn't raise a gallop. If that wasn't bad enough, that was also the day when I decided to dye my hair black and the lads destroyed me. Bobby Robson was doing co-commentary with John Motson and some of the lads had seen him beforehand, and told him to keep an eye out for me. So, during the game, Bobby came out with a line that he might pick me for England's Under-21 squad because I was looking so young.

Then, to make matters worse, the fans got involved. Lester Shapter was the referee and he was famous for his white hair so our supporters started singing: "The ref's got Reidy's hair on." I was definitely regretting leaving the dye on too long.

It was the same at training a few days later when I went in and the lads all started singing Roy Orbison's *Only The Lonely* as soon as I walked into the dressing room. There was no let-up, not even during a game of head tennis, which ended early because they were all wiping the ball after I'd headed it. So much for trying to hold on to my youth.

Howard was more concerned by my performances than my hair and he waited for the right moment before pulling me to one side, at the team hotel ahead of a game at Arsenal. The jolt he gave me meant I knew I either responded the right way, by getting back to the level I'd been at before the injury, or else I would be out. His exact words were: "You've been crap and I can't keep picking you if it carries on" – straight and to the point.

I didn't like hearing that but it got my back up, which was exactly what he had been hoping for. "We've got the Arsenal next, let's see what you're like and go from there." It was a massive game in the context of the title race and Clarkey got the winner with his first goal for us. Most importantly from my point of view, I played well and felt much better than I had for almost a year.

I don't know whether that was psychological due to the manager having a chat with me or whether it was physical, because my body was ready to be pushed, but in all probability it was a combination of the two. Howard had picked his moment and, from then on, I felt great.

My form was far from being the only issue that Howard had to handle, either. Brace had suffered a really bad ankle injury at Newcastle in January 1986 after a bad challenge by Billy Whitehurst and he ended up having to undergo surgery several times. He was a truly great player, a key factor in everything we achieved at home and abroad in 1985, but it doesn't matter who you are or how good you might have been, if you get a horrific injury it takes something away from you.

I wasn't the same player after breaking my leg playing for Bolton against Everton but I was young enough to modify my game, and I don't think Brace was ever quite able to get back to the level that he'd been at previously because he was out for so long. We barely saw him during the campaign and just to compound matters, like me, Neville didn't come back into the side until the season was well under way.

He made his return in a 3-2 win against Watford in late October but, like Brace, he probably didn't get back to his pre-injury levels although, unlike Brace, he'd almost certainly disagree with me about that. Before his injury, Neville had been the best in the world; after it he was merely brilliant.

Howard was managing all of these situations, spinning several fragile plates at one time and sometimes stopping them all from coming crashing down, which made the incessant speculation about his future troubling for all of us. We had lost a great player the year previously and we didn't want to lose a manager, who most of us felt was the best in the business.

It still came as a shock when it emerged that he was going, though, because we had just won the league, and the expectation was that he would look to kick on. However, Bilbao convinced him to take over there and once that move was confirmed, Everton were faced with the prospect of having to replace their greatest-ever manager.

I never asked Howard why he left the club when he did. Like everyone else, I presume that it was due to a longing to enjoy the European game but I wish I would have spoken to him about it at the time just to be able to understand what his thoughts were. You just assume that there will be time to have those chats but life doesn't always work out that way. Not that anyone at Everton would have denied him the opportunity to take on a new challenge. He had more than earned the right to plot his own course and all we could do was wish him well, no matter how disappointed we were to lose him.

The great thing was that he went out in the way that he deserved – as a champion. I know he came back and managed the club a couple more times in the 1990s and things didn't work out the way he would have wanted them to. But there could have been no better way for him to depart than as a manager who had not just won the league championship, but who was good enough to reclaim it two years later.

We won it comfortably as well, by nine points, largely thanks to a run of seven successive victories during spring which allowed us to ease away from Liverpool. Even though they went on to defeat us 3-1 at Anfield in a derby match that will always be remembered for Kevin Sheedy gesturing his "affection" for The Kop, they couldn't prevent us from becoming champions again.

The title was secured with a 1-0 win at Norwich, with Pat van den Hauwe scoring the goal that guaranteed we could not be caught with two games to go. After the game, Jimmy Martin, our legendary kit man, was supposed to be driving the team bus back to Merseyside but he refused, because he wanted to join in with the celebrations. We got another driver to do it and the poor fella had to put up with a slap on the head from Terry Darracott every time we thought he might be going a bit too fast. "Slow down," Terry would say. "Nothing more than 50."

For once, no one wanted to get home. We wanted the journey to last forever. It took us hours to get back and somewhere along the way Ian Snodin fell asleep, which was a big mistake. His missus was due to meet him at a service station to take him back to Doncaster but, as long as he was in the land of nod, he was our property and we could do with him as we wished.

Someone produced a pair of scissors and the lads cut his suit up, even going as far as slicing his belt and shoes up. I don't know how but he didn't feel a thing, maybe it was a case of no sense, no feeling, and as we approached the services all of the lads shouted him. "Snods, Snods, we're here." As he stood up, still half asleep, his suit dropped around his ankles in bits.

If that was a funny ending to a great day, there were fewer smiling faces after we were presented with the league trophy at the end of our next game, at home to Luton. It wasn't that we weren't delighted because the reality was that we couldn't have been happier, but we'd had it off with them in previous matches and that bad blood spilled over after we defeated them 3-1.

We wanted to celebrate but it had been a brutal game, with Peter Nicholas getting sent off for them and it went off in the tunnel. As usual, I made my mark by having a go at big Mick Harford, who had a fearsome reputation, thrusting the trophy towards him and shouting: "Have a fucking look at that because you won't win it yourself." Mick hadn't even been playing so God knows why I picked on him, particularly as he was about twice my size – and worse was to come when we were called up by England at the same time.

Recognising diplomacy is the better part of valour, I spoke to Bryan Robson and told him to get us out on the bevvy, and asked him to have a word with big Mick to smooth things over. We did just that and after about six pints in Switzerland the following year, in a pre-Euro '88 get-together, everything was fine between me and Mick, and he remains a good friend. I just make sure I don't mention anything about trophies when I see him.

Those two incidents – in the tunnel following Luton at home and on the coach after Norwich – summed up the camaraderie that was such a key factor in our league title success. This was a team in which everyone played their part, on and off the pitch, and it had to be because of the number of injuries we had.

There were naysayers who argued that we had triumphed in a poor season, the kind of ridiculous argument that gets trotted out whenever kids do well in their GCSEs or A-Levels, but those of us who were involved know that ours was a triumph in adversity, and that made it even sweeter. From the outside it can be easy to decry the achievements of others but when you are on the inside, and you have seen first-hand how success has been earned, you are able to appreciate it as it should be.

We had a few games in New Zealand and Australia at the end of the season, a trip when we got thrown off a flight because we were legless. The first Rugby World Cup was on and they all thought we were rugby players, which probably tells you all you need to know about our drinking, but the best bit was the week we had in Hawaii on the way back. There was an American football team there and they were all big lads so we had a drinking competition with them and battered them but then they wanted a sprinting competition and we beat them at that, too. The poor Americans were falling all over the place.

That 1986/87 season had been so hard that it showed the need for new blood. So many players had struggled physically, myself included, and there were others, like Paul Power, who were on their last legs, leading me to the conclusion that things needed to be freshened up. It had been a big enough ask to win the league with what we had, so asking us to do it again the following season would have been asking for trouble. Ideally, Howard would have stuck around to oversee another reinvigoration of the squad but his decision to move to the Basque country ensured that the responsibility fell to someone else. That man was Colin Harvey.

In hindsight, there are no shortage of people who say Colin wasn't the right man to succeed Howard as boss, that he was a perfect number two but an imperfect manager. It is easy to say that now but there was not a dissenting voice against his appointment, certainly not within the dressing room, where we all wanted him to step up. Not just for continuity, either. We had all seen enough of Colin to believe that there was no one better placed than him to continue Howard's good work.

The bigger shock came when Colin rang me and asked if I would go on to the staff because Terry Darracott was being moved up and he wanted me to become a coach, as well as carrying on playing. I was uncomfortable with the idea at first and I said to Colin that I knew certain things went on in dressing rooms and I'm not the type to report back to the manager, but he was great about that. "If anything's going on out of school, I don't want to hear it from you," he said. "I'll find out about it anyway." That put me at ease and I agreed to step up. I hadn't planned to do it but it was a good opportunity, so it was a case of seeing how it went.

Getting involved in the buying and selling of players was above my remit, though, which isn't my way of dodging accountability. I just didn't have anything to do with transfers. It's clear we didn't do as well in the market during that period as we had in the years previous, though. We were spending decent money - £2.2m on Tony Cottee, £925,000 for Pat Nevin, £850,000 on Stuart McCall and so on – but the signings didn't work out as well as we would have hoped. In a way, that's a compliment to Howard because he'd set such a high standard when it came to bringing players in and finding value, but it undermined our chances of maintaining the success that we had enjoyed under his management.

One player who I believe would have made a huge difference was defender Steve Bould. Maybe we were too honest because Bouldy asked Colin if he would be first choice, and Colin told him he would be coming in as a squad player. Arsenal were also interested so Bouldy asked George Graham the same question and George, being George, told him he would go into the team. That made Bouldy's mind up for him but when he went to Arsenal, George put him in the reserves!

It was a white lie and players don't like being misled but Steve went on to be really successful at Arsenal so I doubt he holds it against George – I know I wouldn't. The ones who did come in were all good players, but it was hard for them to live up to the expectations of a club like Everton.

Tony Cottee is a great lad and a brilliant finisher who always scored goals but was he up there with Gray, Sharp and Lineker? Probably not. Pat was a very skilful player but did he deliver enough at Everton? Probably not. Like those two, Stuart had a really good career and his impact as a substitute on the 1989 FA Cup final was incredible, but did he do it for Everton week in, week out? Probably not.

At the same time, Liverpool were bringing in the likes of John Barnes and Peter Beardsley, my England team-mates, and I would have loved either of those two but we went down a different route. There was even a suggestion we could have signed Paul Gascoigne from Newcastle United but that came to nothing. I'd actually had talks with them a couple of years earlier after coming back from Mexico. Ian McFaul wanted to sign me and when I spoke to him he told me that his plan was for me to play next to Gazza in midfield.

Clubs live and die by their signings and, as others were bringing in quality, we were struggling to keep pace with them. Liverpool had done better business and they ran away with the league in 1987/88, with us finishing in fourth. All we could do was give them a bloody nose when we prevented them from going 30 games unbeaten and breaking Leeds United's long-standing unbeaten record from the start of a First Division season, beating them 1-0 at Goodison in March.

In that sense it was a good day but, in another, it highlighted that we had gone from being better than Liverpool and going toe-to-toe with them to being in a situation in which we were competitive only on a one-off basis. Not that our relative decline took any edge away from the derby, as the Anfield fixture earlier that season underlined.

It was during that game that I caught Barnesy a bit late and the Liverpool fans all jumped to their feet, showering me with abuse. Among the avalanche of voices, one could be heard louder than the others. "Hey you, you dirty little bastard," came the shout. I looked and saw it was my Uncle Arthur.

He was a warm man, very tough, but an absolute gentleman and he loved Liverpool Football Club. He wanted me to do well, he used to come and watch me play for Huyton Boys and he always took a keen interest in my football career but, on derby day, all bets were off. I wouldn't have had it any other way. "Fuck off Uncle Arthur," I shouted back at him and got on with the game. Only on Merseyside.

That wasn't the only family trouble I encountered that day, either. I did my groin in the second half but managed to complete the 90 minutes. It was something and nothing. I just stretched a bit too much going into a tackle with Steve McMahon and I felt it go straight away. My dad had seen something that wasn't there, though, and after the game his face was like thunder. "He fucking did you there," my dad shouted, but I knew that he hadn't. I told him I'd done it on the stretch but he wanted to fight everyone because his lad had got hurt! Just like when I was a kid, the passions caused by Everton and Liverpool ran high in the Reid clan.

The problem for Colin was that, away from the derby-day skirmishes, Everton were struggling to keep pace with Liverpool and it doesn't matter who you are, or what you've achieved, a situation like that will always lead to you coming under pressure. George Graham's Arsenal were coming to the fore, too, and we were being squeezed out. The horrible side of being a manager didn't really suit Colin because he is such a lovely, genuine fella, so telling people that they weren't playing was very difficult for him to cope with.

He had to leave me out of the side once and I could tell he didn't enjoy doing it. That approach transmitted itself to the players and although none of them took advantage, because we all had far too much respect for Colin to do that, there was a sense that something wasn't right. When that happens, managers have a problem on their hands. For all his brilliant football knowledge and peerless understanding of Everton, when you're in that hot seat you soon discover that it's totally different to being a first-team coach. I learned that the hard way when I went on to become a manager myself.

Coaching was Colin's forte and management didn't suit his personality in quite the same way but we were all desperate for him to succeed. I know there have been instances at clubs when players have got managers out but that wasn't the case with Colin at Everton. If anything, he wanted to succeed too much and we were too keen for him to do well because of the huge respect and love that we had for him. When it comes down to it, we were killing each other with kindness and neither manager, nor players, got what we wanted out of a relationship which, on paper at least, had seemed like a match made in heaven.

The summer of 1988 brought the curtain down on my England career, with the last of my 13 caps coming against Switzerland in a pre-European Championship warm-up. I was included in the finals squad but didn't feature. Bobby Robson ensured me and Viv Anderson, who was also unused, were given a round of applause in appreciation of our commitment to the cause. You can imagine how that went down with the rest of the lads. Every time I went somewhere, even if it was just getting in and out of the lift, they would clap me.

Bobby was just trying to be nice but that killed me. You either play or you don't. The ones who play get the applause. I'm definitely not the type who could not play in a Champions League final, then go and get changed and put myself in the middle of the celebrations. I'm not having a go at John Terry for doing that but it's not something that I could have done.

Considering the bad injuries that I suffered, I'm not disappointed at only getting 13 caps for England. When I was lying in a hospital bed with my career on the line I would have given anything to play for England but looking at it in terms of what I had to offer, I think I was better than 13 caps. I look at it simply, though; when I was a schoolboy I wanted to play for England and I achieved that ambition. That's the main thing. I did what I set out to do.

The following season it fell to Colin to bring my Everton career to a close. The end came in January 1989 and it still hurts me. Not because of the manner of my departure; Colin handled that like the gentleman that he is. What pained me most was that I was having to walk away from a club that I didn't just love, I was absolutely besotted with.

Aside from my family, nothing in my life has ever meant as much to me as Everton Football Club and I count myself as being hugely privileged not just to have represented them, but to have played for them during arguably the greatest era in its entire history. So, bringing the curtain down on that period of my life was only ever going to prompt anguish.

I tried to find a bit of perspective by telling myself that all good things come to an end, and reminding myself that not many players are fortunate enough to have the honour of pulling on that beautiful blue shirt. I even took solace from the number of fans who complained that I was being allowed to leave ahead of my time, even though some of them, as is their right, had let me know that they hadn't been overly impressed with my form during my final 12 months at the club.

They didn't want me to go and I didn't want to leave but I knew that I had to. I didn't know it at the time but my final game turned out to be a 3-1 home defeat to eventual champions,

Arsenal. I didn't complete the match because Colin took me off with 18 minutes remaining. Had I known that would be the last time I graced Goodison Park as an Everton player I would have milked the moment. Colin didn't pick me again, though, so when Queens Park Rangers came in with an offer to sign me and Everton accepted it, I knew the writing was on the wall.

At least there was no subterfuge and no one attempted to pull the wool over anyone else's eyes. Colin had a chat with me, told me he wanted to go with Brace and McCall in midfield and I said I wanted to play first-team football. If that meant going somewhere else, then so be it. He didn't enjoy the conversation but he said that he understood my feelings because he was exactly the same when he was a player, which left us just needing to resolve how I would leave.

Colin went to the chairman, Sir Philip Carter, to discuss the situation, and it was put to me that if I agreed to forego my signing-on fees then they would give me a free transfer. I accepted the offer and QPR got the deal done in no time at all. My departure was that straightforward.

If arriving at Everton had been a battle with contract wrangles, career-threatening injuries, aborted moves and failed medicals all intervening in one way or another, arranging my exit was so uncomplicated that it felt totally surreal. I knew I was getting a good move and I was looking forward to working under Trevor Francis, who I'd played alongside for England. But leaving Everton was a terrible thing for me.

I was a professional footballer and I should have been comfortable with that kind of scenario but Everton had got under my skin – and it still does. To this day, I still get goosebumps when I go to Goodison Park but, as a player, you could multiply those feelings by any number you care to come up with.

So the day I walked away was devastating. I was looking forward to a new challenge but I was doing so in the knowledge that I was leaving part of myself with Everton.

# 12. FROM BIG CITY TO MAN CITY

*'Like everyone else, the disaster had hit me hard but
there was something uplifting about the way people
came together. It didn't take the pain or anger away –
how could it? But it did show how ordinary people
could come together and take strength from one
another, even at a time of tragedy'*

I DIDN'T just want to play – I was desperate to play. Becoming
surplus to requirements at Everton hadn't diminished that
desire. If anything, it exaggerated it.

Having missed so much football through injury and when I
was a contract rebel at Bolton, I knew that I had to make the
most of every opportunity I had to play football. Thankfully,
Trevor Francis believed I still had something to offer and took a
chance on me, even though I was now 32. He even told me not
to worry about the medical, which was great.

Had he not come in for me, my final months at Everton

probably wouldn't have been the best because I wasn't going to be first choice and I'm not great at dealing with those kind of situations. I would have festered on the bench and everyone would have ended up being sick of me so it was probably better for all involved that I left, with at least some people wishing that I had stayed. As heart-breaking as it was, it was best for all. My only subsequent worry was moving down to London, a city that I've always enjoyed visiting but never had any desire to live in.

At first, I stayed in digs at the Royal Lancaster Hotel where I became really friendly with the general manager, a lovely fella called Sala Houri, so when my mum and dad came down to see me play I put them up there. Sala kindly put them in the presidential suite overlooking the Italian gardens in Hyde Park. I'm not exaggerating when I say it was bigger than the council house that we lived in.

When they were checking out I asked my mum if they'd enjoyed staying there and she said it was great, but was disappointed that there hadn't been a kettle in the room. I told her all she had to do was to ring down and someone would bring a cup of tea. I told her that if you don't ring them it would be hard for them to stay employed because that's part of their job. "I never thought of that," she responded. "I tell you what, though, me and your dad enjoyed the fridge."

I looked at "the fridge" and realised it was the mini-bar. They'd gone through the lot! Obviously, I had to pay the bill but it was worth every penny. From an attic in Huyton to the presidential suite of a top London hotel, that's some journey! If you can't enjoy a drink when you've done that, then when can you? I just wish they'd had a kettle in the room.

My first game was a goalless draw against Nottingham Forest but it was another game involving Brian Clough's side a few months later which turned the world of everyone from my hometown upside down. On April 15, 1989 I was playing for QPR against Middlesbrough. It was all still a bit new to me and I was having to get used to not being an Everton player. It was an exciting time for my new club, though. We'd just signed Nigel Spackman from Liverpool and Colin Clarke had joined for a club record transfer fee as well, so the mood was good. We went into the game expecting to win, even though we were at the wrong end of the table.

The pitch at Loftus Road was bumpy and at half-time Trevor had the hump with us because we hadn't really got going. I was listening to the manager but was also distracted because Everton were playing Norwich City in the FA Cup semi-final at Villa Park, and I wanted to know how they were getting on. But before I could find out, my attention was drawn to the other semi-final when someone said there were people injured at Hillsborough. That was where Liverpool were playing Nottingham Forest and then someone else said there'd been some sort of pitch invasion, and there had been fatalities.

I tracked down a television just to the side of the dressing room area and no scores were being given out, it was just a running commentary on what was known. The information was still sketchy and, like a lot of people, at first I thought that it must have gone off. In hindsight, that might seem a terrible thing to think but hooliganism was a big problem and it wasn't out of the ordinary for a game to be delayed because of trouble.

It was only as more details came through that I realised something much, much worse had happened. That process was underway when we went back out for the second half but, even then, I didn't know what exactly was going on. If I had I might not have been able to play because I knew a lot of lads who were at Hillsborough and my mind would have been with them, rather than on the game I was playing in. But as soon as the final whistle went, I raced off the pitch to try and find out more in the hope that things hadn't turned out so bad. They had, though.

"People have died," someone said and, even though fatalities had been mentioned at half-time, this hit me harder because almost an hour had passed and any hope that there might have been misinformation about the severity of what was happening was lost. I spoke to Nigel Spackman because I knew he'd be worried out of his mind as well, but it was too much to take in. How can people die at a football match?

As the night went on, the number of people who were reported dead was growing. With every update, the situation became worse and more difficult to comprehend. Being in London, we were detached from what was happening but still very much aware of it and connected to it emotionally, though it all felt a bit surreal. A tragedy was unfolding involving the people of my hometown, the team that I'd supported as a boy and a group of supporters that included many people that I knew.

The rivalry between Everton and Liverpool is magnificent because it is so passionate and fierce but that night and, for some time after, it was irrelevant. I rang a good mate, Ted Roberts, a big Liverpudlian who hadn't been at the game and he told me the phones were knackered because so many people were trying to get hold of one another. I had a massive mobile phone but they were new out and the only people I could call on it were Paul Parker and the agent, Eric Hall, so obviously back in Liverpool the landline system was being bombarded and couldn't cope with the strain. All I could do was sit and wait for news, and pray.

On the Tuesday, me and Nigel were on a day off so we got a plane up to Liverpool and went to Anfield. It was a place that I had been to countless times as a player and fan but I had never seen it like this. As soon as we walked in I saw the pitch, that beautifully lush, green playing surface being covered with floral tributes, and it sent a chill down my spine. It was the saddest, most wonderful sight you could ever see.

Like everyone else, the disaster had hit me hard but there was something uplifting about the way people came together. It didn't take the pain or anger away – how could it? But it did show how ordinary people could come together and take strength from one another, even at a time of tragedy. There were flowers with red and white ribbons on and others with blue and white. For me, there has never been a greater symbol of either community strength or civic solidarity. It didn't matter who you supported, this was the city's tragedy. While other elements shamefully turned on Liverpool, we were going to stand shoulder to shoulder with each other. Self-pity city my arse.

What I experienced had a profound effect on me and thousands of others, and it is one of the many reasons why the people of Liverpool remain so angry about how we were treated. From Kelvin MacKenzie's disgraceful 'The Truth' front page which rightly finished *The Sun* on Merseyside, to the claims made by Sir Bernard Ingham, Margaret Thatcher's press secretary, that "a tanked up mob" of Liverpool fans had been one of the causes of Hillsborough, we were coming under attack at a time when we were on our knees; how can that ever be excused or forgotten?

I know my city and its people and I wasn't having any of the smears. The truth was to be found in the terrible stories that fans who'd been in Sheffield came back with, it wasn't going to be discovered in scurrilous news headlines or via shady briefings from politicians, who wouldn't put their name to unfounded allegations designed to distract us from what had really gone on.

Thankfully, even though Liverpool was at its lowest ebb, it fought back. As a city, we refused to accept the false narratives and, even though it took far too long for the full truth to begin to emerge, the Hillsborough campaigners, and everyone who stood by them, ensured that it eventually did. They deserve every accolade for carrying the fight. Those who did everything in their considerable power to try to deny them truth and justice are shamed by their actions.

As a player, I could only take my hat off to the likes of Kenny Dalglish and Alan Hansen who went beyond the call of duty in the way they responded to the disaster. They were still comparatively young lads at the time – Kenny was 38 and Alan was 33 – and nothing they had done in their lives could have prepared them for what they were facing. But their actions were totally in keeping with the city and the club that they were part of and the same could be said of Everton.

Again, I wouldn't have expected anything different from my former club but it is only when you are put to the test that you find out exactly who – and what – you are. At the most testing time anyone could ever imagine, Everton and Liverpool found it within themselves to respond in exactly the right way. We have arguments and we have passion because we love football and we want to win but when something really matters, as it did in the aftermath of Hillsborough, we instinctively know what is important, and we know that we have to be there for one another. I just wish we hadn't needed to find out and that the 96 men, women and children who died were still with us.

As someone who'd been brought up in a council house and who had gone on to do well for himself, professionally and financially, I could have been a Tory pin-up boy. A lad from Liverpool who had "got on his bike" to London, who was living it up at the Royal

Lancaster Hotel and who even had his own mobile phone: I was exactly the type that Margaret Thatcher and her cronies were targeting. But whatever the trappings of my success, I couldn't have been further removed from her politics.

I was – and still am – a socialist and I'm proud to describe myself in that way. I've never forgotten where I come from – Huyton, the constituency where Harold Wilson, the Labour Prime Minister, was the MP – and I've never lost sight of the belief in social justice that was instilled in me when I was growing up. That quote Shankly came out with, about the socialism he believed in being about everyone working together and sharing in the rewards, is absolutely spot on.

I couldn't phrase it as eloquently as him so I'll just put it like this – there is more than enough money to go around this world for people to have a good standard of living. So most, if not all, of what Thatcher did at that time repulsed me because it went against everything that I stand for. Hillsborough was one incident that occurred under her government that highlighted her indifference to ordinary people and Orgreave was another.

I was a professional footballer but I wasn't aloof to any of this. Whole towns, villages and communities were destroyed, especially in mining areas, simply because of her attitude to the working class. You were either with her or against her – and I was most definitely in the second camp.

What happened at Hillsborough had its roots in her ideologies. It was about a growing police state and the empowerment of particular forces, the demonization of people from the north and especially cities like Liverpool, and the sense that those in authority could treat them however they liked.

We knew that long before April 15, 1989, but what happened at Hillsborough on that day proved us right in the worst way possible. Some would suggest Thatcher has blood on her hands. I would argue that's too strong but I would say that through her policies and her beliefs she certainly made that tragedy possible.

When something as catastrophic as Hillsborough happens you question everything and you struggle to find importance in things that seemed to matter more than anything else beforehand. Some of the Liverpool players admitted later that they struggled to see the point of playing football during that period and it is easy to understand why, given how closely involved they had been in such a terrible tragedy.

In that context, football is irrelevant, but in everyday life it is one of the most important trivialities because so many of us live our lives through it. So we were always going to pull our boots back on and get back playing but we did so with a renewed and heightened sense of perspective.

After returning from Merseyside I went back to training with QPR at the Harrods Club in Barnes with a feeling that, although football wasn't a matter of life and death, it was a sport which millions of people go to extraordinary lengths to support. Every single player owed it to those fans to do everything they possibly could to bring pleasure and joy. In QPR's case that season, the best we could offer our supporters was relief because we had been in danger of being relegated when I joined and we were all desperate to avoid that.

We had a decent team with David Seaman in goal, although he took some getting used to because he'd turn up to training wearing waders after going fishing. The defence included the likes of Parker, Alan McDonald and David Bardsley, in midfield we had players like Wayne Fereday, Andy Sinton, David Kerslake and Spackers, with Clarkey and Mark Falco up front. So there wasn't a lack of quality. We had good players and, once confidence picked up, so did our form and we ended up finishing ninth, which was more than respectable.

On the pitch I settled in without too many problems, although I was less successful off it because I bought a house in Gerrards Cross and ended up being the only person to buy a London property during the boom years and lose money on it! But I was happy at QPR and even though Trevor was replaced by Don Howe a few months into the 1989/90 season, I wasn't expecting anything other than to finish my career at Loftus Road.

Even when Ray Wilkins came in, and I asked Don whether he would still want me around because he might not want two veteran midfielders in the same side, he put me at ease, saying he saw us working as a pair. That turned out right as we didn't lose any of the handful of games we played together. So there was no real urge to get back to the North West but that all changed when Manchester City brought Howard Kendall back to English football, setting in motion a chain of events which would lead to me being reunited with the manager who I owed so much to.

The first I knew of his move to City came when Howard called me out of the blue. I suppose it would be described as an illegal approach nowadays because he just came out with what was happening with him, and what he hoped would happen with me. "I'm coming back, lad," he said. "Do you fancy coming to Man City with me?" Just to dangle the carrot a bit more, he told me that if I moved up there with him I'd be working as his number two as well as playing.

No incentives were required, though. Howard himself was the big pull. How could I possibly turn him down after everything we had achieved together at Everton? This was an offer that I couldn't refuse but, knowing what I wanted and being able to make it happen were not necessarily the same thing. City didn't have the funds to buy me and needed me to secure a free transfer, or else the move would be off.

I went and spoke to Don and he was as good as gold. He knew what the offer meant to me and why I wanted to go so he gave me his blessing. All that remained was for me to thrash out personal terms with City and I made that easier by agreeing to take a pay cut. So much for "Greedy Reidy."

I probably had a few nights out too many while I was staying at the Royal Lancaster but I had a good time at QPR. Even though I was only there for a short period, I think I did alright for them. I only got one goal while I was there but it was a header against Wimbledon, of all teams, probably the most unlikely one of my entire career. We also had a memorable 3-2 win over Liverpool just before I left, which I enjoyed as much as anyone.

But when Howard came calling I didn't think twice and he made it even easier for me by telling me I wouldn't need to undergo a medical, apart from bending over and touching my toes. It meant I would become one of a select group of footballers who went through their entire career without passing a medical examination. Howard knew there was no point in giving me a test, that I'd almost certainly fail, and it was because of the injuries that a lot of people thought I was finished by the time I reached my early-30s. For all the doubts about me, though, I ended up playing more than 500 games, which isn't bad considering I basically had four or five years out. I was just unfortunate.

That said it did help that I had a bigger heart than 'normal people', as was discovered by medics at Walton Hospital after I'd injured my ribs playing for Everton against Watford. The treatment, so I could make a speedy recovered, involved freezing my nerves around the area – which is when the find was made.

It wasn't that I was missing games throughout my career with hamstring strains or whatever, I had the kind of big injuries that would keep any player out – and I had lots of them. Maybe another manager wouldn't have taken a chance on me at that stage of my career but Howard knew me better than anyone and he understood what I couldn't do. By the same token, maybe I wouldn't have left QPR if it had been any manager other than Howard. That was how strong the bond between us was.

As soon as I walked into City it hit me that I'd joined one of the country's biggest clubs. From the outside, they had sometimes appeared to be something of a basket case because they had so many problems and seemed to be changing their manager far too often. However, from the inside, I realised straight away that they are a massive institution.

The problem was that the quality of the playing staff didn't match up with the stature of the club. When Howard took over, City were bottom of the league, a situation which led him to the inevitable conclusion that he needed to bring players in or else relegation would be unavoidable. That was easier said than done, though. Not only did Howard need to convince the board to part with money to fund the transfers he wanted to make, there was the added issue of the loyalty of the City fans, which meant they didn't want to lose players who had served the club well.

After signing Alan Harper from Sheffield Wednesday, Howard then set up a deal which would see Mark Ward come to City from West Ham, with Trevor Morley and Ian Bishop going the other way. There was already suspicion about Howard, mainly because Mel Machin had done a good job and had presided over a 5-1 win over Manchester United earlier that season, but that transfer deal took it to another level. Bishop had been one of the more popular players but Howard wanted to build his own team and he couldn't afford to worry about who were, or were not, crowd favourites; he just had to make decisions that would be right for the club in the predicament that they were in.

As well as bringing in Harpo and myself, Howard then added Neil Pointon, Inchy and Wayne Clarke to the squad, which gave us a strong contingent of former Everton old boys, something else that didn't go down too well with the City fans. Their disenchantment with what was going on came over loud and clear in a game against Charlton Athletic when Howard brought Inchy on and the substitution was jeered, with the supporters then breaking out into a chant of: "What the fuck is going on?" We were also being nicknamed Everton Reserves, which didn't help matters, and just to put the tin hat on it all, Howard had a fall-out with a journalist called Peter Gardner from the *Manchester Evening News* which meant even the local paper turned against us.

Peter had travelled on the team bus for years and no one had challenged that previously, but Howard wanted the players to be able to have some privacy on the way to and from games and he put a stop to it. From then on Peter didn't do him any favours in his reports. He also had a direct line to Peter Swales, the City chairman, and they would call each other every morning which I don't think was helpful for the club, and it didn't do Howard any favours. But he'd been around long enough to know that if results went well all of these problems would diminish.

That Charlton game in late February brought things to a head. We lost 2-1 and desperate times called for desperate measures. When the training ground at Platt Lane was frozen the following Monday, Howard told us to report to a club called Bowlers, where we sometimes had an indoor session. I said we needed training to be short and sharp, to get everyone bright and on their toes, so I was thinking he'd opt for a five-a-side but he had other ideas. "No lad," he said. "Get the catering manager."

I went and got him and then he said to me: "Get the players' lounge open, get the table tennis going and I want five crates of Budweiser." I was thinking he'd lost it but Howard looked at me, and said: "I've got it, lad."

The lads all came in, wondering what was going on. Howard got hold of a bat, gave me the other one, I served and he hit it back. We only had two shots, one apiece, and he told me to drop the bat and then Wardy had a go. The same thing happened again, a couple of shots and then Howard brought it to a halt. "Stop, mistake, go and sit down and get a Budweiser," he said, and Wardy did as he was told. It was 10.30 in the morning.

After two hours of playing table tennis and drinking Budweiser he sent us home, and told us to make sure we were at it in training the following morning. We were all high on life though so went to Mulligan's, near Manchester Airport, and the party carried on there. We lost our next game at Nottingham Forest – a match which will always be remembered for Gary Crosby heading the ball out of Andy Dibble's right hand before scoring – but we only lost one of the remaining 11 fixtures and ended up avoiding relegation fairly comfortably.

Howard's methods had worked. Whether it was freshening up the squad, making unpopular decisions, challenging the influence of the local press or organising a bevvy when other managers would have been running the bollocks off us, all his calls paid off one way or another because we stayed up.

There will be some who won't approve of the table tennis and Budwieser stunt and, in the context of the modern game, with everything we know about sports science and nutrition, it's hard to imagine anything like that happening now. However, at the time it was the right thing to do.

As an act of man-management and sports psychology it was a

masterstroke because it took all of the tension out of a difficult situation and allowed us to have a bit of fun, at a time when we were coming under increasing pressure. I couldn't believe it myself and I'd been involved in a lot of team-bonding exercises with Howard by that stage. The likes of Paul Lake, Ian Brightwell, Steve Redmond and Andy Hinchcliffe must have felt like they were on a different planet.

There was another time when he couldn't take the team for a friendly at Bury so he called me over to the hotel the night before to work out what system we were going to play. He ordered some wine and after we'd had a glass or two, we set up the team; we had four at the back, four in midfield and three up top! Gary Megson spotted it straight away and said, "That's 12 players," so I jumped in and told him: "You're right, you're not playing!"

That was the team that we'd come up with, though, and all because we'd got pissed before we did it. The lads were laughing but they took it in the right spirit and things like that, intentional or not, helped us to get a real team spirit going. The dressing room became a fun place to be and that was key to our results improving, a process that continued when Howard brought in Niall Quinn and later Tony Coton, two brilliant signings who improved us at both ends of the pitch.

If I was to pick out one fixture which best illustrated how far we had come in a short space of time it would be an away game at Aston Villa on April 1, 1990. They were a really strong side and were going for the title under Graham Taylor's management, while we were fighting for our lives at the other end of the table. If anyone had been having a bet on it, the only choice was a home win but we upset the odds and in doing so, eased the relegation fears that had dogged City all season.

Villa actually went ahead through Gordon Cowans but Mark

Ward equalised from outside the box and I got the winner late on, by being in the right place at the right time after David White's shot came back off the post. Unlike most of the money that had been wagered, there was one lucky punter who predicted the result and won a few bob. That was me.

You were allowed to have a bet in those days, at least I hope we were anyway: I had £50 on a City win at 5/1 so I was even more jubilant than usual when I turned out to be the unlikely hero. A winning goal, three massive points, the pressure relieved and £250 profit, I don't think I had too many days that were much better than that.

The thing that Howard had recognised, and I don't think he's been given enough credit for this, was that City had some really good emerging young players, but they needed more experience and know-how around them to allow them to thrive. That was why he decided to bring in some of his Everton old boys. He knew exactly what he would get from all of us and what we could bring to the dressing room. He had talent and massive potential in the form of Lake, White and Brightwell but he also knew that each of them would benefit from having more proven players around them, especially during a relegation battle.

Had it not been for injury, Lakey would have been one of the best England players that there had been for a long time. He was that good. He had speed, control, pace, a brilliant range of passing, desire and he was a nailed-on superstar. At the time he was getting favourable comparisons with Alan Hansen, which was a big compliment but it wasn't misplaced. I would say that, if anything, Lakey had a bit more devil in him and was probably a bit more attack-minded.

There was one pre-season friendly in Pinzolo, Italy, when we played Bologna and he went on this run, beating one man, then another, then another and finished it off by chipping the keeper. It was one of those moments when you gasp at what you've just seen. I was fortunate enough in my career to share the pitch with some magnificent players, but that was one of the finest demonstrations of talent that I ever witnessed. It was world class and that was the level that I genuinely believe he was destined for. That's why it's such an enormous tragedy, for him and for English football, that his career was ended prematurely.

Paul had already suffered one bad knee injury when I got to City and then he did it again, which was the beginning of the end for him. I don't have many personal regrets from my football career but if I could change one thing it would be that Lakey would have been able to fulfil his potential. No player deserves what happened to him but, in his case, it was made even worse because he was such a great lad and everyone could see that he was a wonderful footballer.

I was in the twilight of my own playing days when events took an unexpected turn, and inadvertently thrust me towards a new career in management. The sequence of events began with a 3-3 draw against Manchester United in October 1990, a game in which they scored twice in the last 10 minutes to draw level, after Howard took me off and brought Brightwell on. I had a massive ruck with Howard afterwards but he claimed he'd had no choice because he needed to save my legs for a League Cup tie at home to Arsenal on the following Tuesday.

I was always moaning but he knew how to handle me, although I was even less impressed when we lost 1-0 to George Graham's side. As usual, I went into a bit of a sulk about the result but I went and had a drink with Howard at the Copthorne Hotel, where we were staying. Joe Melling and Bob Cass, a couple of journalists who we knew well, joined us. We were talking about our game and also about Everton's because they'd lost away to Sheffield United to put Colin under real pressure.

During the course of the conversation, Cassie asked Howard out of the blue whether he would go back to Everton. Thinking it was a hypothetical question, Howard said, "yes" and then Cassie went out to make a phone call. We had no idea who he had gone to speak to but when he came back he told us he'd been in touch with Jim Greenwood, Everton's chief executive. That kick-started a sequence of events which culminated in Howard returning to his beloved Goodison Park.

That was how one of the biggest moves in the history of both clubs happened. There were no agents, no stories planted in newspapers and no manoeuvring behind the scenes. It was just an innocent conversation, a well-connected journalist, a club in need and that was all that was required to put the wheels in motion.

It was all done and dusted pretty quickly and Howard's 11-month spell with us came to an end with him saying that while City was a love affair, Everton had been a marriage. I understood where he was coming from although it didn't help his cause with those City fans, who had been suspicious of his Everton links from the outset.

His final game in charge was against Sunderland and he pulled me afterwards to ask if I would go back to Everton with him. I was tempted, which was inevitable given my own bond with the club, but my main reaction was that we had a big job on at City and things were starting to look up, so much so that we had a chance of doing something there. The conversation went on and after accepting that I wouldn't be leaving City, Howard said he would put in a good word for me to replace him as manager.

That sounded great to me but I also knew that Howard hadn't seen eye-to-eye with Swales so I wasn't holding out too much hope. There had been a couple of occasions when we'd been on away trips and the chairman had told Howard that the club wouldn't pay for the odd bottle of wine that he'd had. Then there was the situation with Peter Gardner, who was very close to Swales, as well as issues with players' contracts that led Howard to believe City wasn't being run as well as it should have been. He thought it was being run on a wing and a prayer and he wasn't afraid of voicing his opinion about what should have been happening.

So while Howard was off to Everton, a decision which might have been a mistake on his behalf, given the way things turned out, I was in the mix for my first manager's job and I had the outgoing boss, who didn't get on well with the chairman, in my corner. With that kind of backing, I should have been a bigger long shot than City had been to win at Villa but even I wasn't backing myself this time.

I knew that I wanted the job but I didn't think my chances of getting it were particularly strong. Not only did I have to convince the City fans that replacing one ex-Everton man with another was a good idea, I also had to win Swales over. On top of that, I was a managerial novice and City were a club with a reputation for chewing managers up and spitting them out. I wanted the job, though. I wanted it badly.

# 13. THE MAINE MAN

*'As many of my predecessors discovered, what City managers wanted and what City managers got during that era were often two very different things'*

"I'LL do it for one game." That was my opening gambit to Peter Swales when he asked me to take over the team temporarily following Howard's departure.

I was half holding a gun to his head because I knew he needed someone in charge for our next fixture, at home to Leeds United, and he knew that if I did okay it might be hard to shift me. We lost 3-2 in a great match and Alan Harper missed a penalty, but the supporters were brilliant and their backing got me the job.

The fans had become sick and tired of one change after another and, for whatever reason, they saw something in me that they liked. The chairman was left with little option but to make me player-manager at the age of 35. It was a fantastic opportunity, more than I could have wished for at that stage of my career, but it was also a bit intimidating. Whereas the man I was succeeding was a proven winner, I had everything to prove.

I looked at what other player-managers had done when they

first got jobs at big clubs and the obvious example was Kenny Dalglish at Liverpool, who took over at Anfield at a similar age, so made sure he had Bob Paisley around to enjoy the benefit of his experience. With Howard in his second spell of marital bliss at Everton, there was only one person I wanted to fill a similar role for me and that was Ian Greaves, because he'd been a great manager and I knew he was also a great psychologist, but he had a bad back so could only commit to helping me as a scout.

Instead, Greavesy recommended Sam Ellis as my number two so I took his advice, but that didn't go down too well with the supporters. He had the reputation of being a long-ball merchant from his time as manager of Blackpool and Bury. Once Sam was in among the lads he was fine, but the reaction to his appointment was my first real insight into the way every decision you make as manager is scrutinised to an incredible degree. I already had a thick skin – how could I have anything else when even the songs in praise of me said I was fat and round? – but I quickly realised that I was going to need an even thicker one, particularly at a club like City, where molehills can be turned into mountains.

My first official game in charge was at Luton Town on November 17, 1990. Going into the last minute we were 2-1 up thanks to goals from Steve Redmond and David White and I was almost counting the points when Keith Burge, the referee, gave them a penalty. It was a foul, Colin Hendry caught Iain Dowie as they competed for a bouncing ball on that ridiculous plastic pitch, so I had no complaints about the decision. What did wind me up though was the way the penalty was taken.

Tony Coton hadn't even set himself when John Dreyer took one step back but, instead of keeping on retreating for a standard penalty run-up, he stepped forward straight away and scored before Tony could even move. Tony went absolutely nuts and chased the referee up the pitch before several more of our players joined in the protests.

The lads were still livid after the final whistle so they challenged Burge again and, having left myself out because I knew I'd struggle with my knees on that surface, I ended up having to walk on to the pitch to drag them away. I could understand their anger and, if anything, I was even more pissed off than they were but I couldn't afford my first game in charge to end with a full-blown diplomatic incident. For once in my life, I had to act as peacemaker, even though I really wanted to be a rabble-rouser.

That was the first sign that I was changing but the more difficult adjustment involved coming to terms with no longer being just a player. In the dressing room I went from being Reidy to gaffer and I'm sure that took a bit of getting used to for the players, too. From being the experienced professional who they could turn to for advice or be on the receiving end of a verbal bollocking when necessary, I was suddenly the fella who could leave them out, and even punish them when they stepped out of line.

Even managers who've been in the game for years will admit that those responsibilities are never easy but they're much harder when you're starting out, especially if you are still playing, as I was. For that reason, I decided I had to delegate. I told Sam that when I was out on the park he had to make the decisions because I wanted to concentrate on playing.

Obviously we discussed things before matches and at half-time but I had to give him some control because, otherwise, I would have struggled to keep the balls I was juggling in the air. I was fortunate in that I had learned from some great managers but it was still a steep learning curve and an unforgiving one, too. In football management no one waits for you to reach a stage when you get good results consistently; you have to deliver from the off.

We did okay on that front, finishing fifth in my first season in charge, and we had some really good results on the way, most notably victories over Aston Villa, Nottingham Forest and Tottenham. We had a strong group and it needed to be strengthened still further if we were going to really kick on but there was always a feeling of instability around the club, that was hard to understand or explain.

I know Chelsea change managers regularly now but they have an infrastructure that allows that to happen without the whole club being destabilised, but City never had that kind of solid setup. The board was a strange make-up of old money and wealthy brewers but Peter Swales dominated everything, a reality that Howard had never been comfortable with.

It didn't make things easier for me in my first job but at least there was someone much worse off in the same city. Alex Ferguson was right under the pump at United, so much so that when he came to a youth-team game at our place he looked lost. That was how strong the pressure was he was under. One of the most resilient figures in British football was actually beleaguered.

Sam and myself called him over and we had scampi and chips with him to show a bit of solidarity, to try and take his mind off things, but I could tell he was under pressure. United had won the FA Cup the previous May after Mark Robins kept Alex in a job with a winner at Forest in the third round that, in hindsight, changed everything. But even after lifting his first trophy in England there were still questions because United were struggling to make a real impression in the league. He ended up knocking Liverpool off their perch, which was no bad thing, but had I known what United would go on to achieve under him there's not a chance I would have given him his dinner!

I liked him straight away, though. He was hard work at times and he was tough and uncompromising but, in terms of how he conducted himself with other managers, I always found him to be incredibly fair. There's no doubt that he was always looking for an edge because that was what made him tick, especially when United were playing their rivals, but he was also big enough to hold his hands up if he got something wrong. After one derby, Alex told the press lads that Neil Pointon had maimed one of his players so I went to have it out with him and he admitted straight away that he'd used the wrong word and retracted it.

That said a lot about him and it was just unfortunate for us, and for every other club in the country, that he put together a group of players that dominated English football for years. One of those players was Ryan Giggs and the first time I saw him was in a reserve-team game at Platt Lane. As he went past one player after another I turned around and stated the obvious to Ken Barnes. "This kid's a good player," I said, and Ken replied: "Yes, we had him but he went to United."

The story goes that money changed hands but without knowing the ins and outs of everything I couldn't possibly comment. All I know is that at one point City had a kid who would go on to become one of the greatest wingers in the history of British football and he ended up being a magnificent servant to United, rather than to ourselves.

Things like that went in Alex's favour but he made the most of every single one of them, and the main reason that he was able to do so was that he had bollocks. He made decisions that were unpopular that turned out to be masterstrokes, he faced down dissent when others might have wilted under pressure and, in doing so, he proved himself to be a managerial great. It would have been better for me if he'd done it somewhere other than United – the Outer Hebrides would have been just about far enough away – but at least he gave me the opportunity to pit my wits against the very best.

That Robins goal was the obvious turning point but Alex was also making things happen, never more so than in the 1990 FA Cup final when he dropped Jim Leighton, his first-choice goalkeeper, for the replay and replaced him with Les Sealey. If that had backfired, he would have been in real trouble. The risk involved in that kind of decision means not many managers would have taken it, but he did, and it paid off for him.

As much as I would have preferred his big calls to have gone against him, because that would have helped City and myself, I have to take my hat off to him. Alex made choices that altered the course of football history and he kept doing it for 27 years at one club. If that doesn't earn respect I don't know what does.

As a kid, Shankly was God to me. It was his charisma. I knew he had it as a kid but it was only when I came across him as a player that I realised just how much he had. It was Peter Thompson's testimonial dinner and he walked into the Pack Horse Hotel in Bolton and, honestly, it was like the messiah had just arrived. I've never, ever seen a room with so much love in it. People adored him. He got up to speak and everyone fell silent because they wanted to hear every single word that he said. This wasn't about football, it went well beyond that. It was about him as a man and the way he saw the world.

There are many other great managers, Harry Catterick is another and his record has somehow been forgotten, but Shankly's charisma set him apart. I always remember him speaking at St George's Hall in Liverpool city centre and coming out with one of the greatest lines I've heard from anyone in football. "You players should be thankful to go out on the pitch to play for these people," he said. That's what I was brought up on. What a man!

Forget whatever allegiance you might have and whatever team you support, that's a manager who you'd love to play for and a man for whom you'd give everything you've got.

I was also fortunate enough to work under Howard, a manager who remains one of the most underrated that we have ever had in Britain. I admired Bob Paisley from a distance and the same went for Brian Clough but when it comes down to it, Alex's longevity and his peerless ability to win trophies marks him out as the finest manager of modern times.

In my first job I was having to take him on at the same time as dealing with the City board. It was like fighting Mike Tyson with one hand tied behind my back. It wasn't long before I took over from Howard that Iron Mike's reign as undefeated world heavyweight champion was ended by James "Buster" Douglas, which proved that even a journeyman has a puncher's chance. I just needed to keep Alex within range.

To do that, we had to buy better players, an ambition that every City manager had for 30 years but found difficult, if not impossible, to achieve until Sheikh Mansour arrived and bankrolled the club in a way that allowed them to compete for the best in the market. United's commercial revenues were the biggest in the country and that allowed them to spend more on transfer fees and wages than most other clubs, City included. This made it even more important that when we did have the opportunity to bring in top talent we made the most of it.

I know that's easier said than done. I realise that sometimes there are situations that are out of your control because players and agents will use your interest to attract another club. But I've always felt that if City had shown a bit more ambition we might have been able to hold on to United's coat tails more than we did. There was investment in the squad and we brought in some good players but there wasn't enough. At the highest level, that is almost always going to result in falling short.

The signing that we missed out on that I most regret was John Barnes. Graeme Souness had taken over as manager of Liverpool and had set about dismantling a squad which he felt was in need of freshening up. His thirst for fresh blood meant a number of players became available for transfer. Barnesy, who I had played with for England and who had become one of the best players in the world while at Anfield, had the kind of individual talent that can transform any team.

He had suffered a few bad injuries by the time we became interested in him. The power that had helped him become a defender's nightmare in the late-1980s was not quite as explosive as it had once been but the ability was still in place. There were few footballers in that era who could master a football like he could. As soon as I found out he was up for grabs I asked the chairman to get a deal done.

He was at the top of my wish-list ahead of the start of the 1993/94 season but I had also urged the club to sign Paul Stewart, Andy Townsend and Geoff Thomas. Those were the four main names on my wanted list – and I got none of them. The only one who we did sign was Alfons Groenendijk for £200,000 from Ajax. In the same summer, United signed Roy Keane for a British record fee and all I can say is you get what you pay for.

I was also left to rue another couple of players who got away. Henrik Larsson was scouted at Feyenoord by Bobby Saxton, who I'd later link up with at Sunderland. I then rang a friend of Ian Greaves' in Holland but he said he wasn't convinced he would be able to handle the physicality of the Premier League. 'Sacko' said he was brilliant but we were not in a position to gamble on someone who might not be equipped for the English game.

At one point I also asked Bristol City about Andy Cole but then Sam Ellis spoke to Pat Rice at Arsenal, where Andy had been as a young player, and told us he was a bit of an awkward lad to deal with. I've got to know Andy pretty well since and not only was he a magnificent finisher, he is also a great person. So that's at least another two top players who we did our homework on – which worked against us.

That's not to say that I didn't make mistakes that cost us, because I did. Just as the club let me down over Barnes and others, I let myself down with a couple of decisions, none more so than allowing Colin Hendry to join Blackburn Rovers. If I could change one thing I did at City it would be that.

The only excuses I can offer are that I was a young manager cutting his teeth in the game and it was inevitable that not every move I made would be the right one. I was at a club where wheeling and dealing meant that you sometimes had to lose a player to bring another one in. The combination of both of those factors played a significant role in my thinking with the decision to sell Colin. I wanted to bring Keith Curle in from Wimbledon but for that deal to happen I had to let one player go. At first I tried to move Steve Redmond on, but nothing materialised on that front so when Blackburn came to us with an offer for Colin we accepted it.

I was having to juggle things around and I made a decision that I have long since come to regret. Colin and Curle would have been an excellent pairing but I did what I thought was best in the knowledge that I could have one but couldn't have both, unless we found another way of bringing money in. But if there's one person in all of this that I don't have to apologise to it's Colin as his move to Blackburn turned out to be the best of his career.

While I went on to get the sack and City continued their flawed attempts to overcome the elite, he won the league under Kenny Dalglish and remains revered at Blackburn to this day. While my decision backfired on me, it paid dividends for him. He deserves all the credit in the world for making the most of being shown the door because not every player is able to do that.

The situation with Clive Allen was different, though. I received criticism at the time; first, for freezing Clive out of the team and second, for allowing him to join Chelsea. As with a lot of managerial decisions supporters don't agree with, there was information that they were not party to that might have influenced their thinking had they been aware of it.

I inherited a situation with Clive that began when he told Howard that he would like to leave the club. It was during the talks that led to Wardy signing and Howard had offered Bishop and Morley in exchange, but it didn't look as if the deal would happen. While this was going on, Clive went to Howard and said he wouldn't mind being used as a makeweight. The gaffer didn't act upon that, and ended up getting the deal done without having to take him up on his offer.

This might have been unfair on my part but that gave me an impression of Clive that coloured the way I viewed him when I took over as manager. Not long after that, I fell out with him and stopped picking him. He's a good pal now but at the time it was difficult, and there was one FA Cup game at Port Vale when I brought him on, he scored and started kissing the badge.

I thought that was a bit much, given he'd wanted to go to West Ham a few months earlier but these are the kind of problems that you will have as a young manager, particularly when you're still part of the dressing room setup and your predecessor has given you a bit of additional intelligence about your team-mates.

That was a difficult situation but at least the complication of being a player, as well as a manager, was becoming less of an issue as my legs started to go. When I realised that was happening I brought in Steve McMahon from Liverpool to do the job that I had been doing in midfield. As important as the job that Macca did for the team was, his arrival allowed me to start putting distance between the dressing room and myself.

Along with Macca and Curle, Terry Phelan was another big signing who went straight into the first team. It was widely reported that the fees for Phelan and Curle were around £2.5m each which, as plenty of people were willing to point out, was a lot of money for two defenders from Wimbledon. I had been talking with Joe Kinnear, who was their manager, but the deal got done at the highest level, with Swales conducting negotiations on our behalf and Sam Hammam looking after Wimbledon's interests. I had nothing to do with the transfer talks so, like everyone else, I took the £2.5m claims at face value when they came out.

It was only when speaking to Joe later that I discovered the initial fee for both players had been in the region of £1.5m each. There were performance-related incentives that could have seen Wimbledon earn another £2m in total, but for those to be realised City would have had to have won pretty much everything, from the Premier League title to The Boat Race!

Still, it made Hammam look like a hard-nosed negotiator and Swales appear to be a big spender. At least the big hitters were happy even if, in the eyes of the watching public, it seemed that we had overpaid. The main thing was that we had got the players. For all of the shenanigans that were going on over my head, I had asked for Curle and Phelan to be signed and the club had delivered. I'd also learned something about the way the reality of fees is sometimes different to the way they are reported, too, so it was a good experience for me.

The most important thing we brought to the club wasn't a player, though, it was stability. We became consistent in our approach, consistent in our results and consistent in the feeling that something was growing. That was reflected in my first two full seasons in charge as we finished fifth in both campaigns, gathering 62 points in 1990/91 and 70 in 1991/92. It felt like momentum was building, particularly with players like David White coming to the fore.

There was a game at Villa in April 1991 when he scored four goals in a 5-1 win and everything seemed possible for him and for us. He was up against Paul McGrath, who was rightly regarded as one of the best defenders in the game, but Whitey destroyed him. His pace, willingness to run in behind and ability to finish meant that I could play him as an orthodox winger, or push him alongside Quinny, and he could do damage. His improvement was representative of the whole team. Although I wouldn't say we looked set to challenge, our progress was significant enough to expect that it would be maintained, given the mix of youth and experience we had.

That confidence intensified during pre-season ahead of the start of the 1992/93 campaign, primarily because Paul Lake was able to be involved again after a horrific run of major knee injuries. That was a major boost for us and I said so at the time, telling the press that it was like having a £3m signing given to me. Like everyone else at the club I was desperate for Lakey to have a run of games without injury, mainly because that was the least that he deserved, after everything he had been through, but also because I knew that if he stayed fit he had the talent to help us go to the next level.

After looking as classy as ever in training and in the friendlies that we played, I picked Lakey for our first game of the season

**Savouring Success:** A year after becoming Sunderland manager I celebrated promotion with assistant Paul Bracewell and the players in April 1996

**Fergie Time:** Getting the better of Sir Alex Ferguson's Manchester United courtesy of a 2-1 Premier League victory at Roker Park, March 1997

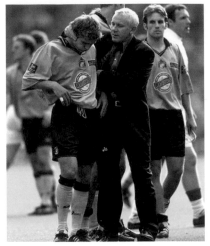

**Final Farewell:** I wave to the Sunderland fans after the final Premier League game at Roker Park, a 3-0 defeat of Everton which kept alive the club's chances of staying in the top flight, May 1997

**Gray Day:** Comforting Michael Gray after the boyhood Mackem's penalty shootout miss condemned Sunderland to defeat in the remarkable 1998 play-off final against Charlton Athletic at Wembley

**Calm Before The Storm:** Six bottles of Laurent Perrier later, I was able to introduce new signing Lee Clark to his – and our – new home, the Stadium of Light, summer 1997

**Champagne Moment:** Celebrating promotion back to the Premier League following a 5–2 victory at Bury, April 1999

**Trophy Time:** Showing off the league championship following the final game of the 1998/99 season, a 2–1 home defeat of Birmingham City, May 1999

THE IRONGATE GROUP

*office product solutions*

ephone: 1332)
5950

Facsimile: (01332)
291311

**Derby Delight:** My typical bench demeanour lets you know that Sunderland are on the way to a 5–0 victory at Derby County, September 1999

**Award Double:** Kevin Phillips and I scoop October 1999's Premier League awards

**Lead The Way:** Welcoming Labour PM Tony Blair to the Stadium of Light, December 1999

**Old Rivals:** Sharing a joke with Liverpool caretaker-manager Phil Thompson at Anfield, March 2000

**Familiar Fury:** A difference of opinion with the linesman during a 1–1 draw with Liverpool, February 2001

**Sinking Feeling:** Niall Quinn portrays my inner woes during a 3-0 defeat at West Ham United, April 2002

**End In Sight:** With Arsenal's Arsene Wenger, October 2002 – the 3-1 defeat brought the curtain down for me at Sunderland

**Poisoned Chalice:** Speaking to the media in the opening weeks of my time as Leeds United caretaker-manager, April 2003

**Smiles Better:** Defeat of Fulham helps Leeds take a step closer to survival, April 2003

**Goodison Woe:** A 4-0 defeat at Everton sets alarm bells ringing, September 2003

**Old Friends:** I greet my former England boss, Sir Bobby Robson, ahead of Leeds United's opening game of the 2003/04 season, against Newcastle United at Elland Road

**Thumbs Up:** Greeting Coventry City fans ahead of the final game of 2003/04, my first as Sky Blues boss, a 2-1 victory over a Crystal Palace side who would be promoted via the play-offs

**Big Adventure:** Overseeing training with the Thailand national side, November 2008

**Back Home:** Assistant-boss to Tony Pulis at Stoke City, November 2009

**Anxious Times:** Plymouth claimed a welcome 3-2 victory at Bristol Rovers, January 2011

**Something To Say:** With the fourth official as Bolton coach, April 2016

**The 'Kids':** A recent picture with Shaun, Gary Anthony, Michael Patrick and Carol Elizabeth

**Close Bond:** Messing around with my grandson Freddie

**My Girls:** A family photo with Carol Elizabeth, Louise and Mum

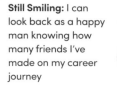

**Still Smiling:** I can look back as a happy man knowing how many friends I've made on my career journey

– the first Monday night football televised by BSkyB as part of their multi-million pound contract with the newly-formed Premier League – at home to QPR. He only lasted an hour though, having felt pressure in his knee. The hope was that this was just the kind of minor problem that is inevitable after such a long lay-off and he was passed fit for our next game just two days later, at Middlesbrough. This time he only got as far as the seventh minute before his knee went again. We lost 2-0 but the defeat was the least of my worries.

It was the third time Lakey had ruptured his anterior cruciate ligament and he had already performed a couple of minor miracles by coming back from a potentially career-threatening injury twice. I feared he would never play for me again, or anyone else for that matter. Tragically, that proved to be the case.

City didn't cover themselves in glory in the aftermath and I know that is something that Lakey rightly remains unhappy about. The decision was taken to fly him to Los Angeles where he would be treated by a surgeon called Dr Domenick Sisto, who had rescued the careers of John Salako and Ian Durrant. Swales even approved a request for Lakey to fly out first class, which went against his usual instincts. In the circumstances he could hardly refuse, even though it had taken a bit of arm twisting on my behalf for him to agree.

But, after the operation, Dr Sisto explained the seriousness of the situation to Lakey and, understandably, he took it badly. Having been in a similar situation as a player I knew what he was going through and, without exaggerating, it is mental torture. Lakey then got in touch with the club, asking for his girlfriend to be flown out but Swales refused to pay for her and wouldn't change his mind. Quinny and myself took a collection in the dressing room to fund her travel costs.

It was bad enough that the players had to pay for something that should have been the club's responsibility. To make matters worse, when the time came for Lakey to return to the UK, he turned up at the airport to catch his flight home, only to discover that his ticket was in economy. I'm no snob, and I know Lakey isn't, but when you're a professional footballer who has just had major knee surgery and you're on crutches, the least you expect your club to provide is a bit of leg room and additional comfort. There's not a chance that modern-day City would treat a top player like that. They would go to whatever lengths necessary to aid his recovery and no expense would be spared. That's not an indulgence, it's basic common sense.

Whatever Swales wasn't, there's no doubt he was a political animal. You don't go from being at Altrincham with Freddie Pye and Noel White to becoming chairman of The Football Association unless you know how to fight political battles – and win them. His two main ambitions after buying a stake in City were to make the club successful and for himself to win power; he achieved the second of those objectives, but not the first.

In the process, he sacked 11 managers and, as one of those, I can pass my own verdict on him and that is that I was never, ever comfortable with him, and never felt I could trust him. That made City a very difficult club to manage. While he left me alone with the team, his willingness to interfere on my behalf had all but evaporated at the end of my third season in charge. We had finished ninth, which was disappointing after what had happened over the previous two years. To make matters worse, United had won the title for the first time since 1967 so Swales's trigger finger began to get itchy.

There were two issues in particular which underlined his growing sense of restlessness. Firstly, he didn't give me any support in my attempts to sign any of the four main players on my wanted list. Secondly, he brought in John Maddock, a journalist who was his mate, to work above me as general manager. It was the perfect storm – United were champions, the chairman's pockets had been sewn up and I was under pressure from above.

Like the 'Swales Out' graffiti that was daubed around Maine Road whenever he changed manager, the writing was on the wall for me, but I wasn't going to make things easy by walking away. Even though we had dropped a few places in the league table, City had established themselves as a top-half team under my management. Why should I lose faith in myself, even if it was clear that my superiors were not backing me as they once had?

My perseverance earned me four more games at the start of the 1993/94 season before I was dismissed. I wasn't helped by a poor start, which saw us take only one point from those matches, but even if we'd dropped only two points it would have been a matter of time before I was let go. It was Maddock, who had only been at the club for five minutes, who advised Swales to sack me and the chairman acted upon his recommendation. 'It may be seen as a panic measure so early into the season but we need to do something to sustain the club's future,' Maddock said in a statement, as if chopping and changing managers was suddenly going to become the panacea for all of City's ills.

Not that these events surprised me. As a manager with little experience I still knew enough about City and the way they were run to know that dismissal was an occupational hazard there, more than at most other clubs. Even before I got the job it felt like they had wanted me to jump through hoops to get it, and it was clear from the outset that those in control of the club had a clear idea of their own importance.

The tone was set when I had to go to meet one of the investors, a fella called Steven Bollin, at Mere, and the first thing he said to me was: "Why should I give you the fucking job?" It wasn't the obvious opening question in an interview but I didn't want him to put me on the back foot straight away, so I responded: "Why shouldn't you give me the fucking job?" At the start, I could get away with that kind of response because I knew that they needed someone to succeed Howard. But at the end they held all the cards and all you can do is accept their decision.

I knew the end was nigh when Swales came to me and told me to sack Sam Ellis. It was a standard move for an over-bearing chairman when a manager is under pressure but I refused. I didn't think it was right that Sam should take responsibility for our downturn in fortunes, and there was no chance that I was going to sacrifice him to try and save my own skin. I know there have been managers who have done that but it's not for me.

Swales obviously didn't take that well and he told me that the fans weren't happy because they thought we were playing the long-ball game, and there had been a couple of incidents when our discipline had been brought into question. So that was our playing style, our behaviour and our coaching staff all being shot at by the most powerful individual at the club, and he was using the supporters to do it.

The discipline issue was a tricky one and I had to acknowledge that. A couple of the players had been caught in what I can only describe as compromising positions with women, and that had provoked negative headlines. I hit back at Swales, telling him he couldn't handle his boardroom, which went down well. We had a ruck about that and I told him that if he was getting involved in the football side of things and making football-related decisions, I cease to be the manager. He obviously agreed with me because he sacked me after just 13 days of the new season.

The fractious build-up to my departure meant there was no element of surprise when it was confirmed. I had been to see Ian Greaves a few days before the guillotine fell and he spelled it out to me, telling me I was going to get sacked and there was nothing I could do to avoid it. I valued his opinion as much as anyone's and his experience in the game, and knowledge of me, meant he was better placed than anyone to assess the situation I was in. In many ways, he was only telling me what I already knew.

Unlike Martin Edwards and the board at Manchester United, who had given Fergie every chance to recover when results were going against him, City's hierarchy wasn't inclined to give a struggling manager sufficient time to turn things around. I probably should have seen it coming before it actually happened and, looking back, it was clear during that pre-season in 1993 that the board wasn't fully behind me.

I bumped into Kenny Dalglish at Manchester Airport one day and he said to me: "It looks like you've got a few quid to spend." I could understand why he thought that, because that was the message that was coming out of the club, and making its way into the newspapers. The briefing was that I had £6m to work with but, ultimately, our outlay was only £200,000 on Groenendijk so God knows what happened to the other £5.8m. I just know that the money never got spent on the players that I had wanted, which was a really bad sign for me.

What made it worse was that I knew that those players wanted to join us. Andy Townsend ended up going to Villa and did really well for them under Ron Atkinson but I had set a deal up for him in strange circumstances a few months earlier, and had expected him to come to City.

We were playing against Chelsea at Stamford Bridge towards the end of the previous season and I caught him late, and he jumped up to have a go at me. "What the fuck are you doing?" he said, no doubt expecting a typical reaction from me. I had bigger plans for him than a verbal spat, though. "You're on a free in the summer," I said. "How do you fancy coming to us?" It must be the only time that a manager has tapped up a transfer target by smashing him on the pitch – but my efforts came to nothing.

I couldn't have done the same with Barnesy because there was no chance of me ever getting close enough to kick him, but I spoke to Souey and, after learning that the asking price was £1.5m, I was hopeful that we could get something done but that went no further, either. The problem was that people other than myself held the purse strings and were also responsible for transfer negotiations so I was in their hands. If they had stopped being convinced by me, which was clearly the case, they were not going to back my judgement.

The way it all ended was not what I would have wanted but like politicians, the career of every City manager during that period only ever ended in one way – failure. That shouldn't obscure from what we achieved, particularly considering that in the first season we finished fifth it was the last time that the club had finished above Man United, before the arrival of Sheikh Mansour almost two decades later.

We were competitive but we didn't quite have enough to make the next step. A few years later Swales admitted that sacking me had been the biggest mistake he had made in football, which was quite a compliment because he wasn't exactly short of errors, but it didn't alter the fact that he had put me out of work. He had been the first chairman to give me an opportunity in management, though, and I'm a great believer that you should be grateful to those who put chances your way, even if you don't always see eye-to-eye with them afterwards.

If the chairman could have given me a top-class midfielder, a forward who was capable of going past people, and one or two others I think our time together would have been more harmonious and might even have taken the club to the next level. Alas, as many of my predecessors discovered, what City managers wanted, and what City managers got during that era were often two very different things.

The league was tight at the time and there was a spell in which Liverpool were in the process of falling off their perch and United were yet to take their place, when supposedly less fashionable clubs had a chance to take advantage of the power vacuum. Leeds United were the ones who filled the void, winning the league under Howard Wilkinson in 1991/92 but there wasn't a great deal between them and some of the other clubs towards the top of the table that season. We certainly weren't a million miles away from them. That had been clear just a month before they were crowned champions when we beat them 4-0 at Maine Road with Andy Hill, Mike Sheron, Quinny and Mark Brennan getting the goals in an outstanding team performance.

Leeds had a very good side but on the day we were unplayable – although we were booed off the pitch by our own supporters because our fans preferred Leeds to win the title rather than Man United! Howard came in at the end and he was wondering how they would bounce back from such a serious setback but they did, which spoke volumes for him and his players. It also underlined how far City had come, and how close we were to being able to compete with the best teams in the league on a regular basis.

So there is perspective and I think, as a group, we did enough to hold our heads high but none of that mattered to those making the decisions. When the time came to make a change, they were ruthless. Maddock was the trigger man and he probably enjoyed giving me the bad news because in the short period that we had worked together, or not as was the case, I hadn't hidden the fact that I didn't like the way he was going about things.

On one occasion, he came in after we had lost 1-0 to Spurs at White Hart Lane and he said: "You haven't done too badly considering you only had 10 men." We hadn't had anyone sent off so I asked him what he was on about. "That Rick Holden," he answered. "It's a waste of time having him out there."

Of all the things he could have done, attacking one of my players was one of the worst. In my eyes, it was a cardinal sin. "Are you having a go at one of my players?" I asked, but I didn't give him a chance to answer. "Fuck off, you fat cunt," I said. "You can't talk to me like that," he replied, but I wasn't about to back down. A line had been crossed. "I just did," I said. "Now fuck off." A few days later I was gone and it was Maddock who gave me my marching orders – but at least I'd had my say.

The worst thing about getting sacked was being out of work. I had been involved in professional football since I was a teenager and I wasn't the type who would take advantage of the enforced break by having a sabbatical or going travelling. I wanted to be out there on the training pitch and I wanted the adrenaline rush that games bring but, by that stage, I had presumed that my playing days were over.

That view changed a month after leaving City when Ian Branfoot got in touch out of the blue and asked me if I fancied playing for Southampton. I went down there and they were in a bit of a crisis, having lost eight of their previous nine games but I got into the side and did okay, only for Branfoot to lose his job following a home defeat to Norwich City at the turn of the year.

There were suggestions – some of them strong – that I might replace him but I ruled myself out on the basis that he had brought me in. It was only fair that I would leave if he was going. A couple of brief stints followed, at Notts County and Bury, and I really enjoyed both, but I was on my last legs by then and I knew I couldn't go on much longer.

As fate would have it, I played the final game of my career against my younger brother, Shaun, in the first game of the 1994/95 season. He was at Rochdale and I was only at Bury because I was helping their manager, Mick Walsh, while he struggled with a few injuries. In that pre-season I'd played when we beat a Man United team featuring Paul Scholes, Nicky Butt, David Beckham and the Nevilles in a Lancashire Cup semi-final, with Mark 'Spike' Carter getting a hat-trick for us.

I was nearly 40 by then and, even though Shaun had been a professional for over a decade, we had never previously come up against one another. I knew Shaun would be looking for me and he knew he wouldn't have to go far to find me because I would be looking for him, too. There were 22 players on the pitch but the two that mattered most in our eyes were each other. There was not a chance either of us were going to give an inch. That wasn't the way we'd been brought up.

We only played against each other for half-an-hour, and it could have been even shorter because the referee had to pull us together after five minutes when I smashed him. We had a little snarl then and not long after he came back looking for a bit of revenge, but I saw him coming and caught him with my elbow. Shaun flipped but I just stood there saying, "Fuck off, you dickhead," as the steam was coming out of his ears.

The referee came running over and the first thing he said was, "What chance have I got?" It could have ended there and then but, as competitive brothers, we couldn't let it lie. Shaun spent the next 15 minutes trying to get me. In the end I had to go off injured, as my sciatica in my back flared up, which was probably best for everyone, especially my mum and dad who were watching in the stand.

To make matters worse for my mum, she ended up getting thrown out of the lounge after the game by Neville Neville, Gary and Phil's dad, because Shaun had got her tickets in the Bury section. It was a great day for them, though. They got to see two of their sons play professionally against one another which, as a parent, must be magnificent.

It was also a fitting way for my playing days to come to an end. It was competitive and the game mattered but I knew I had nothing left, especially as my sciatica had kicked off when Shaun caught me. City had brought my first managerial adventure to an end but I was desperate to start another. I just needed someone to give me another chance and, at that stage, I wasn't exactly inundated with offers.

# 14. RELIGHTING THE FIRE

*'There was a huge passion for football in the area
and I knew that if I could tap into that,
everything else would take care of itself'*

HANGING up my boots was a big thing for me but, by
that stage, my mindset had changed anyway because
I was thinking as a manager, rather than as a player.
The only problem was that I seemed to be the only one who saw
myself as a manager.

For 18 months after leaving Manchester City, I waited for the
phone to ring in the hope a job offer would come my way, but it
never happened. I dipped my toe into the water a few times when
jobs came up but, for whatever reason, I remained on the outside
looking in. It would have been easy to start doubting myself but I
didn't do that. I kept believing that it was a question of the right
opportunity coming along, and being in the right frame of mind
to take advantage of it when it did.

I gave a great deal of thought to what hadn't worked at City. I already knew what had gone well but when you're in the midst of a high-pressure situation it isn't always easy to identify the things you could have done better. Being out of the limelight and away from the hustle and bustle afforded me a period of reflection, which turned out to be a good thing because it served me well.

The main conclusion I came to was that, when you take over at a club, you have to win every battle at the earliest possible opportunity – but there are many different ways to achieve that. There were times at City when I was a bit headstrong, when I would have been better off standing back, taking a deep breath and looking to see the bigger picture.

The other realisation was that there were occasions when it would have helped me if I'd been more willing to view things from other people's perspective. They were little epiphanies for me, the kind you need to have as a young manager because you can only learn through experience. But, unlike as a kid, when next door's phone was ringing constantly (we didn't have one), with scouts from all over the country desperate to get in touch, I was discovering the hard way that out-of-work managers can be forgotten about quite easily. Even though I knew I would be better for having cut my teeth at City I also recognised that, unless someone gave me the chance, the education I'd undergone at Maine Road might have ended up being wasted.

The moment I had been waiting for finally arrived in March 1995 after Sunderland sacked Mick Buxton, who had taken over at Roker Park not long after I had been sacked by City. Sunderland were in the First Division and there was mounting concern that they would be relegated, but when the chance came to take over I jumped at it.

I could see all their problems and I knew the risk – both to my job prospects and reputation – was great but I could also see how huge their potential was. I wouldn't say the decision was a no-brainer because it wasn't, and had we ended up going down I would have had a big job on my hands trying to rebuild my career. But even though the negatives were there for all to see, the positives outweighed them massively. Sunderland were a sleeping giant and someone had to wake them, so why shouldn't it be me?

The first I knew of their interest was when I received a call from Paul Hetherington, a journalist who was also a friend. He told me Sunderland were keen and things just fell into place from there. I met one of the club directors, and the job was offered on the basis that, initially, I would do it for the last seven games on the understanding that, if I kept them up, we would look at a long-term agreement. The problem was, they had lost six of their previous seven and were in grave danger of sliding into the Second Division unless things were turned around quickly, which meant I didn't have time to assess the situation. I just had to trust my instincts, get on with the job and hope for the best.

One of the first things I did was take the squad out to a restaurant called Bistro Romano, armed with £500 of Bob Murray's money. Bob wasn't chairman at the time for tactical reasons – John Featherstone had that role – but he was still the main man, even though he'd had to stand aside after getting a bit of stick from the supporters. It was important that I made the right impression on him at the same time as doing some team bonding.

I achieved the second part of my objective because we had a great time, but I've got a feeling the first part didn't quite work out as planned because we spent £950. I knew then we had a chance of staying up, though, and that was definitely worth another £450 of Bob's money. There was no opportunity to make signings and time was against us so nights out like that were absolutely vital. We had seven games and with morale having been low prior to my arrival, I knew that galvanising team spirit would give us the best chance of avoiding the drop. It's not rocket science by any means but when a team is struggling, like Sunderland were at the time, it is much easier said than done.

On my first full day I put on a short, sharp training session because I wanted the lads to enjoy themselves. It finished with a small-sided game, which was my first real chance to run the rule over the players I had inherited. This was the Wednesday before my first game on the Saturday so I had to think on my feet, and not waste any time doing things that might not make a massive difference. That was why I put my boots on and played at the end of that session. I had to be able to see close-up what I had. I had to be able to work out who was confident and who wasn't. I had to be able to test the players' quality and also their mentality.

They will have thought it was just a game but it was one of the most important training matches I played in. It informed every decision I was about to make. I learned that Richard Ord had good feet but no pace, that Andy Melville had good feet as did Martin Smith, that Craig Russell could run, that a couple of young lads had good energy. I learned that and much more.

On the negative side, I also discovered that Kevin Ball was suspended – which came as no shock whatsoever – and Gary Bennett was injured. However, I had no time to dwell on what we didn't have, I had to focus on what we did have and get the most out of it, which was why I looked to make coming into work as enjoyable as possible.

I got the lads together the day before the game and I asked Gary if he was fit. He told me he'd rather wait until the next day and have a fitness test then but I told him he was out. If I had been there longer I would have given him the extra 24 hours but I knew I had to be decisive and positive in everything I did so that any unnecessary doubts were removed, and everyone knew what they had to do if they wanted to play.

Preparation was all-important and that applied to myself as much as the players, which was why I decided to have a rare early night ahead of my opening game at home to Sheffield United. I was staying at the Seaburn Hotel in Sunderland and, after finishing off a bit of opposition analysis, I went to bed knowing I'd need to be at my most energetic the following day.

It was never going to be the best night's sleep I'd ever had because there was too much at stake but somehow I managed to nod off before midnight, only to be woken up by the fire alarm at two o'clock in the morning. I raced down the stairs, still half asleep, but knowing I couldn't afford to wait and see if it was a false alarm or not.

When I got outside, everyone was a bit disorientated. I noticed two young girls who were really distraught so I went over to comfort them just because, in my mind, that's what you do. I managed to settle them down and by the time we were allowed back into the hotel they were pretty calm, having been given a scare when the alarm went off.

I didn't think any more of it until I was at Roker Park later. The two girls walked in and it turned out they were the daughters of Scott Mathieson, the referee taking charge of our game! There's an old saying in football about giving referees a bit of toffee, which basically means you should always try to find a way of looking after them or praising them without straying outside of the rules, because they might look more fondly on you. Well, without even knowing it, I'd got myself in his good books, which wasn't something that happened often with me and referees.

While the players and their state of mind were within my control, the crowd was out of my hands. Understandably, the supporters were struggling to cope with what they rightly regard as one of the biggest clubs in the country being in danger of slipping into English football's third tier. That was reflected in attendances, which had been as low as 11,000 before I arrived. I hoped the fans would back us and would buy into a new manager who wanted to bring some passion and excitement back, but I knew I couldn't take anything for granted in a situation like that.

However, for the visit of Sheffield United, over 17,000 came through the gate and they backed us with everything they had. Russell's well-taken goal gave us a 1-0 win and while it wasn't pretty, it was effective. The most important thing from my point of view was that everyone on the pitch – and everyone off it – embraced the fresh start and bought in to what we were trying to do. It was exactly what I had been hoping for.

I had taken a gamble by going to Sunderland and if it had backfired it would have become even more difficult for me to get another job, but I had to work. There were negatives – the stadium, although one of English football's most iconic venues, was tired, we didn't have a training ground of our own and there wasn't a big pot of money available to turn things around. But there was a huge passion for football in the area and I knew that if I could tap into that, everything else would take care of itself.

There is a flip side to that kind of fervour in the sense that expectations can rise too rapidly the minute things start going well, but that was the least of my worries. I knew there were supporters who believed Sunderland should be winning the Premier League and that wasn't realistic when I took over, but I would rather manage a club where fans demand the very best rather than one where they fear the worst.

I wanted to fire the supporters' expectations and to allow them to dream again, even though I knew full well that would increase the pressure that I was under. First I had to keep Sunderland in the division because unless that happened the future would be bleak for the club, the fans and for myself. Thankfully, that first ambition was realised as we lost only one of our final seven league games to finish six points above the drop.

As fate would have it, that defeat came at my old stomping ground, Burnden Park, when a late John McGinlay goal gave Bolton a win that could have knocked the stuffing out of us. We responded brilliantly to that setback, beating relegation rivals Swindon thanks to a Martin Smith goal that I regard as one of the most important moments of my managerial career. That strike ensured we were all but safe and we made sure of our survival when we drew at Burnley in a game that was delayed because of crowd congestion.

The official attendance was just over 15,000 but 10,000 of them must have been our fans because they were all over the ground. That was brilliant but it did give me a problem because it meant the players were in the dressing room for longer than is ideal. In a situation like that I knew there was a real danger the tension could build and hinder their performance, so I decided to lighten the mood by telling a joke.

"Have you heard about the geezer whose pregnant missus was having cravings and sent him out late at night to get a snail sandwich?" I asked. The lads all looked at me like I was mad, and they might well have had a point, but there was no turning back. "He goes down to the deli and explains to the shop assistant what he wants, and why he wants it, but out of the blue she asked him when was the last time he'd had sex.

"One thing led to another and before he knew it the husband is invited around the back, where one thing led to another, but he was so exhausted he fell asleep. When he woke up it was seven o'clock in the morning. He legged it back home but just as he was heading towards the path, the gate squeaked behind him as it closed, he tripped and spilt the snails all over the path.

"Before he could do anything about it his heavily-pregnant wife appeared at the door. 'Where the fuck have you been?' she asked but, before she could really tear into him, the husband dropped down to his knees behind the snails. 'Not far now lads,' he said."

It wasn't the best joke I've ever told but it lifted the tension and the lads pissed themselves laughing. That approach wouldn't feature on any pro-licence course or in any FA coaching handbook, but that instinct to relax players is part of management. Of course, you need the tactics, you need the analysis and you need the statistics but you also need to have a human touch because, without it, there will be times when relating to players and getting the best out of them can become a problem. The great thing about that group was the way that they responded to what I was doing, and that was the main reason why we stayed up.

We were still a long, long way away from where Sunderland needed to be, though. When I negotiated my contract with the club after keeping them in the division I told them that I needed £1m to spend on signings if we wanted to give ourselves a chance of kicking on. Having come through a scare they agreed to provide that backing. Even though it wasn't a huge amount of money, it gave me something to work with in the transfer market, which was massively important.

I wanted to make the most of the finances that I had so I brought Paul Bracewell in on a free transfer and also made him my assistant. I got Bobby Saxton involved on the coaching side because I thought we would benefit from his charisma and his knowledge of the game. Bobby was an old school coach, one of the best I ever worked with, and he got on really well with the players. While I was making those changes, I was also on the lookout for a player who could transform the team. I had a look at the squad and there was definitely some quality to work with, but I decided that we needed a goalscorer to set everything off.

I settled on David Kelly, the Wolves and Republic of Ireland striker, but when I went to the board and asked for the money that I had been promised I was told that it wasn't there. I pulled my car keys out of my pocket and handed them over. "I won't be needing them," I said. "I'll get the train back to Manchester because that's me finished here."

There was a panic – and understandably so – because they knew the last thing they needed was the supporters turning on them again after losing the manager who'd just kept Sunderland up. All of a sudden the money that wasn't available, was. Funny that. I'd won the battle but it didn't turn out to be the big victory I'd hoped for because Kelly got injured after a few games and never really hit his stride. That wasn't the point, though, I'd had an agreement with the board and they had to honour it. Thankfully they did, or else I would have been going back home to look for work, and they would have been looking for a new manager.

I had thought that we had enough to be safe in mid-table but the momentum of the previous season continued. It was clear early on that we would be challenging for promotion, which was a massive turnaround in the club's fortunes. The extent of our progress was confirmed over the course of a third round FA Cup tie against Manchester United in which we took them to a replay after drawing 2-2 at Old Trafford. They ended up squeezing past us with a 2-1 win at Roker Park but we had really tested them.

After the game Alex popped his head into the dressing room and said that, on the basis of how we had performed over the two games, we would do well for the rest of the season. Not as well as his own team, mind, as United went on to win the double, but even that achievement illustrated how competitive Sunderland had become. I also knew that it could have been better still because with 10 minutes to go at Old Trafford we had been 2-1 up and United were struggling. Then they got a free-kick and, out of hope more than expectation, they sent the ball into the box. I was thinking, 'Keeper, keeper' but Alec Chamberlain wasn't able to get there and Eric Cantona headed home.

On the basis of that incident, and what I'd seen previously, I decided to go out and get a new goalkeeper and I brought in Shay Given on loan from Blackburn, which turned out to be a great move. He kept 12 clean sheets in the 17 league games he played for us, a key man in our push for promotion.

Shay's presence made a big difference because, with Kelly struggling for form and fitness, we didn't have the match-winner I'd thought we were bringing in when I took the board on. That meant we had to be solid, clever and hard to beat. Shay was really influential on all of those fronts, as were Brace and Kevin Ball, two of my other senior pros and Paul Stewart, who came in on loan, initially, and did so well we signed him permanently.

That combination of quality and know-how, allied with the ongoing improvement of a group of players who could have been playing in Division Two had things turned out differently, fuelled our ambitions. An 18-match unbeaten run, from February 10 to May 5, allowed us to go up as champions. The turnaround had been monumental and it reminded me of what had happened at Everton when I was a player. The revival was built on similar foundations, with team spirit and hard work proving the cornerstones of everything that followed.

This time I was the manager and, although it was more stressful, I was better placed to appreciate the efforts of the players, every one of whom gave everything to take Sunderland back to where they belong.

That run-in included a lesson in dealing with player/manager relations. Dressing room confrontation is part and parcel of football. I know that when it happens now and leaks out it makes headlines but it is a totally normal aspect of the game. If you put every member of any workplace in a room at moments of high pressure, and allow them to speak their mind, what will happen? Whether it's an office or a dressing room, the likelihood is that things will become heated.

As a player and manager I liked that because it showed the people I was working with cared about what they were doing, and were engaged and passionate enough to want to improve. There's nothing worse than a quiet dressing room where people are reluctant to say what they think. That's a negative environment and doesn't help bring out the best in players or get positive results. That doesn't mean things don't sometimes go wrong, though, as the tension can be so great that just one word out of place can change the mood, as I discovered at Grimsby in March.

We were 1-0 up at half-time, having been comfortably the better side, but towards the end of the first half I had sensed that we were letting our foot off the gas a little bit. Half-time was going to be my opportunity to put that right and I didn't want to waste that chance. There's nothing worse as a manager than getting to the end of a game, knowing that you could have got a better result if you had intervened earlier. I was primed for action when the players came into the dressing room.

"Fucking sit down" were my first words and as I started telling them to show more urgency and to step it up, my flow was interrupted by Kevin Ball asking for ice because he'd got a knock. I was in the zone and spoke before I thought. "Shut up, you cunt,"

I said and Bally, who was a hard bastard, jumped up and shouted: "Don't call me a cunt." I thought, 'Oh no, what have I done here?'

Thinking on my feet – partly because I needed to get the team right for the second half and partly out of self-preservation in the knowledge that Bally was about to strangle me – I bought myself some time. "Hey you," I said. "Sit down. You've had your say out there for 45 minutes. We'll sort this out at full time." Thankfully, he sat down and I got the reaction I was hoping for during the second half as we went on to win 4-0 with a really strong performance. However, I spent most of the half wondering how I was going to put things right with Bally.

I ran into the dressing room after the final whistle and as I was in there I heard studs approaching before the door burst open. I was waiting for him. "You were fucking brilliant, you cunt," I said to Bally, and he just burst out laughing. I got away with that one but no matter what went on in the dressing rooms that I was in – as long as it was for the right reasons – I never had a problem with it. If ever there is a place in football where you should be able to say what you think it is the dressing room, even if that does mean that you will occasionally use the wrong words.

We acquitted ourselves pretty well on our return to the Premier League but there were times when the gulf in class that we still needed to bridge was apparent. A 6-2 loss at Chelsea underlined that, but not as much as a 5-0 defeat at Man United on a day when I was indebted to Alex for the way that he reacted to such a one-sided result.

It was the game where Eric Cantona scored his famous chip against us and that goal was symbolic of everything that happened on the pitch that day. Everything they did was at a level that we just couldn't reach. We were crap, but Alex came in afterwards and said: "We would have beaten anyone playing like that." I knew what he was doing straight away. He wasn't bigging his own team up because he didn't need to. He was taking the pressure off a fellow manager, who just happened to be me. That's the measure of the man.

I know he's fierce with his rivals – and rightly so – but a feature of his career has been a generosity to managers when they needed it most. That won't have applied to everyone and there's more than enough evidence to show that he could be ruthless when he needed to be as well, but he definitely saw himself as a shop steward for those of us in the managers' union. That is why he made sure that he didn't put me under the cosh after presiding over a hammering of my team.

Fergie could go easy on me but I couldn't do the same with my players. There was too much at stake for me to accept such a heavy defeat as an occupational hazard of managing a newly-promoted team against one of the best sides in the world. In my own inimitable way, I let the lads know that the way they had played at Old Trafford was not good enough. It was only 12 months earlier that we'd run United so close in the FA Cup and we were a Division One club then, so there was no excuse for our standards dropping to such a degree that we ended up on the wrong end of a hiding.

At times like that, there have to be some home truths and everyone has to have the opportunity to get stuff off their chests. That's what a good dressing room is about. It's not just about popping Champagne corks when you win trophies or achieve promotion, it's about having the desire and the honesty to put things right when they've gone wrong. If that means some feelings get hurt along the way, then so be it.

The beauty is that unless you have a leak, the outside world doesn't get to know when there's been a bit of blood-letting.

You get to let off steam in the knowledge that the only people who'll know about it are your mates, who are in the same room and in the same predicament as you. That is standard practice in professional football but that season at Sunderland we dispensed with convention when the club agreed to participate in a fly-on-the-wall documentary called *Premier Passions*, which was narrated by Gina McKee, the actress. All of a sudden, everything we said would be seen and scrutinised by millions of television viewers, who would see us at our best – and worst.

It wasn't a problem for me and it was good TV for the BBC. Some people looked into it more than was necessary and drew conclusions that didn't need to be made. That's what happens when you open yourself up to that kind of scrutiny so you just have to take any criticism that comes your way and move on. Would it have been something that I would have done through choice? Not really. I'm a great believer in the sanctity of the dressing room and I think that's a place that the public should only see if they're on a stadium tour.

The modern world isn't like that, though. The media wants to have more and more access and they want to go into areas that would previously have been out of bounds to them. Clubs are dealing with that reality daily and they have to try and strike a balance between being helpful and giving too much away. It's not easy, which is why I understood what Bob Murray was getting at when he came to speak to me about the BBC's approach, and suggested it would be a good idea for us to get involved.

From his point of view, this was a chance to give the club a mainstream exposure beyond coverage of our matches, and to open us up to a new audience. I listened to the case he put forward and it was a good one, but I pointed out that there was no way the players or myself would be changing our behaviour for anyone, and that this would be warts-and-all in all that expression means. I also pointed out that I could find myself in trouble because I could see the risks but, ultimately, I knew that the decision did not belong to me, so I said to Bob; "When it comes down to it, you're the boss so if you want it done, it'll be done."

It wasn't my cup of tea and I'd made that clear but it was Bob's club, and he had to make the choice. He decided to go with it and when the crew arrived they told me they would be unobtrusive, which was both a good and a bad thing. On the one hand, forgetting they were there allowed us to get on with our jobs without interruption. On the other, it gave us a false sense of security, which meant there were one or two things that were said that you wouldn't usually say in front of a television camera.

That didn't apply to myself, though. I didn't give a fuck what I said in front of them or what anyone thought of the language I used. No one who has ever been in a dressing room, from Sunday League level upwards, will have been shocked by what they heard. Swearing is part of football culture, and always has been. It is a harsh, unforgiving environment, and the way managers speak to players, and players speak to one another, is well established.

It might have changed a bit now because some of the modern managers like to portray themselves as being more sophisticated, but I guarantee there will still be times when the language used – at half-time and after games – is x-rated. It doesn't matter whether you are Peter Reid from Huyton or Arsene Wenger from Strasbourg, there will be times as a manager when you lose the plot. Sometimes it is absolutely natural because you are furious about a performance and, at others, you have to try and put on a bit of a show to make sure standards don't drop.

In any given situation, be it before kick-off, at half-time or after the game, time is short and tension is high so you have to get your point across as emphatically as you can. There's no point pussyfooting around. You have to get your message across to such a degree that it is absorbed by players who might be tired, who might be feeling sorry for themselves and who might be so revved up that they struggle to take in information. You also don't have the opportunity to have one-on-one conversations with the entire team so you have to speak in a way that cuts across everything, otherwise you may as well just stay outside the dressing room and let them make decisions for themselves.

Obviously, my approach didn't meet with everyone's approval and there was a furore about the first couple of episodes, with some newspapers counting how many times I swore to try to build a controversy around the programme. That made me laugh because, during my career, I've got to know quite a few journalists and some of them swear much more than I do! The difference was there were no TV cameras in their places of work, whereas they were everywhere I went in mine, so I was held up to moral judgement in a way they never would be.

The fly on our dressing room wall showed the world what we were and, regardless of the reaction in some quarters, I am still comfortable about that.

Probably the most notorious episode was the one in which I went for the players at half-time against Arsenal. It was 0-0 and I had a right go at the players. "Keep the fucking ball," was the basic message, and it was hammered home with another liberal sprinkling of industrial language.

Some viewers thought I'd lost the plot because I was ranting and raving but the reality – and I use that word pointedly – was that everything I said and did was pre-meditated. We had two young lads up front – Michael Bridges and Craig Russell – and they were up against Steve Bould and Tony Adams, so I wanted to challenge their mentality. I wanted to get into their heads so that they went back out there and played like men.

In the first half I'd thought they were feeling sorry for themselves because they were having a hard time against two of the most physically-imposing defenders in the league. If we could become a bit more imposing we might be able to get a great result against one of the best sides in the league.

Whether it was down to my colourful team-talk or not, the lads went out and had a right go and we ended up winning 1-0, courtesy of an Adams own goal. So whatever the critics thought of me, I was comfortable in the knowledge that everything I said and did while the cameras were following my every move was with the best interests of Sunderland – and its players – at heart.

The only problem was that my family are from an Irish Catholic background and I had my Auntie Mary on the phone after the first episode to tell me how shocked she was about my swearing. I said sorry to her, but I had no need to apologise to anyone else.

My job was to get the best out of the players I had and I was doing that, which was all credit to them. That they were in the Premier League at all was an incredible achievement and it wasn't as if we had been able to invest vast fortunes to improve a squad which had been so close to being relegated from Division One. I brought in Alex Rae, Tony Coton, Lionel Perez, Niall Quinn and Chris Waddle for around £3m in a period when Newcastle were breaking all kinds of transfer records by paying £15m for Alan Shearer before the start of that season.

They were all good signings one way or another and the quality they brought raised the level of the squad. The problem was that Coton and Quinny both got serious injuries, which weakened us at both ends of the pitch for a big chunk of the season. If they had been able to stay fit, I've no doubt that we would have stayed up but it was much tougher for us when they weren't available, which made it all the more galling when we were eventually relegated by the smallest of margins.

A 3-0 win over Everton in our penultimate game of the season took us to the magic 40-point mark but that was one year when 40 points wasn't enough. When we lost 1-0 at Wimbledon in our final fixture we were relegated, with Coventry and Southampton both finishing a single point above us.

In the weeks afterwards, I drove myself mad thinking back on the games that had cost us. Southampton winning 1-0 at Roker Park was a big one; if we'd just drawn that we would have finished above them. But I knew that injuries had cost us more than anything else. The lads had given everything they had and we had improved so much as a team and as a club but, when it came down to it, a bit of bad luck cost us.

The narrowness of our failure hurt me and it played on my mind, but I was proud of what we had achieved. I knew that I had a squad which was improving, even if relegation was something that we had been desperate to avoid. We were going back to a level that we no longer wanted to be at but my overriding feeling was that we would be taking one step backwards to go two steps forward. If anything, our 'Premier Passions' had intensified.

# 15. OH WHAT CAN IT MEAN?

*'Prolific at one end and parsimonious at the other,
it doesn't get better from a manager's point of view.
We went up not just as champions but as a team which
looked well equipped to compete in the Premier League'*

W HEN Sunderland first revealed plans to move to
a new stadium, the hope was that, when it opened,
we would be a Premier League club. Falling short of
survival by a point meant that when the Stadium of Light hosted
its first fixture on July 30, 1997, a friendly against Ajax, we were
back in Division One in the knowledge that we needed to get
back to the stage that such a magnificent ground deserved.

Bob Murray was clear about what he expected of the players and
myself when he stated that the stadium, "Marked the beginning
of an historic new era for Sunderland." It also marked the end of
having outdated facilities and, for the first time, we actually had
undersoil heating, a basic that most other clubs of our size had
long since taken for granted.

The Bishop of Durham, Michael Turnbull, even came to bless the pitch, which was a nice touch, but given what happened at the end of the season, when we lost the most dramatic play-off final that there has been, I think I would have preferred his divine intervention to come at Wembley.

The stadium was exactly what Sunderland – the club and the area – needed and, even though the groundsman had to dye everything green in the build-up to the opening game because the pitch was in a terrible state, we were delighted to move into it. Roker Park had been one of my favourite away grounds as a player and I loved it as a manager but, in order for the club to progress, we had to move. Bob deserves a lot of credit for taking us into a new stadium and giving the club the best chance possible of growing and fulfilling its massive potential.

That brought additional pressure for the players and myself because we had to make sure that the investment was not wasted. Again, I was given money to spend but, again, it wasn't a vast fortune. With the initial £2m I was handed, which was boosted by a few minor sales, we managed to bring in Kevin Phillips, Jody Craddock, Chris Makin, Nicky Summerbee and Danny Dichio.

At a price of just £450,000, Phillips was arguably the best signing I ever made. Considering he went on to win a European Golden Boot with us, I'd imagine Kevin would consider the move was as successful for him as it was for us. Not that he or I were getting too many plaudits in the opening months of his Sunderland career as, after 15 games, he had scored only four goals and we were in mid-table.

I suppose that was a test of my faith in him but watching him in training I knew it was only a matter of time before the goals came more regularly because his movement and finishing were top class. Once Kevin hit his stride it felt like he would never stop scoring, and he ended that season as the first Sunderland player since Brian Clough to score 30 league goals in a campaign.

Kevin's goalscoring ability was fundamental to the development of that team but he would be the first to admit that, without Niall Quinn, he would not have been as prolific. As a partnership they were perfect, but it might never have happened because not long after Kevin's arrival, Quinny feared his career might be over. He came in to see me one day and said his knee was knackered. He'd had an operation but it still wasn't right, and he was talking about retiring so I persuaded him to go and see a specialist in Bradford.

After that, he began to have more confidence in his knee and working with Kevin gave him a new lease of life. It wasn't as if he ran about too much anyway. All of his best work was done with his head and that was exactly what we needed, given Kevin's ability to get in behind defences and find space in crowded penalty areas. With Bobby Saxton helping me drill the team and getting them as organised as they could be, we knew that as long as we kept things tight at the back we would have a chance of winning any game because of the quality up front.

Things didn't go to plan early on in the 1997/98 season and, after losing four of our first nine games, we were then given a hiding at Reading which led to some of the Sunderland supporters showing their frustration. I could understand that, particularly as we had lost 4-0, and I knew that we had to improve because if a malaise sets in after relegation you can quickly find yourself in charge of a sinking ship.

But, after that setback at Reading, it would be another 16 matches before we tasted defeat again as we established ourselves as one of the best teams in the division. The expectation was that we would be one of the two teams who would go on to win automatic promotion. Our prospects looked good until a game at Easter when the heavens opened at the Stadium of Light and we blew a two-goal lead against QPR. Our home ground didn't feel as if it had been blessed that day because we deserved to take the three points.

Usually if you allow a team to come from behind in a game you've dominated your urge is to slaughter your players for letting a lead slip but I knew I couldn't do that. Had we won that game we would have finished second, ahead of Middlesbrough, but for the second season in succession we were a point short of achieving our objective and we had to make do with the play-offs.

I have mixed feelings about what happened next. Obviously, I was devastated that we were unable to get the job done and that remains one of the biggest and most crushing disappointments of my career. But I still retain a huge sense of pride in what my players gave for the club, even though they ended up falling short. The Play-Off final against Charlton Athletic is regarded as a classic and rightly so, even if it is the last game I would want to watch again. But it took a phenomenal effort from the players – and the supporters – to ensure we got there.

Unlike the final, the semi-final has long since been forgotten by all but those who were involved but, after losing the first leg 2-1 at Sheffield United, it took a special performance – on and off the pitch – for us to reach Wembley. We won the second leg 2-0 on a wonderful night when the Stadium of Light rocked like Roker Park had in its heyday. We then went into the final 12 days later as favourites, even though Charlton had the advantage of playing in their home city.

What took place at Wembley was the stuff of folklore, a match so remarkable and an outcome so dramatic that it transcended football. If I could go back and take a 1-0 win in the most boring circumstances imaginable, I would give anything to make it happen. More than anything, I wish I could take away the pain Mickey Gray felt when he missed the penalty.

Mickey is a Sunderland fan, a great lad and, having had the bottle to step up, he deserves a lot more than to be remembered as the player who cost us that day. It's always easy to look at the player who misses but as a manager I had to focus on what I could have done better during the game. Could I have prevented the game going to penalties?

The one thing that I keep coming back to is that maybe I gambled too much on youth. If I had gone with more experience in the starting XI perhaps we would have been better able to see out certain situations, especially when we took the lead three times, only to be pegged back. At 3-2 up with six minutes remaining we should have seen the game out, and we didn't learn our lesson in extra-time when we went back in front after 99 minutes, only for Charlton to equalise yet again five minutes later.

To make matters worse, Charlton's hero that day was another Sunderland fan as Clive Mendonca struck a hat-trick against the club he had supported all his life, to prevent them from going back to the Premier League. The ensuing penalty shoot-out will live with me forever as Michael became the only one of 14 players to fail to score from 12 yards.

A few days before, we had gone to the Stadium of Light to practise penalties and Michael had been one of our best performers from the spot. I know people say that you can't recreate the conditions of a shoot-out without the crowd and the tension and I have a lot of sympathy with that view but, with so much being at stake, we were determined to leave no stone unturned as we looked to give ourselves an edge.

Mickey was swaggering up to the spot, pinging the ball into whichever corner he wanted it to go into and turning around as if he didn't have a care in the world. So I said to him: "It's a bit different when you have to do it in front of 80,000 people at Wembley." That was a comment that came back to bite me on the arse when his effort was saved, but it felt like fate that it would be him. Not only was he a Sunderland fan, he was only taking one at that stage of the shoot-out because Lee Clark and Kevin Phillips – two of our penalty takers – had gone off through injury.

There is no good way to lose such a vital game but I can't think of many worse than being on the wrong end of a 7-6 scoreline in a penalty shoot-out after leading three times during normal and extra-time. If someone had written a movie script with that many twists, turns and sub-plots, it would have been rejected for being too far-fetched. The ending could not have been more painful for everyone associated with Sunderland, except for Mendonca. We had been the better team and had finished four points clear of Charlton in the regular season, but that counted for nothing.

I went into the dressing room afterwards and all kinds were crying. It was a scene of absolute devastation and Mickey was suffering more than most, not that his plight made any difference to Bobby Saxton, who wasn't the type to allow anyone to wallow in self pity. "Mickey, that's the worst fucking penalty I've ever seen, you useless twat," he said, and the tension was broken – well, momentarily at least.

I got hammered that night. I got on the whisky and, to this day, I have no idea how I got home but, the following morning, I was alert enough to know I had to start repairing what had been broken the day before. My first call was to Mickey and I invited him to my house, to try and lift him but I probably needed boosting as much as he did. Having put so much into winning promotion and falling just short, I knew I had to start all over again, and that is a big ask when you're so disappointed.

What got me fired up again was the attitude of the lads. They all vowed to be even better the following season so that we wouldn't have to go through the lottery of the play-offs. That spirit was infectious and it went through the club and, most importantly, they were as good as their word. Not only did they improve in 1998/99, they reached a level no one would have dreamed possible when we were on our knees in front of the Twin Towers.

We started the new campaign well and, after going top in October, courtesy of a 1-0 victory over Bury, we stayed there. Bobby Saxton, who often got more wound up than I did on the sidelines, thought it was 2-0, failing to notice a Quinny goal getting chalked off, as he was too busy chatting to someone in the crowd. I wondered why he was so relaxed, whistling to himself while I was beside myself, panicking as Bury were throwing long balls into our area late on – and then he was the same when I was delivering a few words in the dressing room post-match, about how we'd battled and how they were the sort of games that won you league titles. He only realised it finished 1-0 when he saw our game mentioned on the TV in the players' lounge afterwards.

That was a very good side. Everyone knew their jobs and we played an exciting brand of football, with wide men attacking at every opportunity and looking to get the ball into the box as often as they could. I kept asking myself how we would do in the Premier League and, the more games we won, the more I knew that stepping up a level would not be beyond us.

We even reached the semi-final of the Worthington Cup and lost out narrowly to a very strong Leicester City side, which gave us another indication of how far we had come. But it was in our own division where our readiness to operate at the highest level was becoming most clear.

To put it bluntly, most of our opponents couldn't live with us and only three teams – Tranmere Rovers, Barnsley and Watford – were able to beat us as we notched up 105 points, a record for that level. Kevin scored 23 goals in 26 appearances, while Quinny struck 18 in 36 and they rightly got a lot of the plaudits, but I was just as happy about what was – or rather, what wasn't – happening at the other end. Goalkeeper Thomas Sorensen, who I'd signed the previous summer, kept 29 clean sheets.

Prolific at one end and parsimonious at the other, it doesn't get any better than that from a manager's point of view. We went up not just as Football League champions but as a team which looked well equipped to compete in the Premier League. I wouldn't say that made our Wembley heartache worthwhile but it definitely made it easier to cope with.

Things couldn't have been going any better for us but, as anyone who has ever worked in football knows, the game has a way of throwing obstacles in your way just as it seems like you have a clear run. In my case, the problem was caused by a t-shirt worn by a Newcastle United fan. Usually that wouldn't be an issue but this time the supporter in question was Lee Clark, one of my senior players and a key midfielder.

It was an unfortunate episode and one which meant I was left with no option but to move Lee on, which disappointed me a lot because he had been a good signing and was one of our most influential players in the promotion-winning campaign. Convincing him to come in the first place had been hard work as his affection for Newcastle was clear, and it was difficult enough for him to contemplate leaving his boyhood club without considering moving to their local rivals. But I got into his agent, Paul Stretford, and managed to talk him into bringing Clarky down to Manchester to meet me at a restaurant called Harper's.

At first, I could tell he was reluctant to be there with me, which was fair enough. Having supported Liverpool and gone on to play for Everton I could at least understand his mindset, even if I hadn't had similar hang-ups about changing loyalties. He told me he was only seeing me out of courtesy but our bottles of Laurent Perrier later he agreed to sign for me. It was one of the best drinking sessions I'd ever paid for, especially as Bob Murray ended up picking up the tab.

I really liked Clarky and he was one of those who was going to be important to us in the Premier League, but all of that changed when he went to watch Newcastle in the FA Cup final against Man United. In the eyes of our fans, it wouldn't have been ideal that he was there at all, but being a professional I could relate to his decision because there are plenty of players who go to see the team they support in big games, and it's never really a problem.

But Clarky didn't just stop with getting a ticket and sitting in the stands, he wore a t-shirt bearing the slogan 'Sad Mackem bastards'. As soon as pictures of him started to appear in the media it was obvious to everyone at Sunderland, particularly me, that his time with us would have to be brought to an abrupt end.

When I next saw him I told him he had to go, it was as simple as that. Our fans wanted him out and there was no way back. He could have been Ronaldo and Messi combined the following season and they still wouldn't have been having him so, when a situation is that bad, you are left with no option but to get rid of the cause of the problem. There are certain things you can't do at a football club – and he'd done one of them. In fairness to Clarky, he held his hands up and accepted that he had to move. It came as a relief to everyone when Fulham came in for him and brought an end to the saga.

In contrast to Clarky, I was still popular with the fans, something that I really appreciated, and they demonstrated their affection for me with a song that ended up making it into the charts. It started off being sung at the Stadium of Light and wherever Sunderland were playing away but it took on a life of its own. Two decades on I can't go anywhere without someone regaling me with it, although sometimes the lyrics get changed if the singer doesn't happen to be a Sunderland supporter.

At least the tune, taken from *Day Dream Believer* by The Monkees, is great, even if the words aren't always complimentary. I've heard it sung that many times that I know the Sunderland version off by heart:

*Oh I could fly without wings,*
*on the back of Reidy's kings,*
*at three o'clock I'm as happy as can be.*
*'Cos the good times they are here*
*and the Premiership is near,*
*so watch out world as all of Roker sings*

*Cheer up Peter Reid,*
*oh what can it mean,*
*to a Sunderland supporter,*
*to be top of the league*

*We once thought of you,*
*as a Scouser dressed in blue,*
*now you're red and white through and through.*
*We've all dreamt of the day,*
*when a saviour would come our way*
*and now we know our dreams are coming true.*

A band called Simply Red And White took it to number 41 in the UK charts in April 1996, which was a magnificent achievement, considering who it was about. This wasn't Elton John singing about Marilyn Monroe or John Lennon singing about Yoko Ono. It was an ode to a greying football manager from Huyton by a group of fans from the North East.

I loved it, though, and it wouldn't surprise me if most of the records that were bought were sold in whichever music shop is closest to my mum's. I even enjoyed it when supporters of other clubs, mainly Newcastle, changed the words so they could have a go at me. Whenever I went to St James' Park I'd hear their version and it made me laugh. "Cheer up Peter Reid, oh what can it mean, to a sad Mackem bastard and a shit football team." Fair play. When I was at Everton I'd go to Anfield and The Kop would be singing, "He's fat, he's shit, he's never fucking fit, Peter Reid, Peter Reid," so none of this was new to me. I always enjoyed terrace banter, even when I was on the receiving end of it.

As far as the Sunderland fans were concerned, I think the urge for me to cheer up was because I looked so aggressive on the touchline. I would get so wound up and engrossed in games that the possibility of me smiling was as remote as the chances of me voting Tory. The supporters latched on to that and turned it into a fun song that caught on, so much so that I can be anywhere in the world and there's a strong chance someone will sing it to me.

I went to Magaluf in spring 2017 to visit a bar which had been Howard Kendall's favourite in Majorca. It was just something that I felt I had to do in honour of him and I sat in his seat and drank Mateus Rosé, which was his favourite tipple whenever he was there. I had a really lovely time, reminiscing about Howard and the great moments that I shared with him. When I left I was away with my thoughts as I walked along the front, basking in the sunshine and a fair bit of nostalgia. Then I heard it. "Cheer up Peter Reid, oh what can it mean..." and the spell was broken.

It happens on planes, trains…it doesn't matter where I go, I'll hear it. Not that I'm complaining. I think it's great, apart from when a stag do of 20-odd lads decide to sing it for the entire duration of a flight and then everyone ends up being sick of it. But if you're in football and you're a high-profile figure, this is part and parcel of it all. You get affection and you get abuse and as long as the latter doesn't go too far, you have to accept it. I've even learned to enjoy some of it.

The Newcastle fans slaughtered me for having "a monkey's he'ed" which was harsh on primates but instead of letting it bother me, I found it funny. When I took part in the Great North Run, which was a wonderful experience, I wore a Sunderland shirt with a monkey's head on the back. I think when people see that you're willing to have a laugh you can gain a mutual respect because that's what football banter, in its truest sense rather than some of the nonsense you see these days, has always been about.

The real beauty of *Cheer Up Peter Reid* was that it showed the fans believed in what I was doing – and they weren't the only ones. After getting back into the Premier League and showing we could more than hold our own at that level, my stock in the boardroom had never been higher. At one stage, Bob Murray described me as, "A Cloughie for the new millennium," an incredible compliment. While I took it with a sizeable pinch of salt, it was nice to hear my boss talk about me in such a positive way. Bob was so impressed that he even decided to take the club off the market after previously putting it up for sale for £2m. "Peter Reid has rekindled my enthusiasm for the job," he said. "The club was for sale, it's not now. We are indebted to Peter."

Considering the state of the club when I took over, we were flying and the season after winning promotion we finished seventh, above the likes of Newcastle, Everton and Tottenham, which underlined how far we had come. We actually missed out on qualifying for Europe on goal difference which was a disappointment, but it didn't check our momentum because the following season we came seventh again. For the first time in far too long, Sunderland had real stability and were well placed to kick on. It remains a massive disappointment that the progress we made during that period was not sustained.

I blame myself for that. It's easy to look at others, to point out what they could have done differently and, in some cases, that is justified. But as a manager of a club that has risen above expectations and created an opportunity to go to the next level, you have to do everything to ensure that happens. I'm not sure I did that because I allowed myself to buy into the chairman's vision of success when I knew we needed to be more ambitious.

The crowd were pushing us, sometimes a bit too much if I'm honest, but that is what happens with fans all over the world. If you perform above expectations, they raise the bar of what is acceptable and that created a new pressure that I had to deal with. But it wasn't as if they were telling me anything I didn't know. Like them, I wanted more. I wanted the team to be better, I wanted to win trophies and I wanted it to happen now, not in five or ten years' time. But there was one game, at home to Everton in March 2000, which pushed me over the edge.

We were drawing 1-1 and the fans were letting me know that they were not happy because we were not winning. I was stood on the line, thinking, 'It's Everton Football Club we're playing and we're in the Premier League, where every result has to be earned', but the expectations of the supporters by then were such that we had to win. We ended up getting the three points, with Kevin scoring the winner, but as soon as the game ended I went in to see Bob because I could see a problem was starting to develop.

He could tell I needed to get something off my chest and before I'd even said anything he started: "Go on, say whatever you've got to say." So I told him. I told him that the expectations of the fans were higher than ever. I told him that we needed to kick on. And I told him that we had to bring in some top international footballers. Bob wasn't on the same page, though. "If we finish fourth-from-bottom every season, I'm happy," he said, and he repeated that message in a meeting with scouts at a later date.

To be fair to the chairman, he was looking at it from the perspective of someone who had been part of a yo-yo club and that had made him crave stability more than anything else. I understood that but I didn't agree with it, and my job was to push, and push some more to make sure that everyone at the club – above and below the manager – was hell bent on making us as successful as we could be.

On that occasion, I wasn't as demanding as I should have been. I had a duty to myself to get more than he was willing to offer but I fell into line, and that was a mistake. At that time, Blackburn Rovers came in for me and I had talks with them but they had just been relegated. Given how well Sunderland were doing in comparison, it would have been a step downwards, regardless of owner Jack Walker's ambition.

I met John Williams, the chairman, and I spoke to Jack on the phone a few times, with both men being really persuasive. But after thinking about it I decided to stay. There was a temptation to go back to the North West, but when it came down to it, things were going too well at Sunderland for me to leave. I just wished the club had backed me more when the time came for us to look to be more than just a team which was a comfortable mid-table side, on the fringes of European qualification.

I made some mistakes with the funds that were made available.

Even though we were still shopping at ASDA when I had been hoping to see what was on the shelves at Harrods, I still should have done better with what I had. Bringing in Lilian Laslandes for £3.6m rebounded on me when he failed to score in 12 league appearances, before we shipped him out to Cologne on loan. Signing him was a mistake but when I'd seen him play for Bordeaux against the likes of Lille, Man United and Celtic, he had done really well, and looked a safe bet. He might have had marital problems by the time he joined us and he was a disaster.

At times he looked like he had never played football but when he eventually went back to Bordeaux he did well for them again, and helped them reach the Champions League. Maybe he was one of those players who needed a certain environment in which to thrive. I also have to question whether I did enough homework on him. I knew him as a footballer, but I didn't know much about him as a character.

The foreign market was opening up and it was easy to get your fingers burned. That happened to me with Nicolas Medina, Tyson Nunez and Carsten Fredgaard in particular. I also missed out on Zlatan Ibrahimovic a couple of times. He was at Malmo when my former Everton team-mate, Andy King, spotted him at La Manga but he ended up going to Ajax. Later on I went over to Holland and spoke to Leo Beenhakker about him but we couldn't get it over the line.

One of the big strengths of the squad was that it had a British feel about it, especially in the dressing room. Maybe I tried to change that culture too much, too soon but there were some big success stories. Stefan Schwarz was a great signing from Valencia, a real class act, and Steve Bould, for a short period. Kevin Kilbane, Julio Arca, Alex Rae and Don Hutchison were also among those who came in and made a really positive impact.

Stefan, in particular, brought quality and top-level experience so it was a massive blow when he ruptured his Achilles tendon playing for Sweden. He was a player who got it easy and gave it easy. As soon as he wasn't there we missed him massively. Don Hutchison was a different type, a midfielder who could drive into the box and get on the end of things, and that made him an important weapon but he was only with us for a year.

I had looked after Hutch financially when he joined and made sure his wages were higher than he had been on previously but he came in to see me one day and told me he wanted to leave. He was only 12 months into a four-year deal so straight away I said to him: "You've been tapped." Hutch claimed he hadn't but I think a couple of clubs had got into him so I went to speak to the chairman to see what could be done, and he said there was no way we could give him an improved deal so soon.

I fully understood that and I told Don that if any clubs were interested in him and could come up with the right money he could go. I spoke to Glenn Roeder at West Ham and Steve McClaren at Boro and he ended up heading to Upton Park for £5m. It was a decent fee but we couldn't replace him and that meant we ended up having to reconfigure our midfield, just when we thought it was settled for the foreseeable future.

The sad thing is that, before all of these problems began to set in, we had looked so strong as a club. There was a spell when we were playing reserve-team games at the Stadium of Light against Liverpool and Man United and we attracted crowds of 40,000 because our second string was so strong. We had Phillips and Quinn in the first team so that meant Michael Bridges and Danny Dichio would play for the reserves along with players like Alex Rae, who was incredibly talented, regardless of the off-field issues he had, and Gavin McCann.

From being a club which looked like it didn't have enough quality to avoid dropping into Division Two when I arrived, we suddenly had a second team that was good enough to win the Central League, creating so much excitement along the way that we were pulling in full houses. That showed how much strength in depth we had but when we needed to push on we didn't. As we discovered to our cost, if you stand still in the Premier League it won't take long for other clubs to overtake you.

That was what happened in 2001/02 when we ended up finishing fourth from bottom, which was a huge disappointment for everyone. In contrast to what had gone before, the whole season was hard work from start to finish. The crowd was restless, which was understandable given how quickly we declined. We only scored 29 goals in the entire campaign, whereas Phillips alone had got 30 in our first year back in the big time.

The following summer I tried to get Robbie Keane in but that didn't work out and we ended up signing Tore-Andre Flo, Matthew Piper, Stephen Wright and Marcus Stewart as I tried to shake things up but, after nine games, we only had eight points. Goals were still hard to come by which meant a 7-0 win at Cambridge United in the Worthington Cup came as a huge relief but it was a false dawn, rather than a new one. After we lost 3-1 away to Arsenal in our next league game it soon became clear that my time at Sunderland was up.

I didn't need anyone to tell me things weren't going well but at a time like that there are no shortage of people ready to tell you what is going wrong, and how much pressure you are under. That goes with the territory but unless the chairman joins in with the chorus of disapproval all you can do is keep your head down, carry on working and hope the turning point is not too far away.

Unfortunately for me, Bob had lost patience and when he called me at home the day after the defeat to Arsenal I knew it was all over. He told me he was going to drive down to Manchester to see me, which was the biggest tell-tale sign of all, and I met him at the Marriott Hotel, where he delivered the bad news. It was amicable and my contract was honoured so I had no complaints about the way that it was handled. I just wished it wasn't ending because I had loved being manager of Sunderland.

Bob then asked me who I thought my successor should be and I put Mick McCarthy's name forward because he would have been ideal. He obviously took my advice because he went and got Howard Wilkinson, with whom he'd shared a box at York Races the previous summer.

When Sunderland released the statement confirming I had left, I was pleased that as well as referencing the chairman's belief that a change was necessary, they also noted my contribution to what had been a really positive period in their history. 'Sunderland is totally unrecognisable now to when Peter Reid walked through the door at Roker Park in 1995,' Bob stated. 'While I know that the recent months have been difficult and disappointing, that should not cloud people's judgement over the many positive things Peter has achieved for the club over many years.'

That meant a lot, particularly as there are no shortage of clubs who turn on managers as soon as they have parted company with them, but I also felt I deserved to be held in that kind of esteem. Not because I think I was anything special; because of where the club was when I found it, and where it was when I left it. I went there and kept them up when they had been virtually down. The following season I won Manager of the Year as we won promotion and although we were relegated 12 months later and lost out in the play-offs the season after that, there was a genuine sense Sunderland was a club headed in the right direction.

We then went up with a record points tally before establishing ourselves in the Premier League. The club's infrastructure also developed which meant that although we were fourth from bottom when I left, we had our own training ground which hadn't been the case when I got there – and a wonderful stadium.

Does all of that make my time at Sunderland a success? That's for others to say but what I can say without fear of contradiction, is that I left that club in a much better position than I found it. The Bishop's blessing definitely helped and so did the chairman's leadership, but I'd like to think that I played my part, too.

# 16. CRISIS CLUBS

*'One day your face fits and everyone thinks you can work miracles, the next you're seen as yesterday's man and a replacement is lined up. It is a cut-throat business and, at times, the treatment of managers can be ridiculously harsh'*

CERTAIN headlines stick in your mind and there is one that comes back to me whenever anyone mentions my time at Leeds United. "The worst job in football?" it asked. "Leeds United, who would manage them?" I would, and I am proud to say that I did.

As a club, it had taken a few knocks when I took over from Terry Venables, and the financial strain that it was under made it an impossible job. But if I was offered the chance to take over at Elland Road again and the circumstances were exactly the same, I wouldn't hesitate.

Maybe that makes me a glutton for punishment, a football addict who cannot kick the habit no matter how bad the fix is, but I look at it another way. There are only a limited number of truly great clubs and if you have the opportunity to manage one of them, you grasp it with both hands. If things don't work out, then so be it, but you have to give it a try.

I've also always been a great believer in the notion that beggars can't be choosers. Having been out of work since being sacked by Sunderland I wasn't in a position to pick and choose my next job. I was on holiday in Abersoch when the call came.

I had been at Anfield the previous night to see Celtic beat Liverpool in the UEFA Cup so was in a good mood. Peter Ridsdale rang me out of the blue to tell me Terry was going and asked if I fancied taking over. I looked at Leeds' position in the table, fifth from bottom with eight games to play. Then I read up on their financial situation, which had been a big story for months, and saw that they were around £80m in debt.

Logically, it was anything but an attractive proposition but the same could be said of me in the eyes of some Leeds fans, with one telling the press that my appointment would go down like a lead balloon if it was confirmed. With that in my mind I took the only option available. I signed on the dotted line and agreed to become manager until the end of the 2002/03 season.

Aside from needing a job, there were two major factors that led me to take that decision. The first was that I knew I would be in a no-lose situation. The club was in a mess but it wasn't of my making. If they did go down under my management, the responsibility would lie elsewhere. The second was even more important. I went through the squad and even though they had been forced into selling some of their best players – Rio Ferdinand, Robbie Keane, Jonathan Woodgate and Robbie Fowler being the biggest losses – there was still so much quality in the ranks that I knew if I did a decent job I would keep Leeds in the Premier League.

Time was against me, though, and my first fixture in charge came only a couple of days after taking over. But what went in my favour was that it was away to Liverpool which meant that my trip to Anfield to support Celtic on the Thursday turned into a scouting mission for our game on the Sunday.

We lost 3-1, but after going 2-0 down we had shown a bit of character to get back into the game thanks to Mark Viduka's goal. But, as the game was in the balance, a big decision went in Liverpool's favour and Huyton's second favourite son, Steven Gerrard, put the result beyond doubt. The thing that stuck in my mind most, though, was The Kop singing Ridsdale's name. This was where Leeds were at as a club. They had become a bit of a laughing stock and with morale at rock-bottom I knew it was going to be difficult to turn things around.

To make matters worse, I hadn't managed to strike up an immediate rapport with my best player, Viduka, who was a complex character as well as being hugely talented. I had a pop at him at half-time at Anfield, telling him that he had to get hold of the ball more so that he could be a focal point for the whole team, but he just looked at me like I was a piece of shite.

As the rest of the players filed out of the dressing room I pulled him and told him the only reason I'd had a go was because he was my best player, which was true, but it seemed as if my attempt at psychology hadn't worked because he didn't do much in the second half. But the big man went on to get 10 goals in our last seven matches, including a hat-trick in our next game against Charlton. Regardless of how difficult he was to handle at times, his form was key to Leeds avoiding relegation that season.

I saw both sides of him when we played Fulham and he scored twice after testing my patience before the game. I had told the players to get to Elland Road earlier than usual because I wanted to have a proper team meeting but Viduka strolled in late, having also been late for training the previous day. I wanted to read him the riot act but I knew that was out of the question because we were relying on him so much. All I could do was use the carrot and the stick. "I'm going to fine you, but if you get me a couple of goals I'll let you off," I said, and he went and won us the game.

As much as his poor timekeeping was a problem, I knew that as long as he was scoring goals and keeping us out of trouble, that I had no choice but to put up with it. Had I made an example of him he might not have reacted well and we could not afford that. Again, this isn't the kind of approach you will find in a coaching manual but it is the kind of dressing room logic that is absolutely crucial in top-level management, especially if you are in a dire situation as Leeds were at the time.

In spite of the pressure we were under – on and off the pitch – we picked up some really good form and when we went to Arsenal in the second-to-last game of the season and beat them 3-2, any lingering doubts about our survival were removed. Arsenal were going for the title and they were a brilliant side, so much so that the defeat to us was the last league game they would lose for almost 18 months. On the day we had too much for them, with Harry Kewell and Viduka doing most of the damage.

The talent that those two had was there for all to see but our unsung hero was Lucas Radebe. I only got to work with him for a short time and he was an absolute warrior, with his desire to get results lifting others at a time when we might have gone under without being able to count on someone with such an infectious attitude. On top of that, we had two fantastic goalkeepers in Paul Robinson and Nigel Martyn, Ian Harte and Gary Kelly in the full-back positions, James Milner, Nick Barmby and Stephen McPhail in midfield and Alan Smith in attack.

In many ways, it was a bit perverse that a squad featuring so much talent had been at risk of dropping into the Championship but the combination of Leeds losing their best players, and the financial cloud that the club was under, had sucked so much positivity out of the place that they ended up needing to be rescued. I was just glad to do my bit and I knew that even if I wasn't offered the job on a permanent basis I would be able to walk out of Elland Road with my head held high.

As it was, I had done enough to be given the job. I was handed a 12-month rolling deal, having won over the board and some of the supporters during my short time at the club. Ridsdale had left under a cloud by then and been replaced as chairman by professor John McKenzie, who was a nice person but knew little about football. I told the professor that it was crucial that we kept our best players if we wanted to build on what we had done at the end of the previous season. He agreed with me on that but, within a couple of months, Kewell had moved to Liverpool and Viduka had tried – and failed – to join AC Milan.

Kewell was a big loss but his contract situation was becoming a problem. The club was not in a strong enough position to allow him to run his deal down and leave on a free the following summer and the decision was taken to cash in, which I understood. Viduka was more of a problem because he thought he was going to Milan, who had offered a couple of million to take him on loan, but the deal collapsed and the big man didn't accept the outcome very well.

On top of that, the financial pressure we were under meant we couldn't afford to keep two top-class keepers on the books. I thought Martyn was slightly better than Robinson, so wanted to retain him. David O'Leary was in charge of Aston Villa and he came in for Robinson, with a £3m fee being agreed, but personal terms proved an issue and the deal was in jeopardy. Knowing we needed to bring funds in if I was to be able to make any kind of impression in the transfer market, I suggested to professor McKenzie that we should use £500,000 of the fee to make up the shortfall in Robinson's wages because we would still be banking £2.5m, but that idea was rejected. Nigel, who wanted first-team football, ended up joining Everton, where he did really well.

While good players were going out, the only ones coming in were on loan, apart from Jody Morris, who joined on a free. We got Jermaine Pennant, Zoumana Camara, Didier Domi, Lamine Sakho, Salomon Olembe, Roque Junior and Cyril Chapuis in on short-term deals because the loan market was the only place we could afford to shop. We also had to let Eddie Gray and Brian Kidd leave the coaching staff to reduce the wage bill so finances were dictating everything that we did – and not for the better.

The feelgood factor that had emerged at the end of the previous season was proving to be unsustainable as the harsh reality of our "resources" for the forthcoming campaign became increasingly clear. Everything seemed difficult and the situation wasn't helped by Viduka leaving nobody in any doubt about his mood during a pre-season friendly against York City, when the referee told me to take him off before he sent him off.

He was sulking and, in a way, I couldn't blame him because he was a top player and he deserved better than what was going on. But that applied to everyone on the playing staff, and it didn't help anyone when motivating him became such a big problem. With so much going wrong and so little going right it was clear by mid-summer that we were going to struggle. I always like to be positive but there was a growing sense of doom and it was hard to see a way out of the mess that we were in.

Of the loan signings we made, my biggest hope was that Roque Junior, a World Cup winner with Brazil, might offer us something but in increasingly desperate times even the desperate measures were not paying off, and he struggled in English football. He was a good footballer but it was just too quick for him. As far as the fans are concerned, he has gone down as one of the worst signings in the club's history as he picked up four bookings and one red card in the seven games he played, a run which saw us lose six and concede 24 goals.

I felt sorry for him, though. He came into an impossible situation – for him and for us – making his debut at Leicester within eight hours of signing because we were desperate for bodies. He had only just got off a plane after playing two World Cup qualifiers for Brazil but we had no choice but to plunge him in at the deep end. Leicester scored two goals in the first 25 minutes and it was an experience from which he never really recovered. It wasn't his fault that his dream move to England turned sour. He was the wrong player at the wrong time, but it wasn't as if there were better options available. We had no money to spend and good players were looking to leave, rather than join us.

To make matters worse, the pressure of being at a big but under-performing club started to get to some of the younger players. Pennant got into a bit of trouble off the pitch which attracted negative publicity Leeds could have done without, after the problems Jonathan Woodgate and Lee Bowyer had been involved in previously. That summed up where we were at. Nothing was going well. But it was on the pitch concerns were growing most as we won only two of our first 11 league games.

With results like that I knew I was under pressure and professor McKenzie wanted to sack me in early October only for Allan Leighton, the vice-chairman, to talk him out of it. But when we lost 6-1 at Portsmouth I knew that would be the end, and that was how it turned out. I got the call from Trevor Birch. Leeds had American bondholders and after the defeat Trevor told me they weren't happy and I said I could understand that, because they were worried about going down, and that was that.

I had questioned the players' attitude after the game, which was inevitable after such a heavy defeat, and while they didn't do themselves any favours that day, in retrospect I wish I hadn't done that. They were just beleaguered and who could blame them? They were at a club which had lost its way as a result of its own mistakes and, when things continued to go wrong, the only solutions they were able to come up with were to sell the best players, and keep on changing managers.

The chances of Leeds' fortunes improving by replacing me were slim, given the new manager would also have no money to spend, but that stark reality did not prevent the axe from falling. Maybe I had been guilty of having delusions of grandeur. Perhaps I expected too much of myself because I had kept Sunderland up when I first went there, and thought I could do it again at Leeds? Terry Venables, someone I regard as a brilliant manager, had been unable to stop the rot so that was a warning in itself. After I left, it didn't get any better so that suggests the problems lay somewhere other than the manager's office.

I could take being sacked and, in some ways, it was inevitable, but I also believed it would change nothing – and that feeling has turned out right. In everything other than their current status, Leeds are a Premier League club, but the way they have been run for far too long would shame a non-league outfit. As happens far too often in those situations, it's left to fans to pick up the pieces.

My regret with Leeds is being at a great club at the wrong time. The support is amazing and I still look at the club as a whole and visualise how big they could be if they lived up to their potential. It didn't work out for me but I still want them to do well because a strong Leeds United would be good for English football.

Once bitten, twice shy? Not in my case. I had only lasted eight months at Leeds but, even though my experience there had ultimately been disappointing and also eye-opening, despite having spent the entirety of my working life in football, I still believed that I had something to give if the right offer came my way from the right club. Again, the usual process of waiting for the phone to ring took place. A few opportunities came up that didn't really excite me, but after Coventry City sacked Eric Black in the spring of 2004 I was contacted by their chairman, Mike McGinnity, who told me he thought I was the man to take them up to the Premier League from the Championship.

As with Leeds, I looked at the financial situation, which wasn't good, but I was excited by the idea of managing another club that had ambitions of winning promotion as they prepared to move into a new stadium. In that respect, it was a similar situation to the one I had inherited at Sunderland, but it did not turn out quite the same way.

I thought I knew exactly what I was letting myself in for as it was clear from the outset that we would have to sell to buy, but I still felt that if the club allowed me to do that we would have a decent shot at winning promotion. I wasn't the only one who thought that, either. After we beat Sunderland on the opening day of the 2004/05 season hopes were raised that we could be competitive – but it turned out to be a false dawn.

In many ways, that win encapsulated everything about my stint at Highfield Road, as nothing was as it seemed. Reality started to set in at the end of August when Tottenham came in for defender Calum Davenport, which set a chain of events in motion that resulted in my eyes being fully opened to the conditions that I was working under. We were playing West Ham at home and Calum's agent wanted to pull him out of the game to protect him from injury. I refused because, although the player wanted the move, I needed a good result – and we got one, a 2-1 win.

I was in my office afterwards with Adrian Heath, who I'd brought in as my assistant, when in walked Alan Pardew, who was managing West Ham at the time. He asked about Calum, which I thought was strange because it was clear to everyone that he was destined for Spurs. That wasn't my problem, though, and my main concern was ensuring that I got Stern John in, having agreed a £250,000 fee with Birmingham for him in the knowledge that Calum would fetch around £1.5m. I had said to Mike that I would sanction the sale as long as he guaranteed me the proceeds and he agreed to that, so everything looked set.

Calum joined Spurs, as expected, but then moved to West Ham, one of our Championship rivals, on loan which came as a disappointment to me but explained why Pardew had been so interested in him. I got Stern John and I needed a couple of other players, with a centre-back being the priority, but out of the blue I got a call from someone at the club telling me that the bank had taken the rest of the money. In the space of that brief telephone conversation I knew that all of the plans I had made had gone up in smoke. Rather than being a repeat of my Sunderland experience, it was starting to feel like a re-run of what had happened at Leeds, and it was a struggle from then on.

It was also another example in dealing with agents. It's like anything else in life, you get some good ones and some bad and the key is knowing how to deal with them. Some will go to extraordinary levels to get what they want for their players and I understand that, because it is a short career. As a manager, though, there are times when you have to stand up for yourself and your club.

There was one occasion when I was having a discussion about

players with Willie McKay and it didn't go well. As things got heated, Willie told me he would get his lads from Glasgow to pay me a visit so I told him I'd get my lads from Liverpool to pay him a visit. It was, "My dad's bigger than your dad" stuff but we ended up having a laugh about it, and got things done.

In this instance, though, I did feel let down by Coventry because I had been told something, and the exact opposite happened, so I started to wonder what I was doing there. To be fair to Stern, he came in and did well, which gave everyone a bit of a lift, but there weren't too many other bright spots. Chief scout Bob Shaw had told me about a young Irish lad called Stephen Hunt, who had been let go by Brentford. Trusting Bob's judgement, I brought him in to see if he was good enough for us. It only took a few training sessions for my mind to be made up and in one of those Hunt had a set-to with Michael Doyle, which I really liked.

I went in to see the board and asked them to bring him in on wages because there was no transfer fee, but my request was rejected and Hunt went on to join Reading, where he did really well. He was a feisty character and he would have been perfect but such was our financial situation that we looked a gift house in the mouth, and another club benefited from our failure.

The same thing happened when Niall Quinn told me about another player, Shane Long, who had caught his eye in Ireland. Again, I went to the board and, again, there was nothing doing. That was the moment when I realised that I didn't stand a chance. The squad wasn't good enough to achieve our objective of promotion and the club didn't have the money to improve it, but still the expectation was on the manager to get results.

I was unable to do that and, by the end of the year, I'd had enough. I'm not a quitter – if anything, everything I've done in my life suggests the opposite – but this really had turned out to be an impossible job. Four successive defeats had left us in 20th place and there had been a few "Reid out" chants which I understood, even if I didn't think the fans were being fair.

I went in at the start of January and told the club I'd had enough. Inchy offered to go with me because that's the kind of lad he is but I told him to stay put, and he ended up succeeding me. I know he was trying to be loyal but it was right that he carried on. Even though he was also accepting a poisoned chalice, I hoped that he would succeed in a way I'd been unable to.

It would be five years before I managed in England again and the reality was that, unfairly or not, my reputation had been damaged by a perception that I had failed at Leeds and Coventry. I understand that and I knew the risks when I took both jobs but if people were prepared to look a little deeper, I'm pretty sure they would come to the conclusion that there wasn't a manager in the world who could have made a success of those jobs at that time. I was just the one who learned that the hard way.

It's because judgements can sometimes be so harsh, and because managers often take responsibility for the failings of others, that it is so difficult to turn jobs down. One day your face fits and everyone thinks you can work miracles, the next you're seen as yesterday's man and a replacement is lined up. It is a cut-throat business and the treatment of managers can be ridiculously harsh.

The most severe case I have experienced involved my old mate, Sam Allardyce. When he took over as England manager in 2016 he was the right man for the job in every sense. He had worked his passage in a way that others hadn't, he had gathered an extraordinary amount of experience at the highest level and he had the respect of his peers and the players who would be working under him. Every box was ticked and yet he only lasted for one game.

Even now I think of the circumstances behind his departure

and it makes me angry. I have to declare an interest in this because Sam is a close friend but, even when I ask his biggest critics what he did that was so wrong that he had to lose his job, they struggle to come up with a good answer. That's because there isn't one. Beyond the media noise and The Football Association's failure to sit tight and back their man when he needed it most, there is no valid reason why Sam isn't still England manager a year later.

Sam was foolish, he knows that. He allowed himself to get caught up in a newspaper sting while trying to help a couple of friends, and it ended up costing him his dream job. But I would question the motives of the journalists who sought to put him in a compromising position, and I would question the reaction of his employers who could – and should – have stood their ground, in the knowledge this was not a case of gross misconduct.

In my career I have had a great relationship with a lot of journalists and I have always counted the likes of Paul Etherington, John Richardson and the late Bob Cass as friends. They have a job to do and that means, sometimes, they will upset us, but because they do it the right way they carry a respect that goes beyond their profession. That's why I think it's sad that journalists from *The Daily Telegraph* set out to dupe Sam. Even when he didn't give them the smoking gun that they had been looking for they still published in an attempt to damn him.

When the story broke I called Sam because I wanted to tell him not to go but I couldn't get hold of him because he was in talks with The FA. It was during those discussions that it was decided he would leave his post. I know Sam isn't everyone's cup of tea but he didn't deserve this to happen. The only good thing that came of the entire sorry saga was that he bounced back, keeping Crystal Palace in the Premier League and reminding everyone what a brilliant manager he is.

Fairness isn't something that any manager can rely on. All you can do is take jobs, try to make the best of them and hope for the best. That's what I did when I returned to management in England when Plymouth Argyle offered me the chance to take charge in 2010. I had followed up a spell in Thailand with a stint as Tony Pulis's assistant at Stoke, which I enjoyed because Tony is another manager whose ability isn't recognised as much as it should be, simply because there are those who don't like his style.

Had Plymouth not come in for me, I would have happily carried on working with Tony but the chance to be the main man, to make the big decisions again, was too tempting to turn down. I realised straight away that I would be fighting fires again because Plymouth were in financial trouble but I have to admit I hadn't recognised that they were about to be engulfed by a raging inferno, and I wouldn't even be armed with a hose. Had the extent of their problems been clear to me I probably wouldn't have taken the job but I'm glad that I did, because I learned more about myself there than I did anywhere else.

I met Sir Roy Gardner, who had been a director of Man United before investing in Plymouth, and he outlined his vision for the club which included plans to build a new stadium as part of England's 2018 World Cup bid. On the surface, it seemed exciting but the reality was different. My fears, that all was not as it seemed, grew just a few days after taking charge. I tried to use the club credit card to book a flight to the south coast from Manchester and it was declined.

During pre-season I had to accept pretty much any offer that came in for our players, but it paled into insignificance in comparison to what followed in March 2011 when the club went into administration, with debts of £13m. Suddenly there were winding up orders and the future of the club was in doubt.

The players were in shock and to put the tin hat on things, we were docked 10 points as a punishment for going into administration and that left us at the bottom of League One. I thought things couldn't get any worse but they did, when I arrived at training one morning and was confronted by a scene of desolation.

Some of the players had their heads in their hands and others were on the phone to their wives and partners, passing on what was obviously bad news. It was then that I discovered they had been told there was no money for them to be paid. I had encountered some problems in football before but this was on a whole new level. Some of the lads didn't even have money for their digs so I helped out where I could. I paid a heating bill for the club and I also had to give my brother, Shaun, a few bob because he had come down to help me out and the wages that he had been promised hadn't materialised.

It really hit me and it really hit all of the lads. How could they be expected to do their jobs properly with all of this going on? How could they possibly focus when they would walk into the Portakabins at Home Park and discover that 10 people, who they had been working alongside, had lost their jobs? At times like that football really doesn't matter. I was picking teams and getting ready for games but for the first time in my career I really didn't feel like doing any of it.

Then the administrators came in and they were put up in a very nice hotel, on however much an hour, while we were going to extraordinary lengths just to get from one day to the next. I will always be grateful to Harry Redknapp and Tim Sherwood, who helped me out with loan players, but there was only so much that anyone could do to help.

I ended up selling my runners-up medal from the 1986 FA Cup final which fetched around £4,000 at an auction, with the proceeds going into the players' pot, but we were relying on charity. In one case, a supporter contributed £400 to pay for our travel costs for a game at Hartlepool United. It was all hands to the pump but we had too many crushing blows in such a short space of time. Ultimately, the 10-point deduction cost us our League One status because we were relegated on 42 points, just six short of safety.

We then had to try to rebuild and in our first game of the following season we fielded 10 new players but the situation was a total mess, and we lost our next eight matches. It was then that Peter Ridsdale, who had been brought in as club adviser at the height of the crisis, met me in Manchester to tell me that they were letting me go. I know I had done everything right and my motive was always to do the best I could for Plymouth Argyle, but I'm not sure certain people at that club can say the same. I made mistakes at Leeds and possibly also at Coventry, but at Plymouth I did everything in my power to help a stricken club.

It was an amazing experience, in some ways because it confirmed my view that it is ordinary people, rather than owners, who make football clubs. The fans stopped that club from dying. Despite the mismanagement of others, they kept their club going.

I have won things in my career and I have represented my country at a World Cup, but what happened at Plymouth was real life and I am proud to have played my small part. It took me back to where I'm from, to a background where no one has much but everyone pitches in and pulls together to keep heads above water. For those reasons, I don't believe that going to Plymouth was a mistake. If another big club that was in financial trouble came to me and asked me to take over, I would probably jump at the chance. That's just who I am.

# 17. THE ELEPHANT MAN

*'I put the ball down, clipped it to the far post and the centre-forward headed it in. Simple. The players all started laughing, though, so I brought the interpreter in and said to him: "What the fuck are they laughing at?"'*

I THOUGHT I had seen it all as far as pubs were concerned. I have witnessed bar-room brawls that would not have been out of place in a Western. I have seen lads buy and sell everything from legs of lamb to widescreen televisions that would be too big for most walls. I have also watched a reporter from *The Sun* newspaper being escorted off the premises when he tried to approach me for an interview.

All these instances – and many, many more besides – took place in The Quiet Man in Huyton, an infamous ale house which fully deserves its place in Merseyside folklore. But as much as I loved the place, and spent far too much of my time there before it closed down, I had to travel to the subcontinent for my most unforgettable experience in a pub – and I wasn't even drunk.

I was sat having a quiet beer in a bar in Mumbai when I heard a thudding sound outside. At first, it was quite faint but it kept getting louder and louder until I decided to put my pint down to go and see what kind of beast would be making such a noise. I looked out through the door and there it was, walking down the street without a care in the world – an enormous Indian elephant out for a Sunday evening stroll.

I actually did a double-take when I saw it but I knew I wasn't hallucinating because I was only on my first pint. Other than witnessing Sam Allardyce sporting Cammell Laird boots, I can't think of any other images that will live with me as much as this one. It was totally surreal.

That was why I went to India, and to Thailand before that. I had spent most of my life in the north of England and while I loved the place, I always had a desire to experience other countries and cultures. Football gave me the opportunity to do that, to go out to two magnificent countries and live as I had never lived before. Like the elephant striding down the street, everything that I saw and heard while I was out there left a lasting impression on me.

I was in my early 50s when I went to Thailand, and my late 50s when I had a brief stint in India. It was a period in my professional career when I could have gone on the media circuit or waited for a manager's job to come up in England, but opportunities like those are too good to turn down. They are about work, first and foremost, but they are also about life. I had no second thoughts when either job came up.

It wasn't as if I had given any thought to managing in Thailand. I went out there in 2008 to take part in a veterans' tournament with Viv Anderson and a gang of other lads and my main thought was that it was going to be the usual jolly boys outing, which was a good thing as far as I was concerned. We were in a bar one night and a fella approached me and asked if I would speak to him about a job. It was an unusual way of going about things but I was out of work and had nothing to lose so, having had a few sherbets, I decided to hear what he had to say. The next thing I knew he put a call in to Worawi Makudi, the president of the Thai Football Association, to arrange a meeting with me. It was during those talks that I agreed to take over as manager.

I hadn't managed since leaving Coventry but I didn't have an itch that I needed to scratch or anything, although I did want to get back into football if the right opportunity came up. The reality was that this was a job that intrigued me so much that I felt I couldn't turn it down. The way that it came about, totally out of the blue, added to the feeling of excitement, and what really added to my sense of fascination was that I didn't know any of the players who I would be working with.

I had never been in a situation like that before because English football is like a village so, no matter what club you turn up at, it's highly unlikely that you will be meeting everyone for the first time. With Thailand it was totally different. The players might have known who I was but I certainly didn't know them. I went in with a blank piece of paper and an acceptance that I was going to have to learn quickly if I was going to make the job work.

For that reason, I brought in Steve Darby, a Scouser who had coached in the Far East for many years. I knew I was going to need his local knowledge and also his cultural understanding because everything about Thailand was totally new to me. The first bits of advice he gave to me were straightforward but demonstrated the differences between the way I would be working, compared to the way I had been used to working.

He told me that I couldn't bollock anyone because that isn't the done thing, and neither could I walk around the dressing room with my bollocks hanging out because that isn't acceptable, either. I wanted to say, "Bollocks to that," but I stopped myself. I had gone to Thailand so I was going to have to adapt to their cultural quirks rather than the other way around. It wasn't easy, though, and I let my standards slip one day when I came out of the shower and walked into the dressing room with my bollocks swinging all over the place. That was normal in England but it didn't happen over there, and all the lads just fell about laughing.

It was just great to be working again. I had been linked with all kinds of jobs and every time a manager got sacked I was featured on the shortlist to replace him. Whether I was a long shot or a short-priced favourite with the bookmakers, I never got further than the talks stage with clubs. Taking a job 6,000 miles away from home meant I was out of sight and out of mind but that suited me. It allowed me to get back to the basics of coaching with a team that was 115th in the FIFA rankings, a side ripe for improvement because the talent and the desire to be better were both evident from the moment I arrived.

I tried to get to grips with some of the basics of the Thai language but I found it difficult. That wasn't a major problem in general because a lot of the people I came across spoke English and, if they didn't, we found a way to communicate, but it made life difficult on the training ground.

I didn't know any of the players by name and, even if I had, I would have struggled to pronounce them so I resorted to calling the lads by their numbers. Then I found out what their nicknames were so I wrote them all down, memorised them and used them in training instead. I had Car, Mooey, Coal, Cop and a goalkeeper called Boy. From that point on I was okay in the main, although the language barrier remained a problem, which I was never able to fully overcome.

The players were technically good and there were certain things that they could do to a really high level but there were other elements, stuff that I would say is basic in the English game, that they struggled with. There was one occasion when I was putting on a session and the idea was for them to put the ball to the back post. It was a bog-standard drill and I hadn't expected any problems because all they had to do was run to a cone and back, and then knock the ball in. One of the problems that I had encountered was that they were trying to walk the ball in at times so I wanted to show them that, when the time was right, we could go a bit more direct.

Mooey went first and he battered the ball out of play. Then the next lad did exactly the same thing. I was stood there, wondering what was going on so I decided to take matters into my own hands. I put the ball down, clipped it to the far post and the centre-forward headed it in. Simple. The players all started laughing, though, so I brought the interpreter in and said to him: "What the fuck are they laughing at?"

He asked them and they told him that, when I was telling them to hit the far post, they thought I meant the corner flag! At least their crossing was more accurate than I'd thought because if they had been aiming for the far post I would have had big problems. As it was, the collection of balls that had gathered around the corner flag suggested I had a group who were capable of knocking a ball into the far post, just as long as they knew which one.

It was because of those kind of cultural misunderstandings that Steve became so important to me but he couldn't do much to sort out my biggest frustration which centred on having balls, cones and bibs available for training. I would tell the staff that I wanted everything in place for the following morning because I wanted to put on a particular session but, when I got there the next day, nothing would be in place, but they would smile at me and tell me it was going to get done.

I couldn't have a go at them because they were so genuine and eager to please but there was a 'mañana' culture which meant things would get done at a time that suited them, rather than when you needed it done. The contrast with England, where training ground staff ask, "How high?" when a manager says, "Jump", couldn't have been more pronounced and I struggled with it at times. But I was the one who had gone into their culture, not the other way around, so I just had to accept the way things were and get on with the job.

Results were good. We reached the semi-final of the Asian Cup and although most of the lads were only earning around £170 per week, their technical levels were high. The local press complained that I didn't smile enough but that was hardly something new. We won the T&T Cup, beating Vietnam in the final, and there were plenty of signs that the team was making solid progress.

For someone who was regarded as a bit of dinosaur in some quarters at home, I introduced a lot of sports science into the national team setup, bringing in a core stability programme, working on diets and using video analysis. Before I went there, quite a few of the players had chilli beef and fried rice as their pre-match meal so I put a stop to that, because it didn't give them the right nutritional balance.

Despite my reputation, I had long since revolutionised my approach to what I ate and drank. I had gone from being a kid who had steak, toast and a pint of milk, which was the most ridiculous pre-match meal, to having fish and then porridge with milk and honey. Football evolves and you have to change with it but it wasn't until I was with England in the mid-1980s and I had a conversation with Ray Wilkins, who was then playing at AC

Milan, about how the players in Italy looked after themselves, that I took on board the importance of eating and drinking the right things at the right times.

He told me all about the pasta they would eat and the amount of water they would drink, and how it was designed to give them a physical edge. That struck a chord with me so when Arsene Wenger took it to the next level in this country, after taking over at Arsenal, I understood what he was doing and why he was doing it. I still enjoyed a bevvy at the right times though. It was too late for me to change everything and there were some things that I wouldn't have altered, even if I could.

I would be out on Saturdays after games and sometimes I wouldn't get home until four o'clock in the morning. Everton had a reputation for being a club where the players socialised a lot and that could be taken two ways. Obviously, it's a good thing that the players were spending time together away from the pitch but, for the critics, it could be used as a stick to beat us with.

We were far from being unique. Sir Alex Ferguson famously went in and tackled United's drinking culture after taking over as manager but I can remember playing against Liverpool in a testimonial for Alan Kennedy's brother at Bury in the early '80s, and their players had been on the ale all day. This was one of *the* great Liverpool sides and I was guesting on the other team, but we couldn't get the ball off them.

Rightly or wrongly, it was part of British football and we didn't half win some European trophies during that period, so it can't have been all bad. Would Everton have been as successful as we were if we didn't have the camaraderie that was built up when we were socialising? I honestly don't know. I would argue that we had the balance right. There would be no drinking within 48 hours of a game but, afterwards, it was absolutely fine.

The other element that shouldn't be overlooked is that it brought players together from rival clubs, something that doesn't happen anywhere near as much as it should in the modern game. I'd kick hell out of someone and they'd do the same to me but afterwards we'd have a pint in the players' lounge. Bryan Robson was a great one for that. It was the done thing and it definitely worked for us.

I did have a few nights in Thailand when I got on the whisky and it ended up being a bit heavy because Bangkok is a place built around having fun, which suited me just fine. But I got myself really fit and the entire experience of living out there was positive. My home was an apartment at the Grand President but I travelled around the country and saw some beautiful places like Chang Mai and Chang Rai.

I fell in love with the country and with the people because they were so passionate about their football and so welcoming that it became easy for me to feel at home there, even though I was having to get used to different ways of working, and all of the other issues that come with working abroad. We took the team out to Vietnam, Japan, Saudi Arabia, Jordan and other places so, as a life experience, it was magnificent.

It was while I was in the Middle East that I took a call which stopped me in my tracks and brought the feelgood factor that I had been enjoying to an abrupt halt. Ian Greaves, my old manager and mentor at Bolton, had died. I was a youngster when I met Greavesy and he was a massive inspiration to me in football, but it was as a man that he really stood out.

He had me up against the office wall at times and he called me a "shithouse rat" more times than I care to remember but, as a human being, he knew how to relate to me, and how to get the best out of me. Socially he was brilliant and we became so close that he was like my second dad. So, when I heard that he had died, I was absolutely devastated.

We had flown over to Qatar to train ahead of a game in Jordan and it was while I was there that the terrible news came through. For once in my life, football came second and I headed straight back to the airport to catch a plane home.

I didn't just want to be at his funeral, I knew I had to be there and I still regard that trip as one of the most important I have ever taken. I needed to pay my respects to a man to whom I owed so much. I needed to grieve and I needed closure. Had I stayed with the team in Qatar none of that would have been possible and I would also have been left with an enormous sense of regret that probably would never have gone away.

Even though I managed to get back, it still hit me hard but at least I was there for his final journey, and the turnout at the church was magnificent. I still miss him now, though. I know it's a natural cycle and you lose friends along the way but I do miss the likes of Greavesy, Howard, Bob Cass, Keith Pinner and Andy King because they all played a big part in my life. The only way I can deal with them not being around is by counting my blessings that I was lucky enough to know them.

Once I got back to Thailand, the little difficulties continued to build up and it was while on another trip home that I got a call from Mike Morris, my mate who is also an agent, and he told me that Tony Pulis wanted to have a word with me about a job at Stoke. Tony told me he wanted me to become his assistant and I accepted the offer. The problem was that I had enjoyed my time in Thailand so much, and had been treated so well, that I didn't want to leave the Thai FA high and dry.

I told them about the situation and they were not happy because I was only 12 months into a four-year deal. I offered to combine the two jobs, returning to Bangkok for every international break to take charge of the national team. They were not keen on that idea, though, and my contract was terminated in September 2009, bringing my Thai adventure to an abrupt end. But at least I was leaving them with an improving team that had lost only two of the 13 matches they played under me.

I stayed in touch with Steve Darby and almost five years to the day after leaving Thailand he called me about a job in another country. This time, the opportunity was in India, as Mumbai were looking for a new manager and Steve thought it would be a chance for us to work together again.

Zico, the legendary former Brazil player, was managing a side out there and so were David James and Marco Materazzi. The more that I looked into it, the more I realised how ambitious the Indian Super League was, with several high-profile players also being signed, including Luis Garcia and Robert Pires. When the formal offer from Mumbai came my way I gave it some thought but it didn't take me long to decide that I wanted to give it a try.

In the end, I was only out in India for three months but I loved it. I stayed at the Palladium Hotel in Mumbai, which was a really opulent place in a wealthy part of town, where the well-heeled could go shopping at Gucci or eat at fine restaurants. But as soon as you walked out of that vicinity you would be confronted by the kind of poverty which shocks you.

I come from a background that would be seen by many as impoverished in comparison to some standards but it was nothing compared to this. I would go for walks because we were spending a lot of time on the road getting to and from games. I wanted to see Mumbai up close, without being stuck behind a glass window going 30 miles an hour down the road. The people had nothing and begging was endemic.

There was a girl with one tooth selling coconuts to try and make ends meet so I would make sure I passed her whenever I was out and I would buy one for 100 rupees, which isn't a great deal of money. She would smile as if I had just given her the crown jewels. That was the strange thing about India and it was something that I haven't experienced anywhere else, certainly not to the same extent, even though the people had so little. It didn't take much to make people happy.

The football infrastructure, in terms of the training facilities, wasn't great but the players were determined to do well so we made the most of what we had. Nicolas Anelka was a big help on that front, even though he missed the first three games after signing for us because he was banned. I know he has a certain reputation but I found him to be a great lad. I loved him. He liked to keep himself to himself, which I was aware of before I worked with him, but he got really involved in training and did everything he could to help the Indian lads, which reflected well on him. He was 36 by then but it was obvious to everyone that he had been a top player and, even though he was a bit introverted, I found him brilliant to work with.

Freddie Ljungberg was there, too, but he didn't kick a ball for me because he had a calf injury and although he'd been a terrific footballer for Arsenal, I didn't get to see it. Had it been down to me, he wouldn't have been one of my choices but I wasn't picking the players we signed, which made it a bit difficult. However, it was an exciting period for football in India.

The Premier League is massive out there. When it's a nice day you will see Manchester United shirts, Chelsea shirts, more Everton shirts than Liverpool, everywhere you look there are symbols of English football. I went to watch a Merseyside derby at a Liverpool supporters' club and the passion was unreal. I got a bit of stick, which was fine, and I made sure I gave it back with interest when Phil Jagielka scored a last-minute equaliser to give Everton a draw at Anfield.

The football is an ongoing project but the place – and the people – were what fascinated me most. Maybe I had become cocooned in my own culture, which meant experiencing other ones was an even bigger eye-opener than it might otherwise have been. It was similar in Thailand, where I would go into the mountains and come across places with no electricity, home to indigenous tribes that I hadn't even heard of before, never mind seen.

The one thing that I was familiar with was the national sport. India is a cricket country and I am a huge fan so it was a huge privilege for me to meet Sachin Tendulkar, the legendary Indian batsman, while I was out there. Along with hearing and seeing an elephant walking down the road, that was the kind of once-in-a-lifetime experience that wouldn't have happened unless I'd decided to broaden my horizons.

Considering my only childhood holidays were days out in New Brighton and Rhyl, football opened up the world to me, and I will always be grateful for that.

# 18. LOVE AND LOSS

*'Whatever the sacrifices I've had to make and however great some of the disappointments have been, I know football has been incredibly good to me and my family'*

IN my career I went through some traumatic times, moments of physical agony when I suffered serious injury and periods of mental torture when I wondered if I would be able to play again. All pale into insignificance in comparison to when I discovered that my daughter, Louise, had cancer.

As a footballer, I was prepared for things to go wrong because anyone who plays knows the risk, but there was nothing that could have prepared me for the worst news I have ever received. To make it even worse, if that is possible, Louise had only got married in October 2016. She was looking forward to a wonderful future with her new husband, Dan, who is a great lad, when her world came crashing down without warning within a couple of months of one of the happiest days of her life.

Like all dads, I have always tried to be strong around Louise but when she came to see me, and told me what the diagnosis was, I felt like I had been knocked down by a steamroller. I can't imagine how hard it must have been for her to stand in front of me and tell me that she had cervical cancer. I know parents who have had to deliver similar news to their children, and that is bad enough, but for a daughter to have to tell her father, in the knowledge that he dotes on her, is something that I can't even contemplate. Obviously my first reaction was one of shock but I also knew that I had to pull myself together for her sake. I just said to her: "You'll fight this, girl, you'll be alright."

I had a million and one questions but I knew this wasn't the right moment. This was a time for me to be there for her in whatever way she needed. One of the many brilliant things about Louise is that she is incredibly methodical and practical so she started going through the options that had been outlined to her.

One of them involved surgery, which would have allowed Louise to keep some of her eggs but there was an additional risk so I told her that, no matter what she decided, the most important thing was that she put her own health first. I know that is easier said than done, especially as she had plans to have children with Dan, but she thought about all of the alternatives and eventually came to the conclusion that she would have a total hysterectomy.

I have always been proud of Louise. Even when she was just sitting there as a kid I was incredibly proud of who she was, and that she was mine. That feeling grew as she got older and became a beautiful, wonderful young woman. But the admiration I had for her as she battled cancer was so powerful that I can't even begin to describe it. Even after she had been given the all-clear the doctors came back and told her that the best way of having complete insurance would be to have chemotherapy.

That hit her psychologically because she had thought she was through the worst of it and this meant a bit more suffering on top, that she hadn't been expecting. To make matters worse, she had an allergic reaction after her first two chemotherapy interventions and she also put a bit of weight on because of the steroids and lost her hair, which meant she had to wear a wig. It has been incredibly tough for her but, no matter what she has gone through, her personality and her determination to get better have been so strong that it has inspired me. There have been times when I have been really down about it all and Louise's spirit has lifted me, which might be the wrong way around, but as a dad I'm not really built to see my little girl going through a bad time.

When I saw her after she had the operation, that was when it hit me hardest. Not surprisingly, she was crying and asking for me but the emotion I felt at that moment, a powerful mix of relief that she had come through the surgery and concern about her situation, meant I had to go out of the room to sort myself out. I just wanted to take her pain away.

It was the same feeling I had when she was seven or eight years old and she had toothache for the first time. I wanted to suffer on her behalf. 'Give it to me,' I kept thinking. 'I'll deal with it so you don't have to.' But I knew there was nothing I could do beyond being there for her. I had to leave her in the hands of the experts, and hope and pray for the best possible outcome. As a parent you always like to believe that if your kids are in any trouble you will be able to help them but, in this situation, I was powerless.

Thankfully, we had the wonderful doctors and nurses of the National Health Service to step in to do what we couldn't. The treatment and care Louise received at the Christie Hospital in Manchester was first class and my admiration for everyone involved in looking after her is absolute. I wouldn't have wanted it to happen in this way. In fact, I would have wanted it to happen in any other way but this, but it has confirmed everything that I have always believed about life in general and about the NHS, and the welfare state in particular. I have never understood the argument that we should cut our vital services, that treatment should be available on the basis of cost, rather than need.

How can market forces be allowed to have a significant impact on whether people are able to get better? This isn't about being left wing – which I am – or right, it is about basic human decency and a willingness to do whatever we can to look after people. I know we need a thriving economy and we need the City to do well, and I also get the need for businesses to make profits. But I don't understand why the NHS is not looked after more.

When I was a player at Everton we would visit Alder Hey Children's Hospital to see the kids and it used to shake me, but it also made me admire the medical staff who looked after them. They need all of the resources that are available to be able to make a difference and, as a society, it is our duty to help make this happen. That should be an absolute priority and after seeing what Louise has been through, and how much care she has needed, it has convinced me more than ever that the NHS, and those who work in it, should be cherished because the reality is that they save lives all the time. I can only thank them from the bottom of my heart for saving my daughter's.

In a situation like the one Louise has been in you have to take any positives that come your way, and one of the things that has lifted me is that I've been able to spend a lot of time with her. I would give anything for the circumstances to be different but, having missed a lot of her growing up, it is a small consolation to be in her company as much as I have. The reality for footballers – and this isn't a complaint – is that the game takes up so much of your time that family life inevitably suffers, and it gets even worse if you go on to become a manager. If you're not training, you're travelling to matches and staying in hotels. If you're not scouting, you're doing press conferences, sorting out contracts and making public appearances. It really is all-consuming.

I was living in Yarm when I was manager at Sunderland and that meant that I was away for most of Louise's formative years. I would get back home whenever I could, and usually that meant weekends after games, before heading back up the motorway early on Mondays.

We took the decision that Louise would stay with her mum, Barbara, at our family home in Atherton while I lived near Sunderland because the nature of football – and management – is that you never know how long you will last. You have a contract and ambitions but the reality when I took the job was that I might only have lasted a few months if things didn't go well.

In the end, I was there seven-and-a-half years but at the time we took the decision we had to do what was right for Louise, and that meant prioritising her stability and education. It was the right choice, too, because under her mother's guidance she developed into a wonderful young woman. No matter how much I wish I had been around more, I know that keeping Louise at home had a positive effect on her. That's the side of football people outside the game don't really see but it is a reality for everyone in it. When Louise got married I used my speech to say that the beautiful and magnificent woman sat in front of the guests was a great credit to her mum because I hadn't really brought her up.

It might actually have been for the best that I wasn't always around if my initial ventures in fatherhood are anything to go by. The first time I was left alone with Louise, our Shaun was with me and within an hour she'd filled her nappy. We were looking at each other as if a volcano had gone off and there was no way of stopping the lava because neither of us had a clue about what to do. I started to open the nappy but I'd only loosened it a little bit when I recoiled in horror at the thought of what was about to confront me. "No way," I said. "You'll have to deal with it."

The baby was rolling around on the mat but Shaun wouldn't do it either and, in the end, I had to hold her while he ran and knocked next door to get my neighbour, a lovely woman called Joan, to do it for us. So much for the Huyton tough guys.

Apart from when Shaun tried red wine for the first time, or ended up eating a bar of green soap thinking it was an apple, I've always been lucky to have my family around me. Along with Howard Kendall and Ian Greaves, my mum and dad were my biggest influences. One of the greatest privileges of my life was that they were able to share the good times with me.

I was also a big influence on them before I was even born, though, and I've never let my mum forget it. She married my dad at St Dominic's Church in Huyton and it was all because of me, although I was oblivious to it at the time and for many years afterwards. It was only when we had a big 'do' for their silver wedding anniversary that it dawned on me. I said to my mum at the time: "Silver wedding? I'm 25." She said: "We got married on February 14, 1956," so I counted the months out on my fingers. "February, March, April, May, I was born on June 20!"

Later on, I made a speech and I couldn't resist having a bit of a crack. "Mum and dad, what a brilliant achievement to make it to 25 years married. To commemorate this momentous occasion I've done a bit of research and it snowed on the day you got married. Then again, I should know because I was there!" My mum was mortified but everyone else cracked up. I owe my parents so much that I know I could never repay them.

As well as bringing me up, they also reared my three brothers, Michael, Gary and Shaun and our wonderful sister, Carol, and they did it brilliantly, working all the hours God sent to make sure we didn't go without. My dad worked at Stoves in Whiston from the age of 14. He worked on the lines at first and went on to be a charge hand. His three basic shifts were 6am-2pm, 2pm-10pm and one that became known as, "Don't make a fucking noise" because he had to sleep through the day, having worked during the night. He always worked in asbestos and when he died they thought that was one of the causes.

Mum worked as a biscuit packer at Huntley & Palmers in Huyton and then as a bread packer at Sayers, among other jobs. She was a grafter and she had to be because she knew that relying on dad's money could be a risky business. Often when he finished his shift on a Friday he'd go to The Green Dragon for a pint and have a few bets but sometimes he would keep on going and, before he knew it, his wages would be gone.

My mum would get really upset and rightly so but, looking back, I've got a bit of sympathy for my dad because his job, and the hours he worked, were so hard. I can't blame him for having a blow-out after spending an entire week in a furnace, but it would have made our lives a bit easier if he'd found his way home with at least some money left.

Holidays were day trips to New Brighton, although we did have a day out in Rhyl once. That was all we could afford but the lack of money never bothered me. Firstly, I never knew any better because everyone where I grew up was in the same boat. Secondly, I had football and as long as someone had a ball – and we had somewhere to play – it felt like I didn't want for anything. The game brought everyone together and that was still the case when I joined Everton years later.

On the day it happened, my mum and dad sat everyone down to make an announcement. My mum told them all that they had to act normal and no one else was to know, and then she came out with it: "Your brother has signed for Everton" and, within minutes, everyone in Huyton knew! Apart from my mum and myself, I don't think anyone was happier than my Uncle Jimmy. He was so committed to Everton that he wouldn't even allow red tomatoes on his plate so he was delighted.

Once, after a game at Everton, I went out with a really good mate of mine, Farjo, and we got absolutely hammered so I went back to my mum's afterwards to get my head down. I slept downstairs on the couch and when I woke up I was freezing so I said to my mum, "Put the heating on will you," and she told me that they didn't have any. I rang Farjo and told him to get me a plumber, a boiler and a load of radiators.

I was living in Bolton so hadn't realised but my mum hadn't mentioned it either, which tells you a lot about her. So, whatever the sacrifices I've had to make and however great some of the disappointments have been, I know football has been incredibly good to me and my family, although I'm not sure Shaun would always agree. As well as having to come through the ranks at Rochdale being known as "Peter Reid's little brother" and having to put up with the comparisons, he also had to suffer for having a sibling willing to speak his mind, regardless of the consequences.

The incident that best sums that up came when Shaun was at Chester, then owned by American businessman, Terry Smith. Smith came over to watch a game while I was at Sunderland and he wanted to scout himself, instead of leaving it to the professionals. I was having a drink with Bryan Robson and spotted Smith, and went for him. Unbeknown to me, he had asked Shaun to go with him to scout as well but he'd pulled out because he had training first thing the following morning.

I had a right go at him because of his treatment of Kevin Ratcliffe, who had been manager there and had done a really good job. On top of that, he'd made Shaun first-team assistant-coach and captain of the midfield, while also appointing captains of the strikers and the defence. It was an absolute car crash and I made no attempt to hide my anger.

Shaun was oblivious to all of this and he was at home when his mobile started going at about 11.30pm. He picked it up and all he could hear was this irate Yank effing and blinding. "I've never been so fucking embarrassed in my life," he said, among many other things as he went off on a mad rant. After trying to calm him down Shaun realised he wasn't going to get any sense out of him so he cut him off.

He went into training the next day, still none the wiser about what had gone on the night before, and all of the lads were in bulk laughing. Smith had been down about six times asking where Shaun was so my little brother went to see him in the boardroom, not knowing that the volcano that was about to erupt in front of him had been caused by me.

Smith's face was crimson red and blue veins were bulging in his head. "You God damn arsehole," he said. "I went to the game last night and saw your brother with Bryan Robson, so I went over to introduce myself and he made a cunt of me." Shaun was biting the insides of his cheeks to try to stop himself from laughing but it wasn't easy, and he ended up getting only half of the story.

As soon as he came out he rang me. "What did you say to him?" he asked and, seeing as Smith was his boss, I thought I had a duty to tell him the full details of what had happened. "I said to him, 'Don't you dare try to shake fucking hands with me. You've just sacked my mate, a Wales international, a Cup Winners' Cup winner, and you've come over here from America and think you can just do as you please. Fuck off!'" He didn't speak to our Shaun again for about 18 months.

At least Shaun knew what I was like and that meant he was never really surprised whenever I went off on one. There was even one occasion when he saw what was coming before I did. Not that prior knowledge made any difference; he knew he just had to stand back and let me get on with it.

I had been asked to take charge of an England legends team which played Germany at Reading's Madejski Stadium in May 2006, and I decided to take Shaun down with me to help out in the dressing room. It was a charity game and I was delighted to be involved but on the journey down south something kept nagging away at me. One of my players was a certain Boris Johnson and Shaun knew my opinion of him. Like me, he was wondering whether I would be able to keep them to myself.

As most people have now realised, Johnson is – as Nick Clegg once referred to him – a mop-haired buffoon but the people of Liverpool had already come to that conclusion, having been on the receiving end of his brand of politics. Regardless of the reason why the game was taking place, I knew I wasn't going to be in a charitable mood towards him. My anger had been caused due to an article which appeared in *The Spectator* magazine a couple of years earlier that had accused drunken Liverpool fans of causing the Hillsborough disaster, and claimed the city had subsequently been consumed by self-pity.

Johnson hadn't written the piece, Simon Heffer later admitted the hatchet job was his, but he had commissioned it as editor and then ran it, besmirching the reputation of my hometown and, worse still, causing unnecessary distress to the Hillsborough families. He would later apologise but, by then, the damage was done.

The thought of having him in my dressing room was offensive to me and, at first, I thought about pulling out or asking the organisers to tell Johnson that he couldn't take part. But then I realised that this was an opportunity too good to miss.

As soon as he walked into the dressing room I went for him. "Hello Peter, Boris Johnson, pleased to meet you," he said. I wasn't in the mood for pleasantries, though. "I've been meaning to have a word with you, you twat; having a go at Scousers, who the fuck do you think you are?" You could hear a pin drop and the likes of John Barnes, Richard Ashcroft, Nigel Benn and Sean Bean were all open-mouthed. I could tell he couldn't work out whether I was pulling his leg because he was half-smirking and half-shocked but I wasn't messing. "You are a fucking disgrace," I said, and the tirade continued. He shit himself.

Not surprisingly, team spirit wasn't the best after that and I was tempted to leave him on the bench but I brought him on for the last 10 minutes and regretted it, when he flattened Maurizio Gaudino with a ridiculous tackle that caught the media's attention. What the papers didn't know was that, as well as reading him the riot act beforehand, I read it to him again afterwards.

After all the furore over that article he still managed to go on to become Foreign Secretary. He couldn't even be diplomatic and respectful to people from his own country and yet, he was given the responsibility of flying around the world representing the UK at high-level government talks. How is that possible? He knows what the people of Liverpool like myself think of him, though, so that is one small consolation, even if I want to kick the screen in every time he appears on television.

Shaun still sees the funny side. As I had erupted, he was stood in a corner a safe distance away, having realised what was going to happen. Quite rightly, he didn't even try to intervene. He just stood there smirking and let nature take its course.

Shaun was useful to have around at times because he could be my eyes and ears when I wasn't there. There was one time when he was recovering from an injury so he came up to Sunderland to work on his fitness, and spent most of the time in the gym. He was in there one day with Chris Makin and Niall Quinn and the pair of them were just going through the motions. Quinny was on an exercise bike but was more Chris Foy than Chris Hoy, while Makin was doing sit-ups as if he had all day to do 50.

Suddenly, Quinny's going like the clappers on the bike and Makin is trying to break the world record for sit-ups in a minute, all because I was about to walk in the door to check on how they were doing. I muttered something uncomplimentary at them and went on my way, and Quinny gave the game away after I'd gone. "He's fucking horrible when you're injured," he said to Shaun, not that he needed anyone to tell him that.

When Sunderland drew Chester in the Worthington Cup in 1998, Shaun became the enemy but I've never seen my dad so proud. It was Shaun's first game back after doing his cruciate but I couldn't afford to think about his fitness so there was no chance of us going easy on him; we had to win the tie. I told the lads to make the pitch as big as we could and to keep on shifting the ball, but I made a decision which I came to regret.

I had been planning on leaving Kevin Phillips out but he wanted to play because he was in good form so I put him in, and Nick Richardson caught him with a late one. We didn't know how bad it was at first and when I found out he'd fractured a metatarsal I was devastated. The only consolation was that Shaun hadn't been the guilty party. I would've chased him back to Chester if he had been! I made sure Nick knew what he'd done and although he was supposed to be playing on the right he ended up switching to the left, to get away from me on the sideline.

We went through comfortably over the two legs but the result didn't matter to my dad, it just meant so much to him to have two of his sons involved in a cup tie at the highest level. I only had to see the look on his face to realise that – it was the same one he wore when I won the FA Cup with Everton 14 years earlier. Football and family were everything to him so having him around for an occasion like that meant a great deal to us as well.

Dad died in February 2006 and his loss still affects me. I was out of work and Sam Allardyce was letting me train at Bolton to keep my hand in. I was there when I got a call from Shaun, telling me Dad had suffered a wobble and was in trouble. I shot down to Whiston Hospital but then he got transferred to Walton Neurology Centre where he had a brain scan, and it soon became clear he'd had a massive stroke. He was basically brain dead and the machine was keeping him alive so I spoke to mum and we decided to get a priest. It was horrendous, especially when he took his final breath, but at least we were all there when it happened.

As a family, we also took solace from the fact he had still been around to celebrate his 50th wedding anniversary with my mum. He'd first taken ill in the December but it obviously meant so much to him that he hung on to enjoy that day, with her and us. I was off the ale but he wasn't going to let me mark the occasion without sharing a drink with him. "I've got some of that pink Laurent Perrier stuff that you like," he said, and I was determined to resist, but he kept on badgering me and in the end I had to give in. I had a couple with him and it was the best couple of drinks I ever had because the next day was the beginning of the end for him. The police had to close the roads for the funeral because that many people attended. To see how much esteem he was held in meant a lot to all of us, but I still miss him.

The same goes for Howard Kendall who died on October 17, 2015. Everything that happened on that terrible day remains so vivid in my memory and that is simply because of the profound effect he had on my life. I got a call from Ray Parr, Howard's mate. He asked me if I was alright and I said I was fine, and that I was on my way to the game because Everton were playing Man United at Goodison, and I was really looking forward to it.

It felt like small talk, though, as if he had something more important to get off his chest and he was just building up to it. Then it came. "I've got to tell you something," he said, and straight away I knew something was badly wrong. "The gaffer has passed away." I couldn't take it in. "Fuck off," I replied, as much out of denial as shock. I couldn't take it in. Ray could tell how much I was struggling with what he was telling me and he just said: "I'm really sorry, Peter, but he's died."

It was then reality started to dawn. Howard was gone. I'd like to say I know what my first thoughts were but I haven't got a clue. I just know I was devastated and I'm not ashamed to say I shed a tear, in fact, I shed many. This wasn't just the death of a football manager, it was the loss of someone who believed in me when others didn't, a person who took me on the greatest journey of my football career, a mentor, a friend, a funny, warm individual.

As the memories flooded back, none more so than the image of his beaming face when we won the FA Cup, my sense of anguish grew. I wondered if I should even go to the game because I was in a state but I quickly dismissed those thoughts. If there was one place in the world I needed to be that day it was Goodison.

I was in Derek Hatton's executive box but before I went there I headed to number 9 Goodison Road, where Ray entertains guests on matchdays, and Howard had a seat there, an old boardroom seat with the Everton motif on. The chair was empty except for a blue rose that had been placed on it. Seeing that set me off again.

I headed over to the ground a couple of hours before kick-off and the atmosphere was one of the strangest I've ever experienced. Goodison is usually bouncing when United visit but on that autumn Saturday afternoon it was subdued and sombre. How could it be normal? The greatest manager in Everton's history had died and yet life, in this case a football match, had to go on.

We got beat 3-0 but I've never been less bothered by a defeat. In many ways, the game was irrelevant. With flags flying at half-mast in Howard's honour and images of him beamed on to the big screen before kick-off it must have been almost impossible for the players to focus on the job at hand. The club had been shaken to its foundations and the supporters had turned up to pay tribute to Howard, rather than to roar their team to victory.

A lot has been said about Howard after his death and while he did enjoy a drink, as I do, he was also a brilliantly warm person and that is one of the main reasons why he socialised as much as he did. He was always there for his players and I'd like to think he knew that we were there for him. The spirit that he created at Everton in the 1980s lasted for the rest of his life and still lives on. It takes a special, unique person to be able to do that and for that reason he was one of the most significant people in the lives of so many of the players who worked under him.

I've long thought that his ability as a manager has been overlooked and so too, to some degree, have his qualities as a human being. But those of us who were lucky enough to get close to him know how remarkable he was, and that's why a day doesn't pass when I don't think about him.

If there is a good thing, besides his legacy, which will be appreciated by Evertonians for generations to come, it is that on the day Howard was laid to rest the bond that he had created between the players was there for everyone to see again. We met at the Hilton Hotel in Liverpool city centre before heading up to the Anglican Cathedral, where the funeral service was taking place, and it felt like a family reunion.

As soon as I walked in I saw Andy Gray at the bar and the first thing he said to me was: "Come on, Champagne, Laurent Perrier." I responded: "I'm speaking at the funeral," but, even though I protested, I already had a feeling that resistance was futile. Andy just looked at me so I asked him if he was speaking and he just said he couldn't have done it, but he wasn't giving up on me. "For the gaffer," he said, and at that point he had me.

We raised a glass – or several – to Howard and I can say without fear of contradiction that he would have liked that. This was a send-off from his own band of brothers, done in a style that captured exactly what we were about. We won more than enough and we brought the glory days back to Goodison but while success can come and go, the camaraderie that developed will never die. That is testament to a genius called Howard Kendall.

He is – and was – one of the greats, and my only regret is that he never had the chance to become even greater because of a tragic situation that was out of his control. But he is still the most successful manager in Everton's history and that, in itself, makes him an absolute legend. I just wish he was still around to reminisce about the time that we spent together because it was such a special period in all of our lives.

I know it's natural that you lose people along the way, especially when you reach the age that I am now, but every now and then it dawns on me that three of my biggest mentors – my dad, Howard and Ian Greaves – are no longer around, and it does hit me hard. It's taught me to cherish every moment, none more so than the ones I spend with my family, especially Louise.

# POSTSCRIPT: FUTURE ROLES?

*'Now I'm in a position to pass on the benefit
of my experience, good and bad, and having
learned so much from some of the game's greats,
I feel I have a moral duty to share whatever
knowledge I have picked up along the way'*

THERE have been times in recent years when I have wondered if I would ever reach the stage when I no longer need football.

I have had a fantastic career – as a player and manager – and travelled to parts of the world that I didn't even know existed when I was a kid growing up in Huyton. And I have been blessed with a wonderful family including a cherished grandson, Freddie, who I dote on.

But every time I ask myself whether the time has come to call it a day, I know in my heart of hearts that even though I'm now in my early 60s, I still haven't lost the football bug – and maybe I never will. So when I took a phone call from Paul Cook, the Wigan Athletic manager, early in the summer of 2017 asking me if I would go in to help him out I jumped at the chance.

I could quote Michael Corleone in *Godfather III* and say that just when I thought I was out, they pulled me back in, but I would only be kidding myself. I pulled myself in at the first opportunity I could because football is all I have ever known. I still love the game as much now as I did when I was five years old, kicking a ball along Wimbourne Road.

Wigan was the club which allowed me to use their facilities to keep my fitness when I was involved in a contractual dispute with Bolton. If they feel I can help them in any way I will do so. Cooky is a great lad and he shares many of the traditional football values that I hold dear, so I didn't hesitate when he asked me to get involved. Now I'm in a position to pass on the benefit of my experience, good and bad. Having learned so much from some of the game's greats, I feel I have a moral duty to share whatever knowledge I have picked up along the way. I know how helpful that can be because I know what it is like to be desperate to learn things from people who have been there and done it.

The best example I can give was when I was fortunate enough to spend some time in the company of the late, great Sir Matt Busby. We used to have a family do every Boxing Day and he was friends with some of my relations, so I'd sit down with him while he had a scotch, and I'd just listen. This was the man, the icon, who built a team from the rubble of Munich.

Like anyone who gets to ask questions of a managerial legend, I wanted to know who Sir Matt thought had been his greatest players at Manchester United. In my own mind, I already knew the answer. George Best would be his number one. Besty was the best player I had seen at Anfield. There was one game in December 1969 when United were wearing all white and he was as majestic as their kit. I was shouting, "Kick him, kick him," but Liverpool couldn't get near him because every time they thought he was in range, he would just drop his shoulder or feint and then glide away. He was untouchable.

Liverpool had some great players out there as well – Emlyn Hughes, Ian Callaghan and so on – but Best was too good. United won 4-1 and I was devastated. Only a couple of years earlier, United had come out wearing blue and he got two that day, the second one was a header, and I was thinking, 'I hate this fella,' but what a footballer he was. Like most, I didn't like him because I knew he could hurt my team but I respected his talent, and that was what was going through my mind when I sat with Sir Matt. His deep voice will live with me and as soon as I mentioned Besty, his response was instant. "What a player," he said.

So I asked if he was the best and Sir Matt said, "It might have been Duncan," referring to the legendary Duncan Edwards, who was tragically cut down in his prime as one of the victims of the Munich disaster. What a player he must have been if Sir Matt thought he was maybe better than George Best.

Ian Greaves, my manager at Bolton, had been at United as a player. He was left out of the squad which was involved in the disaster in Munich, and had a similar opinion. That's two people with a great knowledge of the game. I can only imagine how good Duncan really was.

But listening to people who know the game is what allows football knowledge to be passed on from one generation to the next. Now that I'm the one with white hair (the dye hasn't been used since Wimbledon...) and the experience, I have a duty to share it with anyone who thinks it might be beneficial to them, just as people like Sir Matt shared theirs with me.

But I can't help thinking that the modern generation is being blinded by science. As well as the buzz words and phrases like "pressing", "between the lines" and "inverted wingers", there is a spin put on to the game which takes away from the one reality that never, ever changes – just as was the case when I was coming through. It is still all about the players.

Every Saturday night Bill Shankly would call Sir Matt and ask if he could buy Denis Law. Why? Because he was a great player, and the great managers recognise that great players make the difference. They don't overcomplicate things or discuss their own systems and tactics as if they are reinventing the wheel. They get the best players they possibly can and then create the conditions for them to perform.

Cooky doesn't need much advice because he understands football and recognises what he needs to do to be successful but if he seeks my opinion, I will tell him what Howard Kendall and Ian Greaves always told me and what I have always believed since I was a kid – it is all about players. And I count myself hugely fortunate to have been one.